Building Resilience Through Contemplative Practice

D1547444

Recasting burnout as a crucial phase of service, *Building Resilience Through Contemplative Practice* uses real-world case studies to teach professionals and volunteers unique skills for cultivating resilience.

Viewing service and burnout as interdependent throughout phases of stability, collapse, reorganization, and exploitation, the book uniquely combines elements of adaptive resilience theory with contemplative practices and pedagogies. Drawing on the author's extensive experience working at the intersection of service and contemplative practices, this is the first book to demonstrate how and why professionals and volunteers can reframe burnout as an opportunity for resilience-building service. User-friendly case studies provide tools, skills, and exercises for reconstructive next steps. Chapters address personal, group, and structural levels of service and burnout.

Illuminating the link between adaptive resilience and burnout as a normal and useful phase of service, *Building Resilience Through Contemplative Practice* is a necessary resource for professionals and volunteers across a wide range of service settings.

Bobbi Patterson, PhD, M. Div, is professor of pedagogy in the Department of Religion and the Graduate Division of Religion at Emory University. A well-known speaker and presenter on burnout and resilience, she has helped create, direct, and reorganize a range of community-partnered service experiences and programs for over fifty years.

"A must read for anyone engaged in volunteer service or in the helping professions! *Building Resilience Through Contemplative Practice* offers a fresh and hopeful perspective that positively reframes burnout as an adaptive phase of thriving service. A gem of a resource that grounds and renews through inspiring case examples and practical and heartful exercises. Written by a deeply wise and compassionate teacher, Bobbi Patterson, who walks the talk and uniquely understands Christian and Buddhist contemplation coupled with a life of service."

– **Susan Bauer-Wu, PhD,** President, Mind & Life Institute

"This is a book that provides the balm of perspective for those whose careers or volunteer commitment focuses on serving. Rather than give in to burnout, Bobbi Patterson's deep insight is that burnout is part of the cycle of service leading to resilience. Reading this book should not be yet another task undertaken by those already burdened; rather, it should be embraced as a hopeful and compassionate refuge at the crossroad where service and contemplative practice meet."

– **Joseph Favazza, PhD,** President of St. Anselm College; widely known expert on pedagogies of community-engaged learning

Building Resilience Through Contemplative Practice

A Field Manual for Helping Professionals and Volunteers

Bobbi Patterson

Routledge
Taylor & Francis Group

NEW YORK AND LONDON

First published 2020
by Routledge
52 Vanderbilt Avenue, New York, NY 10017

and by Routledge
2 Park Square, Milton Park, Abingdon, Oxon, OX14 4RN

Routledge is an imprint of the Taylor & Francis Group, an informa business

Library of Congress Cataloging-in-Publication Data
A catalog record for this title has been requested

ISBN: 978-0-367-13376-4 (hbk)
ISBN: 978-0-367-13377-1 (pbk)
ISBN: 978-0-429-05815-8 (ebk)

Typeset in Bembo
by Swales & Willis, Exeter, Devon, UK

To Joe
Who calls me
Barbara

Contents

Figures

Acknowledgments

Service and burnout have taught me a lot about acknowledgments. Acknowledge when service's attitudes and actions come to fruition. Acknowledge when burnout's attitudes and actions come to collapse, even devastation. Acknowledge that both nourish resilience. Webs of people, creatures, and places brought these lessons to life for me – too many to name, but the memories burn bright. Deep gratitude.

My first steps into serving followed my mother's trail-blazing work as a young public mental health social worker in South Carolina. In her matter-of-fact voice, she told stories of driving on the sandy dirt roads of the coastal islands to visit families requesting help for their children and elders. My grandmother – Nana, I called her – set the path for my mother by directing a regional Red Cross Office in the piedmont of the state. Both women rooted service in relationships before engaging their training. Pragmatists and women of faith, they admitted the work flourished and failed. I found that truth compelling and hard to take in until service and burnout showed the way. My brother's resonant path as teacher and professor delivered content while building community. He teaches me still. My father's thick psychiatric career traveled through high and very low years of American public mental health. His mother's career in nursing and father's pharmaceutical gifts pulled his curiosity to the healing arts of heart and mind. Watching him play ping-pong on Sunday afternoons with patients left to survive in huge public psychiatric hospitals set a direction I tried to keep. From him and my mother, I learned to assume that every person has an interesting story, one of pain and promise. Take the journey together. Stay in reality.

This book wandered in the back of my mind for over twenty years. Two formidable forces coerced it forward. The Religion and Ecology Collaborative, an urgent vision of graduate students in Religious Studies, Becky Copeland, Johannes Kleiner, and Liz Whiting-Pierce, reconnected me with Professor Lance Gunderson. In conversations, seminars, monthly colloquia, and a retreat, they brought adaptive resilience theory and models to life, including – for me – the life of serving and burning out. Lance Gunderson's willingness to continue tutoring me over many years not only enriched my understanding but fostered laughter and friendship. I am grateful for it all and responsible for any misrepresentations of Adaptive Resilience, which inspired this book's approach.

Allison Adams, the second force, invited me to apply to The Center for Faculty Development and Excellence's "Scholarly Writing and Publishing Fund," which she directs. She offered clear and helpful advice for my application, and I always felt her cheering me on. The funding connected me and the project with Cecelia Cancellaro, an editor-agent and founder of Word Literary. Like her firm, she specializes in books that engage public issues, diversity, and social change. With her deft clarity, she unraveled my confused writing. With her smart yet light touch, she suggested small turns in the text that greatly improved it. Cecelia's professional and personal approach also helped me avoid unnecessary drama. We kept working and the book's vision flourished.

Cecelia served as the book's agent, and now the book is here. Gratitude to Anna Moore, publisher with Routledge, and Ellie Duncan, editorial assistant, both consummate professionals who made me feel welcomed and kept this project on track. Sioned Jones, a sharp-eyed and creative copy editor, and Caroline Watson, a quick-responding production editor, well moved this manuscript through its final paces. Still, the final manuscript including formatted diagrams and images as well as citations, indexing, and bibliography would not exist without the creative smarts of Elaine Penagos, a graduate student colleague whose attention, kindness, and hard work turned details into finished text.

The book draws on more than forty years of volunteering and professional service work with a range of community partners. During those years countless people taught me lessons that became these chapters. I can only name a few. Volunteer Emory's founders, Wendy Rosenberg Nadel and Debbie Genzer, gained support from my boss, Don Shockely (university chaplain) and further interest from President Jim Laney. Their inspiration helped me find ways to link my earlier work in community-based service and ministry with this new job as associate university chaplain of Emory University. Sammy Clark, the university chaplain of Oxford College of Emory University, tutored me in student group volunteerism as we partnered with others for nine service trips in the United States and abroad.

Ira Harkavay and Keith Morton welcomed me to observe and learn from their academically-engaged service partnership programs. Their models profoundly informed my development of Emory's first academically grounded, community-engaged courses called Theory Practice Learning. Michael Rich and Vialla Hartfield-Méndez tutored me in asset-based approaches and more. Vialla continues to nourish and hone my skills for participating in the creation of transformational and democratic relationships with community partners rather than solely transactional ones.

Other Emory colleagues through the years invited me into broader service venues. Nadine Kaslow, for example, director of the Grady Psychiatric Unit and founder of the NIA Project, urged me to teach compassion meditation to suicide attempters. The Compassion Based Cognitive Training protocol created by Lobsang Tenzin Negi became our intervention. His presence and teachings continue to enrich my spirit and actions. The staff of the Wabash Center for Teaching and Learning in Theology and Religion, Nadine Pence, Paul Myrhe, and Tom Pearson, encouraged my explorations of pedagogies of place and community-engagement. Their full support of an eighteen-month Mid-Career Colloquy for faculty engaged and interested in community-partnered teaching and learning opened new insights for my own work. The impacts of those sessions under the insightful leadership of Joe Favazza, the aesthetic intelligence of Joy Bostic, and the pragmatic smarts of Tom Pearson drew me deeper into the wisdom and power of breakdown for building resilience.

Jim Hoesteroy, a department colleague, read and wrote with me as this book took life. Kristin Phillips, Sherryl Goodman, and Arri Eisen encouraged me through times of doubt. Tracy Scott remains a solid source of wit and healthy boundary-setting.

Colleagues from the Religion Department kept my spirits high and my mind joyously engaged. Thanks to all, especially department chair, Gary Laderman, who gave personal and financial support, and Joyce Flueckiger who believed in my ideas and approaches as did Laurie Patton and Wendy Farley. Toni Avery, our able department administrator always offered time and a listening ear. She let me sit with her in her office that late Friday afternoon when I signed this book contract.

Graduate student colleagues writing regularly with me in Emory's Matheson Reading Room, Meredith Doster, Nicole Symmonds, Cara Curtis, Emmy Corey, Shari Madkins, Norah Elmagraby, Charles Barber, and Marianne Florian, and others, kept the work coming through good effort and loving spirits. Karen Stolley, my long-time writing partner, and generous friend, urged me to trust the power of this vision of service and burnout and work diligently to write well. She inspires! To all, great gratitude.

Linda Bryant, a spiritual teacher for over fifty years, matures my understandings of Christian faith as compassionate, shared work for community-based social change. Don Saliers, who honed my liturgical sensibilities, also keeps me spiritually grounded. The mentoring and teaching of Roberta Bondi and her writing cultivated my love for the Christian Desert Mothers and Fathers. From time to time, Barbara Brown Taylor and I shared a cup of coffee and kept asking more questions. Carol Newsome continues to say yes when I holler for help. We share a contemplative practice group with Peggy Courtright, my life-long spiritual and everything friend, and Nancy Baxter, who quickens my life and ministry on its own terms. Other practice partners, especially Peggy Barlett and Dayle Hosack, and the extraordinary group of people that meet weekly on Wednesdays on campus teach me how to link stillness with strength in everyday living and service. I bow to them all in gratitude for their contributions to the contemplative core of this book.

The brothers of the Society of St. John the Evangelist welcomed me as a first-year graduate student at Harvard over forty years ago. They do their best to draw me on in the deep journey of love that is Love. Their capacities to root in the ancient traditions of Christianity while speaking to contemporary life and issues inspires me. Through workshops, trainings, and countless retreats, I am practicing hope as I pray for transformation. My director of many years, James Koester, Superior, offers steady companionship, insight, solace, and laugher. We both like working with the earth and its creatures. I'm still learning to let myself be caught up in the richness of good news that takes flesh and action.

Our household, meaning Joe's and mine, is life with dogs and dear friends. Lobo, our current husky, regularly beckoned me away from the self-preoccupation of writing a book. Joe Patterson's presence in my life leaves me speechless – most of the time. I find it hard to express how his intelligent, matter-of-fact approach to life grounds me. His aesthetic and ethical sensibilities fill our lives with beauty. And I make it every day because of his love.

Preface

Facing Burnout

The Debate

Rachel Sanders, an African-American woman, poured coffee from a Thermos decorated with yellow and gray swirls, the colors of her son's high-school basketball team. She hoped the caffeine buzz would help her cope with the roar of high school debaters rehearsing their arguments in every corner of the university's student center. Getting up before dawn, she drove 200 miles from Alabama to Atlanta to deliver three debaters, including her daughter, to this regional tournament. While the teams competed throughout the day, she planned to dive into her novel, an escape and reward. But not yet. Requests kept coming. "Ms. Sanders, can you please hand me my book bag?" "May I have my *other* file box?" "Can I leave my coat with you?" Each question fueled her own internal debate, which had been getting louder over the last weeks. How much longer could she serve as the school-wide coordinator of all debate team travel? What began as an easy task had become overwhelming. Why did she feel so trapped and resentful? Didn't every good mother support her children's activities?

The original "yes" to this service counted on other parents' willingness to share the driving. Everyone agreed. But the plan and the promises fell apart. Increasingly, she pleaded for help. Each adult offered a good reason for saying no "this time." But there never seemed to be a "good time." Some never returned her phone calls. For three years, she had held this position. No one else would step up; her resentment and despair grew. She tried propping herself up with pep talks. They now fell flat. This was her fifth long-distance trip in seven months. She sought solace in memories of the first year's drives. The girls' excitement bubbling forward from the back of the van eased the tedium. Older now, the girls mostly slept, leaving Rachel to her own thoughts.

This morning, as the miles rolled by, Rachel obsessed over the new demands of her son's basketball commitments. How would she juggle her husband's high travel job, her own work with a small financial services firm, and her children's schedules? One more request for another file box brought her back to the student center. "Drink your coffee and start reading," she muttered to herself handing over the box. She felt so cut off from any joy in this service. Had her mother ever felt like giving up when serving as the church's carpool coordinator all those years? Maybe her mother's faith buffered the burnout, but her faith in herself and service was waning. Turning her eyes back to her book, the pages went blank. She felt burned and hated admitting it. She wished she could abandon this service. But in her family, only the self-absorbed and uncommitted burned out in service.

On the other coast of the United States, the blood pressure of Sal Darman sky-rocketed. An urban, white male non-profit social worker, he directed a state agency coordinating children's healthcare. After twelve years in the job, he still could not fathom how the single swipe of a newly elected governor's pen could erase one fourth of his budget. Months of lobbying to keep barely adequate funding levels just dead-ended. He texted the Governor's Chief of Staff who tried to soften the blow. "Don't take it personally, Sal." But Sal's doctor disagreed. It was personal. Sal's blood pressure continued to sky-rocket. Staff raises would again be postponed not because of work poorly done, but because of politics. How many would quit this time? Should his administrative team try to regroup and refocus energy on fund-raising rather than lobbying? His mind began flipping through the Rolodex of options: new grants, more volunteers, quit.

That option appeared more frequently lately, quit. Previously pushed to the unthinkable, nothing a career social worker would do, the idea of leaving now drew him. Stymied by his own hurt and frustration in the face of another budget blow, he stared out the cracked windows of his office onto a narrow downtown alley. Exhausted, feeling without options, he told his secretary he was going to lunch. Dodging the packed sidewalk outside, he sensed he could not go back. But the decision rested less on the current news and more on his growing realization. He had burned out.

Lessons Never Learned

When we read these vignettes, they seem overly dramatic. We want to problem-solve. Point these people to additional resources. Give them extra time off. Shower them with more praise and thanks. All these strategies reveal two fundamental problems. First, we believe good people do not burn out in service. Whatever is happening, it is not burnout. Or if we sense it might be going in the burnout direction, we want to work to stop it. Good people serving with others don't do that, they don't burn out. That's the second fundamental problem. It's not acceptable to include painful losses and numbing anger when we talk about service. These topics do not belong to suitable service scripts. No surprise that skill sets for handling breakdowns go missing. Also missing are guiding values for self-care, healthy limits, and working through service conflicts rooted in political and economic realities. No wonder when service gets rough, we deny, fudge, or blame others. We find no other sources of help. This book changes all that. It takes burnout seriously as a phase within the normal cycles of service. Each chapter presents a real-world service experience and provides a set of values and skills that have the ability to move us into and through service burnout with resilience.

Service as Usual

Think about your own experiences of losses and breakdowns in the midst of doing the work you love. My first queasy recognition of burnout involved a bright-eyed second grader whose parents worked multiple jobs to pay the bills. He and I enjoyed our time together though he often missed our after-school sessions. I understood. I had worked in urban settings for several years and knew something about the struggles families like his faced. So, I kept driving the thirty minutes to his school. Every child deserved support and he was a very funny and creative kid with assets many might have overlooked.[1] We kept at it for over a year.

When I met with the school counselor for our annual assessment, I learned that my tutee had missed over fifty-five percent of his after-school sessions. She had kept count; I had not. He also missed that meeting. I shared what I knew. Sometimes he left school immediately to help care for his younger siblings. Other times, he had required appointments with other programs providing the family support they needed. Sure, sometimes, he just didn't come – too tired, too unfocused, wanting to play – to be a kid. His work was deteriorating academically. The counselor did not like the trend. I got that, but his teacher and I wanted to keep at it. So, we had a meeting with his family, teachers, the counselor, and him.

Things got better for a few weeks, but then, he began to miss sessions. By now, we were almost a year and a half into our after-school relationship. The commute traffic grew. I grew weary with it, especially when he did not show up. I had no information about handling the growing debate in my head. Should I keep coming? Should I continue working with the school, but with another child? Might his schedule free up and his focus sharpen? Was I just being selfish? I struggled, of course, with the thoughts of failing him and failing the narrative of good service. How to approach it? What to do? Without principles and tools, I just kept dragging through as best I could. I now know I was living the collapse or burnout phase of service.

Burnout corners us. The old script calls this "caring more about me than the service" or "unwilling to give up when it's called for." On the page, service burnout seems obvious – though we might still pull back from calling it burnout. When it happens, we do not ask ourselves what's going on or how we think and feel about the growing gap. What have you done with such thoughts? Where did you put these feelings? Why? Would you bring this up with a co-volunteer, a supervisor? Did you do some reflective writing just for yourself? What happened to that? Maybe, if you're like me, like most of us, you just keep going. We repeat the story we've been told with no idea how to tell a different story of service *and* burnout. Until this book.

Narratives of Service

The story of service has a long history in the United States. Early settlers arriving on America's shores and encountering indigenous American Indians brought high hopes. They expected to find rich land to cultivate, opportunities for trade, and freedom from persecution. Colonies like Massachusetts broadly organized life around a particular religious tradition joining spiritual expectations of material life with heavenly success. A good deal of colonial era success rose from ethics of shared resources and work among the colonists. These actions and philosophies, many of them brought from Europe, planted the roots of America's broader public service legacy. Models of service held by American Indians and immigrant minorities from Europe and South America also contributed. Enslaved Africans brought their own legacies of community sharing and service. These enabled them to survive chattel slavery. The emergence of our young nation in many ways depended on these forms and ethics of giving back to one's community.

As Spain, France, Holland, and Great Britain lost power over American colonies, the young Republic legally separated religious teachings from democratic secular life. Yet, service remained a shared space reinforced by many religious communities and encouraged by those in public service. We morally expected public, shared contributions to our thriving democracy. Service became a public ethic, a civic duty. Various types of service emerged and adapted, some born of economic, social, or political goals and some born of issues such as child welfare, the care of mentally ill people, and support for American Indians. Regional differences impacted values and assumptions about service. Quakers' work in eastern, mid, and upper states' prisons or Baptists' service to migrant families in the mid-west remind us of the breadth of models and assumed values. Protestant visions of the new nation working together for common goals impacted civic visions of community service as core to covenant life.[2] By the mid-1800s Alexis de Tocqueville, a famous French sociologist and political theorist who visited America, identified volunteering and professional service as key features of the American way.

Protestant revivals nourished visions of service organizations, which came to life during that period from boarding houses for those committed to grain-dominant vegetarianism, to those serving newly arrived immigrants. Jewish and Roman Catholic service organizations also arose particularly providing support for immigrants facing prejudice and persecution. Orphanages for Irish-Catholic children and Jewish immigrant social services grew new forms of American volunteerism and professional service societies. Private schools, volunteer groups, and rural retreat centers offered alternate forms of family life and spiritual practice across the country. Government-driven services also grew including early versions of minimal support for people living with disabilities. Unjustly, government programs displaced American Indian children from their families under the auspices of civic duty. Our story of service is wide and deep, drawing from complex agendas, hopes, and actions, and always intertwined with themes of renewal, sacrifice, support, and control. Each and all claiming their place as part of the heart of our thriving democracy.

Homeland-focused Protestant missions took that American spirit into poorer urban areas, the region called Appalachia, and beyond our shores to international mission sites. These service stories often mixed service with conversion and education, sometimes including vocational training. In the latter half of the 1800s, YMCAs and YWCAs signaled new modes of community-based service specifically informed by Christian values. The 1900s birthed The Boy Scouts with other scouting programs to follow. Local Black and White businessmen fostered an array of service groups meeting local needs across the country. Some of these helped foster national and international service organizations like Rotary International and Kiwanis International. By the mid-twentieth century, the Ys emerged as campus-based generators of youth movements for Christian service aligned with and then turning into movements for civil rights, racial justice and eventually women's rights. A whole new generation of service organizations emerged.

What had been a religiously inspired and civically driven narrative continued to grow and revised itself toward more secular and humanistic understandings and expressions of civic duty. Today's tech generations build on these narratives, supporting service through internet-spread calls to engagement through crowd-funding sites. They focus on U.S.-based, as well as global, service opportunities, all advocating the ethics of giving back to others. Our American story of service remains ubiquitous from local battered women's shelters, to regional movements for environmental justice, to major sports leagues, like the National Football League, all focused on service for the common good.

From different sources fostering diverse intentions, American service organizations embraced many versions of service-optimism.[3] They shared an assurance that civic giving would enrich and strengthen democracy. It's a proud and much richer story than these pages can tell. But along with that potent and resource-full narrative came another expectation that stretched the story toward fantasy: truly committed people sharing service do not burn out. The light shines on the destination, the outcomes, *not* the journey. We tell stories of perseverance. The narratives do not explain the breakdowns, the washouts, the damages *unless* there's a full recovery leading to an "even better" situation. Everything works out because we do not quit. The realities are much messier – and we do burn out. And within the collapse, we can change, recalibrate, even rebuild the next phase of a service cycle.

Stories of Service

Because the story of service deeply impacted my life, the content of this book matters to me. I came to service early and often. My maternal grandmother, Nana, deeply influenced my ways of seeing the world. She stood in a twentieth-century lineage of religious, southern women who considered it their faithful joy and duty to work with poor families, particularly her "neighbors" as she called them. I never heard Nana talk about structural injustices, either defending assumptions that kept people and resources "in their places" or criticizing them. As the regional director of the Red Cross, I find it difficult to believe that she did not understand the harsh consequences of class or race based structural injustices in her area. But she never discussed these realities with me. She focused daily on real people's situations and stories, a choice she had the privilege to make. She worked hard to meet needs and if she could even exceed them. Mozelle Stanton, my nana, was a woman of her time and region. Yet, she did break some long-held assumptions. A 1950s local newspaper story about her Red Cross work stated that she did her job "as good as a man." As many professional women of her day, she walked through her office door every morning promptly at 8 a.m. to begin the day's journeys down dusty dirt roads of her local counties. In her two-door black Chevy tank, as we later called it, she went full throttle into daunting work – as good as any man. I know because I rode with her on many a blisteringly hot summer day – no air conditioning, only windows. I witnessed the complex web of shouted greetings that met her at the steps of broken-down trailers. White, black, and mixed Cherokee families took us into their homes, sometimes serving us pie and peaches, while receiving Red Cross provided clothes, shoes, school supplies, and medical referrals.

My paternal grandmother died when I was one. Sadly, I did not know her, but I have her nursing textbooks full of skillful notes taken in the margins. She was a model student who loved science and became a lead nurse in a small southern city hospital. She also founded and managed a popular hot dog stand, which she cleverly located across the street from the hospital. Her famous and unique hot dog chili marked my family's Sunday after-church lunch *every* week. My maternal grandfather was a quiet, gentle business man who listened to my stories. My paternal grandfather was the town pharmacist. In their tiny southern town, the town Mayor's phone number was 1. The Police Chief's phone number was 2.

My grandparents basically served as the local doctors. Their phone number was 3. Night or day, I came from people who helped.

My parents' careers in public mental health more directly set the stage for my service involvements. Having achieved her master's degree in social work at twenty-four, my mother's thesis focused on social work and psychiatric interventions. She addressed the then new technique of electric shock, but from social work perspectives. She met my father when they both chose to work at a large, state-run psychiatric hospital. By the end of her career, she directed the foster family program for a large urban county in Atlanta. She combined excellent administrative models with deeply personal caring for the parents and children she supported. Locally, she honed a legacy as a change-maker.

My father trained in psychiatry at the University of Pennsylvania where new national models of public mental health were being created and tested. His career focused on clinical psychiatric care in public hospital settings. He drew often on the arts, adding color to beige hallways, tearing down the high brick wall around the facility and building a chapel. He oversaw the building of a new wing using innovative architecture emphasizing community-life for in-patient treatment. A warm and caring man, he contributed to new forms of patient care and healing, including his personal commitment to show up on Sundays and take anyone on for a rousing game of ping-pong. My parents strongly supported my brother's and my activities in school, church, and the community often assuming positions of leadership, meaning, they stayed in the trenches to get jobs done. We had our serious family struggles too. But serving with others kept us more balanced.

My brother and I currently work in academic institutions, which we've always considered our community; places where we receive the thrill of ongoing learning and try to give back in our teaching, relationships with colleagues, and activities with campus life. We were raised on the concept of vocation. One has skills and interests that come along with your DNA code. Discern them. Put them to good use. Enjoy them. These lessons were rooted in our intellectually-oriented Presbyterian church, which we understood to be a "covenant community." Yes, my mother was the real deal. She raised us in the Westminster confession, a reformed confession of faith and doctrine. No "Presbo-Baptists" in our family, her term for ill-educated and confused Presbyterians. My brother and I memorized two catechisms. Our church family claimed an entire city block of Columbia, South Carolina's downtown. We were there often singing, learning, worshipping, and having fun. Our head minister held extra degrees and delivered complex academically-informed preaching.

"Witness" in this context meant service. My mother viewed other forms of conversion witness negatively. "Don't talk," she would say, "Do something!" Jesus' name in our household existed only in bodily form, service. Any other godly talk belonged solely to private prayer. Nana said the same thing. When John F. Kennedy gave his inaugural challenge, "Ask not what your country can do for you. Ask what you can do for your country," we easily took it to heart. Although Kennedy may not have fully envisioned the movements that came to fruition in the 1960s for racial, women's, and gay rights, his call to service contributed to the broader rekindling of the fires of democratic engagement. Emboldened and enacted under the leadership of The Rev. Dr. Martin Luther King, Jr., activists at Stonewall, and women like Ella Baker, these flames also fostered the Special Olympics, Habitat for

Humanity, the first Food Banks – including Atlanta's, founded by my friend, Bill Bolling, and new visions for community-based mental health.

How did you come to service? Was it through family tradition, membership in a service organization, religious commitment, or something else? Students I've worked with taught debate to inner city teens and fell in love with service. Friends from my swim team coach local athletic teams. Maybe you thrived while staffing a children's education day in your local community garden. Some of us come to service because our companies expect it, sponsoring tutoring programs or river or park clean-ups. Perhaps your church hosts a soccer league, or your mosque has organized a domestic violence shelter for women and children. In my neighborhood, a Jewish temple has long-sponsored a homeless shelter. Perhaps a teacher inspired you as he linked classroom content with community-partnerships for change. Service draws us in so many ways. Yet, we never receive training or advice about how to talk honestly and move into and through all the phases of service, including the one we call burnout.

Leaving the Household of Service

That gap became tactile for me on a sultry Sunday afternoon in downtown Atlanta. As I leaned against our family's first car, an old blue Chevy Malibu, I watched trash blowing against a rusting chain link fence. I felt stymied too. Waves of steamy summer heat rose from the asphalt under my feet, which stretched forward to a brick apartment building at the far end of the parking lot. Once an elegant downtown address, the building's pedigree had faded. So, had mine having just turned down a career-changing job as the first Director of The Atlanta's Women Prisoners' Housing and Re-Entry Program. My fifteen years in community-based work, as volunteer and professional, now officially tanked. I had no choice. Every time I drove into that lot or wove my way through the interior renovation's sawhorses and debris, my skin burned. Not a mild disease, but a spreading singe, one that escalated from early days of stinging to recent sensations of lightning streaking up and down my arms. The visceral, insistent message proved inescapable, a fire, but without purpose or direction.

Why the burning, I kept asking myself? What could be more engaging than co-creating with women a first-ever residential program designed for self-empowerment beyond prison? I never got to that question. The fire took over and demanded all I had. I tried being rational. I suggested to my physician-psychiatrist father that I might be developing a neurological problem. He didn't buy it. He curtly suggested I go deeper. But I did not know how. Eventually, the burning collapsed my capacity to choose. I felt emotionally and spiritually cornered and full of self-blame. I lost track of the story I was supposed to tell. So, I just stepped out of the narrative of service. I left the household of giving back with others. I thought it was for good.

Households: Keeping Us in Reality

I learned about that metaphor of service as household life several years later. What I assumed was my service-ending burnout left me saddened, angry, and curious. Although I didn't recognize it then, I began piecing together the ideas, values, and tools that would eventually become this book. One source inspiring the actual writing of this book came a number of years later when I read the pioneering work of

Eugene Odum, a founder of the field of ecology. In his book, *Fundamentals of Ecology,* he emphasized the interrelating and interdependent dynamics of life systems.

The metaphor of a household helped him convey the ways these complex interactions work together to shape a flexible and resilient life system. The whole is the parts and as these interact, the whole is greater than the sum of the parts. There's magic in life systems, but part of this magic involves breakdowns and collapse. More on that later. Odem's perspectives signaled a field change in environmental sciences. I found his model useful for thinking about my own household and life experiences. The Patterson household of one husband and dogs goes along pretty well until someone gets really sick or someone changes a job. Then, ordinary tasks start to wobble and emotions run higher. If the car breaks at this point, the wobbling shifts into a hell breaking loose.

But I get ahead of myself. After that searing and stymieing experience with the Transition Center, I did stay away from service-centered positions and volunteering for a while. That space of rest at a distance helped me slowly regain my footing. I suppose my history with service shaped a strong enough foundation that the household did not collapse as I assumed it would. I had time to remember my own service histories beyond those of my family. I thought about my training in urban ministry at the Harvard Divinity School, courses in urban planning and negotiation at the Kennedy and Design Schools. Classes in ethics and pastoral care also helped me in my fieldwork, helping to run a federally-funded meals program for elders in the Central Square area of Cambridge. My first jobs in urban ministry in Jackson, Mississippi in a neighborhood-based social services center and then the Episcopal Cathedral enriched my understanding of regional differences in urban service resources and needs. Our move to Atlanta offered my first work in an addiction treatment center, eventually as a family counselor. And after two years, I applied and got a new job as a university-wide chaplain at Emory University in Atlanta. That position emphasized connecting the campus to Atlanta. I knew how to do that having run urban summer programs while living in a downtown neighborhood known as Bedford Pines, which has since become gentrified.

My work at Emory over the last thirty-five years continued to involve service despite my changing positions. Beginning with the community partnerships I helped form during my Chaplaincy work, I joined a service trip initiative developed with the dearly beloved Oxford College[4] chaplain, Sammy Clark. For nine years, we co-led three-week service trips in areas of the United States, South America, and Africa. Preparatory reflection for these trips helped us conceive how and why we served with others and post-trip reflection provided real world litmus tests of our models. A short time as Emory's Dean of Students added even more insights as I worked with a plethora of student-founded service initiatives including Emory's nationally recognized service program, Volunteer Emory.

Having moved back into service, I never forgot that harrowing day in the parking lot and the sting of burnout with no story, no model. Figuring out another way of understanding the real complexities of our service and burnout household lives kept nagging at me. Even as I shifted into my current work as a professor in the Religion Department, I continued serving. As Emory's first Director of Experiential Learning, I created the Theory Practice Learning Program along with a group of dedicated and engaged faculty. We strived to bring classrooms, pedagogies, and community partners together for shared work that communities prioritize. Simultaneously, I worked with colleagues in the Religion Department to revitalize and redesign our Internship Course and programs to more strongly link academic training with community-engaged agendas and actions. This work continues in a richer and more university-wide form through the innovative leadership of Professor Vialla Hartfield-Méndez, a faculty member in the Department of Spanish and Portuguese and director of Engaged Learning first through the Center for Community Partnerships and now through the Center for Faculty Development and Excellence (CFDE). Professor Hartfield-Méndez and I have co-taught the first graduate level community-engagement course through the Laney Graduate School at Emory, which works with other community-partnered research, service, and scholarship ventures organized through Engaged Learning in the CFDE.

Over the last seven years, my academic interests have focused at the intersections of Religion and Ecology and Contemplative Studies, specifically in Christianity and Buddhism. The Religion and Ecology work happily raised my initial alliances with Emory's Environmental Sciences Department to a higher level. Specifically, I began working more closely with Professor Lance Gunderson, an internationally regarded scholar of Environmental Studies and a leading expert of Resilience Theory. In undergraduate and graduate classes, I began to co-teach with Professor Gunderson or by myself, the life systems model called Resilience Theory. That model became the key to my redefinition of burnout as a natural and adaptive phase of ongoing service cycles.

Without necessary periods of breakdown or collapse, life systems cannot reorganize and adapt to continually shifting contexts, resources, and needs. No household is static or stable all the time. Stability is not permanent. Change will happen, but what I learned from Resilience Theory that is even more important is that change enriches system capacities. Though real damage happens, forests burn or species die, a life system cannot maintain its adaptive capacities to recalibrate or redesign. Without failures life systems, including service, ultimately will fail. They lack resilience because they aren't training for it. Imagine trying to stay healthy and strong without working out. When we do our workouts, we're breaking down small portions of our muscles, which urges them to rebuild, to get stronger. Service, to be healthily adaptive and resilient, does this too.

All of us have experienced the truth that service changes. Sometimes the changes come from without the system. Sometimes, they arise within. Many of these changes hurt. They damage. They trigger collapse. But this book tells a new and different story about service collapse; one the embraces it as part of the process of building resilience. The need is *not* to ignore burnout, but to get with it. And to do that, these chapters and their real service stories provide and explain values, tools, and skills for moving into and through burnout as part of cycles of service. You will learn how to work within the rubble of those breakdowns and discover still-available – even newly released – resources for rebuilding service. Burnout offers materials for rekindling our flame for giving back with others.

Cycles of Resilience

As I began connecting Adaptive Resilience Theory with my ongoing search for a truth-telling approach to service and burnout, I agreed to help a friend take a group of urban African-American boys to hike in the mountains. Marianne Skeen, a local and national leader in the Appalachian Trail Conservancy, wrote grants and co-developed this program with a local community-based after school and enrichment program. Our group walked a five-mile trail to the "Len Foote Hike Inn," a backcountry lodge in the foothills of North Georgia. On the way there, we shared many adventures identifying animals, enjoying views, and working to make it to the top. By the later afternoon, we made our destination and unpacked. Meeting in the simple lobby of the Inn, we joined an environmental talk-demonstration by the Hike Inn's Educator.

She showed us the gardens and grounds telling us about the area's plants, animals, and seasons. Then she invited us to follow her into the basement to see how the Hike Inn "recycled." Heading down the stairs, the lead boys hesitated on the bottom steps moaning with loud "uuuugggghhh's" and "ooooooooeeeee's."We jerked to a stop like dominoes up the stairs. Slowly and with many assurances, the Educator got us all into the basement. We gawked at the sight. The boys simultaneously expressed their disgust. The basement floor held 5 wooden beds settled on simple wooden legs. Each approximately 6 feet by 3 feet and about 1 foot deep, they were packed with paper and other debris. Upon closer observation, which the Educator encouraged, we saw *many* active worms. Roiling hordes of them were eating, digesting, and expelling their body waste.The Educator informed us, "These worms produce the best dirt money can buy."

She went on to explain the details of this process while the boys groaned, stepped back, and grabbed at each other. Once expelled from the worms' bodies, paper and other debris became fertilizer for the Inn's vegetable and ornamental gardens. "We're eating that?" one boy nervously asked as others guffawed. The Educator assured us that all food was well washed, but yes, we were eating healthy food born of "that." Now loud protests from the boys filled the room. When I taught experience-driven courses on Religion and Ecology, I heard the same resistances to recognizing breakdown as sources of life reconstructed or changed. The class' exercises of observation, touch, and listening, urged us to engage difference as stories of collapsed possibilities. So, I did not flinch as these boys exclaimed that they would *not* eat *anything* tonight – no matter what! The terrors and marvels of processes of breaking down and rebuilding vividly revealed particular and basic insights of Resilience Theory.

Breakdown and Waste Created Food

Of course, it was not all magic in this worm bed of roses. Even there, worms get sick. They die. They get poisoned by inks and other unrecognized toxins. Sometimes the collapses are unexpected and alternate next phases emerge.That particular worm bed can adapt and recover. Sometimes not. Some nights the staff forgets to turn the beds leading to more serious problems.Yet amid the range of flux and flow, the beds, overall, do their amazingly reliable resilient work. And when one fails, there's learning to be had, which informs another stage of best practices.

Later that night in my bunk musing over what we had seen and learned, I thought about a recent conversation I had shared with my father. In his early eighties, then, he was suffering with age-onset depression. The struggle had taken its toll, and though he could make jokes about the irony of a psychiatrist *experiencing* depression, not just treating it, days and nights were hard. His second wife, Rosemary, a former psychiatric nurse, shaped a daily schedule for him providing activity and structure. Typically, people living with depression benefit from this. Understandably at times, Dad resented and resisted the structure. But Rosemary kept up the heat, for which I was grateful. More than once during my visits he turned to me scowling as Rosemary called from another room insisting he go out and get the paper, or get on the treadmill, or feed the cat. He verbally resisted, "In a minute"; "OK, soon." Eventually, she would explode and with lively off-color language tell him to get up and get going. At that point, he would turn to me with his eyes almost twinkling, something we longed to see. And he would whisper to me, "She's keeping me in reality. So, I get up off my butt and go."

Burnout is a normal phase in cycles of service. The breaking down work of those worm beds ain't that pretty in process, but the next phases produce materials and energy-transferred food for gardens. So too for service. All the pieces come together and hum – for a while. Then something wavers, additional break downs occur. We and our work get thrown into shattered and seared stuff, collapsed budgets, broken relationships, our own exhaustion. Before this book, this phase signaled failure, the end of service, no options. Here's another perspective: move into the searing and shattering to discover alternative choices. If we reject this approach, breakdowns will eventually destroy service as we knew it. We will burn out, but not because we were "bad." We burn out because we denied burnout is real. We resisted living with and through it to reorganize, rebuild, or discern what we needed to alter, reorganize, or let go. This book teaches why, when, and how to develop the values, tools, and skills that keep service resilient and thriving.

Notes

1 To understand the differences that an asset-based approach can make in community-engaged partnerships, see Kretzmann and McKnight, *Building Communities from the Inside Out*. The charts found on pages 34, 43, and 44 highlight assets that particular community groups bring to community change work. Often these contributions and forms of leadership go overlooked or ignored.
2 Thuesen, "The Logic of Mainline Churches," 34. For many Protestants, this perfection mirrored Christ's actions, sacrificing on behalf of others.
3 Ibid, 33.
4 Oxford College is the original Emory campus and now offers two-year Associates degrees as part of the Emory University system.

References

Kretzmann, John P. and John L. McKnight. *Building Communities from the Inside Out: A Path toward Finding and Mobilizing A Community's Assets.* Chicago, IL: ACTA Publications, 1993.
Thuesen, Peter J. "The Logic of Mainline Churchliness: Historical Background since the Reformation" in *The Quiet Hand of God: Faith-Based Activism and the Public Role of Mainline Protestantism*, edited by Robert Wuthnow and John H. Evans. Berkeley, CA: University of California Press, 2002.

Chapter 1

Rewriting the Story of Service and Burnout

When I slowly returned to service after my scrape with burnout, I decided to gather stories from others who had similar experiences: what it felt like; what people thought about it and themselves; who they told and how they described it; and where their burnout experiences took them. I want to know more about what happened to me. I held no illusions. I knew their stories might provide cover for burnout. They might call it something else. Some did. Some did not. But all of their stories took me in a direction I had not fully expected. They confirmed that I now needed to tell a different story of service, one that included burnout.

Meanwhile, my faculty responsibilities expanded to include working with graduate students. Three smart and creative students who took an American religious cultures seminar I taught asked me and a colleague from the Environmental Sciences Department at Emory, Lance Gunderson, to co-teach a class on religion and ecology the following semester. A dabbler in these fields due to my own love of being outdoors, I relied fully on Lance Gunderson, an internationally recognized ecologist. It was during this seminar (and a follow-up course) that Lance introduced us to Adaptive Resilience Theory (ART), a life and social systems model that became central to my work on burnout.

From an ART perspective, system collapse or breakdown is a crucial phase for long-term thriving.[1] All healthy life and social systems cycle through phases. One necessary phase for building resilience is collapse, and for our purposes here, burnout. From a very basic Adaptive Resilience perspective, a single cycle of a life or social system is composed of four phases: *stability, collapse, reorganization*, and *exploitation*. Systems go through many such cycles. Sometimes phases veer from their usual order. The theory began in case study data and continues refining itself through actual examples. These clarify and demonstrate how, when, and why each phase fosters aspects of adaptive change. Specifically, the collapse phase, burnout, cracks open previously untapped, even trapped or ignored, materials and energies. The breaking down or apart offers the system a kind of test. Is it resilient enough to conjure next steps, or new or revised configurations? ART views collapse as possible, released creative potential, the stuff of resilience. Continual stability eventually weakens a system's adaptive capacities. Healthy systems require these disturbance phases. See the basic model in Figure 1.1.

To translate this to service, burnout is a naturally occurring phase of an adaptive and resilient service system. Not a sign of linear no-return failure, burnout's painful pressures release potential for transformative reorganization. Tough times, even collapse, contribute to resilient thriving. Hard to imagine, right? When all hell is breaking loose, useful stuff does too? Yes. The pain and struggle still sears. The system's

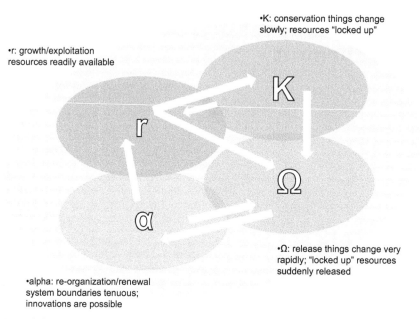

•K: conservation things change slowly; resources "locked up"

•r: growth/exploitation resources readily available

•Ω: release things change very rapidly; "locked up" resources suddenly released

•alpha: re-organization/renewal system boundaries tenuous; innovations are possible

Figure 1.1 Resilience Model. From *Panarchy*, edited by Lance Gunderson and C. S. Holling, Figure 2-1, 34. Copyright 2002 Island Press. Reproduced by permission of Island Press, Washington DC.

meltdown causes real problems. But, if we can keep our heads, bodies, and hearts from only flailing or fleeing, we'll discover untapped or reconfigured resources. Burnout's potential plummets if we cannot value the change that birthed them.

Stability is *not* the only sweet spot of service. Resilience approaches highlight that we can't know precisely how or what kind of adaptive states might emerge after a breakdown. But while in it, we can learn to trust and support the process, ourselves, and our service partners and communities. To stick with a resilience approach requires honesty and trust at every level of the system. That trust can help us settle into what's actually happening with serious interest, even kindness, rather than panic. The principles and practices in this book explain how to embrace this approach and its work. We can choose to rebuild while rooted in difficult realities. We do not have to panic or judge ourselves or others, but we need resources for that work. This book finds them in the principles and practices of contemplative traditions in forms that anyone can embrace, secularized forms. Much more about this in the next chapter.

The following two case studies, one more general and one more detailed, demonstrate how, when, and why an adaptive resilience approach works and how contemplative values and actions contribute.

A General Case Study

Let's imagine we live in a community with a growing population of people struggling to survive without shelter. A group of us decide to open a soup kitchen to provide one healthy meal a day, five days a week. We feel conflicted, but responsibilities for seven days a week overwhelm us. The response is strong from other community groups including several willing to offer space and kitchens. After a number of months, we begin to serve and get to know people facing homelessness. Steadily, the numbers grow and we reconfigure our work to meet the demand. As relationships deepen, we feel we cannot ignore other service needs, especially lack of basic toiletries and clean clothes. So, we open a small clothes closet and begin collecting soap, shampoo, and toothpaste from local volunteer service organizations, Kiwanis Club, Rotary, etc. Initially, the good people bringing these items also help us organize our distribution area. But within months their number wanes. Donations continue to roll in, but no one consistently restocks the shelves or hands out the goods. We worry about this, but have no answers. We're all working at the max. Even as some pitch in extra hours to help stock this area, pressures mount. One core volunteer leaves. Others are starting to burn out.

Still working from the old model of service with its straight-line growth, we expect demand will only escalate. We worry that our commitment will not match the demand. We need more volunteers. And volunteers who will stick. To use a natural systems analogy, our service to people without shelter began as an open field with lots of potential. Soon, what we cultivated in that field did so well, we planted a few other things. Meanwhile, other plants simply arrived by natural selection. The natural trend suggests ongoing growth. But in fact, natural systems do not just keep exploding and expanding. At some point, the system will be stretched beyond its capacities. Or a natural disaster, a forest fire, will hit. The system will be derailed from ongoing growth. It will have to adapt, find other strategies for thriving. We believed otherwise. We believed not only that we could just keep expanding, but also that we *should*. Of course, we could not match the steady growth.

If we had known about and embraced a resilience approach, we would have seen a very different picture. Even at the first signals of breakdown, we would pause to assess. The number of volunteers is going down. A few people are burning out and leaving. Time to be honest. Our service is outstripping our capacity. Of course, even using the old model, smart service directors might try to pace growth of service. But growth remains a good and expected thing. So, even if you're slowing down, keep growing. A resilience approach stays in reality. Periods of steady stability, including ongoing growth, will eventually hit a collapsing point. So, what to do that fosters adaptation? You could convene a conversation with all the stakeholders including guests, local neighbors, volunteer supporters, and involved city officials.

The agenda of such a gathering: face our limits, recognize our emerging breakdown. Then the questions make sense because they're rooted in reality. Can we draw more from the volunteers and staff we have? Can we recruit new volunteers – enough of them? How much pressure can the space tolerate? How will we keep the supply of toiletries and clothes going up? With these questions on the table a range of options emerge – again, rooted in reality. Is it time to limit our service? Is it time to temporarily stop and rethink our model? Do we terminate service completely or can a downsized program go on? Do we need additional experts, new construction, better funding approaches? All of these recognize that collapse is emerging, but at this point, it has not flipped the system into full-on burnout. Real choices await.

This story of service does not assume that we can do whatever service asks of us. This narrative embraces values of giving, but it is not a moral tale of unending selfless dedication to the point of collapse. Resilient service assumes that our service system will not continue as is. Something will trigger a reversal, a blow-out, a stop. We will burn out; and likely you've experienced this painful reality. Likely, you've lived this story and the counterintuitive old approach of denying or turning our backs on impending collapse. We choose the fantasy of limitless capacity and disturbingly with a semi-righteous tone. Pressures build. Programs and people break down. Burnout.

From a resilience perspective, our soup kitchen can re-learn service as including burnout. We can adapt instead of linearly pressing forward no matter what. Now's the time to learn from the smaller collapses and alter our goals and actions. We can build adaptive responses focusing on the interplay of change and persistence, unpredictability and predictability.[2] These are next steps, but of a new kind compared to the old endless trudge forward when times are bad. When we deny burnout, we cork the flows of adaptive capacity building, and our service systems and our lives turn brittle and unresponsive. We need service and burnout systems that can "experience wide change and still maintain the integrity of their functions."[3] Working many different factors and operating over several different scales (both spatial and temporal), we can learn that breakdowns generate different adaptive cycles.[4] We can give up the old story and discover alternative approaches to offering services to people living without homes.

With this adaptive resilience lens changing how I viewed service and burnout. I dove into more case studies of life systems adapting after crises.[5] Those narratives expanded the range of factors contributing to burnout. Sometimes, our emotional wiring is so over-stretched that it breaks loose and so does all hell. Other times, the work disintegrates because translations of local needs fall on deaf ears at state or regional levels. Burnout can arise from team tensions, an inability to get on the same page or to positively leverage real differences among team members. People get to the same destination from multiple angles. Burnout corners that diversity instead of treasuring it. In other cases, space issues alone can collapse good work.

The case studies taught me to pay more attention to details, those tell-tale signs of impending burnout or barely glowing resources amid the rubble of collapse. So often, we're drawn to the dramatic blow-ups of service burnout. But it's often at the finer levels of service strain that we discover the linchpin pieces that do not require a lot of work to begin rebuilding. For example, in an elder services setting, tensions between volunteer medical students and full-time staff continued to escalate. What was triggering the slowly growing failure of a program that originally had more volunteers than needed and now struggled to find help? The details reveal a small but very sore spot: outdated forms and too many of them. The students said nothing because they did not want to disrespect the staff who seemed utterly wedded to those forms. The staff didn't even recognize that the forms were an issue. They just saw the number of volunteers dwindling, which meant fewer volunteers becoming irritated filling out more and more antiquated forms! In a good effort to just keep going, the old story, burnout, grew – though unnamed. Once we finally found the issue, buried in the glowing coals of burnout, we began to reorganize and go forward.

Other cases of burnout are much tougher to move through. They remind me of what ART calls a systems flip. When a collapse overwhelms a life or service system, it can literally flip. An example is a section of the Everglades shifting from salt to fresh water. Usually, some massive disturbance is required to set off a flip, such as a hurricane or a major human-generated event, like construction of an entirely new sub-division nearby. Such serious upside-downing of our service world changes everything. My burning skin, for example, signaled a system flip for me. Service felt out of the question, out of the picture. But in ART, even something as dramatically altering as a flip is not without next steps needed for system survival. Change is dramatic, but the Everglades are still there. Even flipped systems experiment with and reconstitute their way back to stability.

A More Detailed Case Study

These are simpler examples. How does ART work in more complex situations? Here's a service story.

A professional psychotherapist volunteers weekly to lead an education and sharing group for Latina battered women. Two years into this service, she notices she feels uneasy and irritable about twenty-four hours before the weekly meeting. What's the issue? A few come quickly to mind: the weight of the women's pain, their daily struggles to find work and deal with anti-immigrant attitudes, and the tricky negotiations to integrate newcomers with those who regularly attend. Then there's the local government officials who want to develop the run-down shopping center where this group meets in a storefront space. She knows this will lead to further gentrification of the area, a very mixed bag of opportunity and exclusion.

These challenges bothered her, but she doubted they were the source of her unease. One week, about two hours before group, a phone call came, and the pieces of her puzzle fell into place. The paid babysitter who cared for the women's children during the meetings cancelled *again*. The psychotherapist understood the reasons. The sitter's own children were sick. Her car wouldn't start. Her other part-time employer who paid better needed her. The time the psychotherapist set aside to plan the group's work that night was hijacked by this emergency. This frustrated her, especially that the pattern kept repeating itself. The psychotherapist now realized that every week, as she settled into final planning for the evening, she also began to dread that the phone would ring. No babysitter. Extra work to do. That dread began creeping into a grey irritability that she took to the group each week. She tried to hide it. She had been leading the group a long time. How could she stop now?

Using the old story, the psychotherapist would assume it's OK to notice frustration and unhappiness around the babysitter issues, but the service must go on. The group work matters most. The women cannot be let down. Knowing this script heightened the therapist's internal conflict. But let's shift the lens and see where the story goes. A first step recognizes that the feelings and conflicted thoughts, as well as the additional work, signal a phase change. As she felt herself moving towards the edge of service-ending despair and anger, she could have asked more questions. She could have avoided flipping into full-bore denial with an eventual dead-end in burnout. A resilience strategy keeps asking questions rather forming pre-emptive conclusions. Did having to find a last-minute babysitter really detract from her session preparations? Yes. Had her growing resentment eaten away her joy and commitment? Yes. With more honesty, the therapist is learning the content of her next steps. And that content builds from the recognized reality that things are not working like they need to – for her and for the group.

Note that this resilience approach does not erase frustrations. Even with more honesty about the breakdown, the therapist faces tough decisions and extra work. But the very different approach of ART through breakdowns instead of avoiding them relieves some of the self-condemnation that only makes things worse. The emphasis is on investigation, not blame. The work shifts to discovery rather than cover-up. Even termination of the group counts as a possible reorganizing step. Reality counts more than a fantasized story of service that does not, cannot quit. Experience with ART shows that this honesty frees up more mental space and less energy wasted on placing blame. Resilience expands options, which can become quite concrete. For instance, when the babysitter for the program calls to cancel, that's just reality – not blameworthy or denial-worthy. The therapist can choose in that expanded space to put the phone down and wait. Breathing instead of pretending. Accept the trouble as it is. It's part of the process.

A classic contemplative phrase puts it this way, "Don't just do something; sit there." Take in what's happening without needing to fix, resist, or grab it. It all takes practice and those practices are described in this book. Resilience builds from reality, including burnout. It does not tell an either-or, dead-ending story of service. If your shoulders start to crank up as you realize burnout is at work, it's good to notice. They've probably responded like that for a while. Yes, move towards the burnout rather than deny or avoid it. That's where service has gone. That's the phase you're in. But it's not a dead-end, though it may be very painful, as I found out. Insight, and sometimes even the insight to stop the work arises at this point, which can feel like ruination at that moment.

Accusations against self and/or others comes rushing in along with escape plans, bartering with the future, and other avoidance strategies. Sharon Salzburg, a well-known and expert contemplative teacher, encourages us to let all that arise while we keep breathing. When your attention wants to run from the debris to strategies for getting out of it, pause and bring yourself back to what is: the babysitter keeps canceling which upsets the therapist. The emphasis in resilience is generosity in the face of reality. It takes practice. But if we stick with this response, like sticking with any other good regime, our capacities to be adaptive grow. Burnout will occur but we won't be cornered and stymied. Hurt, singed, and mad, yes, but still resilient. We gain strength to look for opportunities rooted in altruistic understanding and rebuilding.[6] Let's imagine the psychotherapist used an adaptive approach, and in that pausing decided to ask the program director for an appointment.

Hearing her out, the director asked a few questions to clarify details. Surprising the therapist, the director suggested she bring the problem to the group. Initially, the therapist resisted that strategy, feeling the group members were already dealing with too much. Her problems did not count as much. The director got curious about her response. "That seems pretty one-sided to me. Do *you* know their capacities better than they do?" Care-taking plays no role in reorganization. Compassion does, but compassion depends on honest back and forth conversation. The therapist was reading minds and choosing self-denial. Truth-telling helps when moving through burnout because the truth opens up what needs changing or adaptation. The director asked pointedly, "So what will help your present situation? Continuing to hide your distress? Pretending the chaos inside doesn't matter?" The two sat in silence. Then, the director added, "I suggest taking your problem to the whole group as a next step. They have stakes too, including stakes in you. How about letting go of the self-sacrificing. Invite them in to the disruption you feel."

It took a second conversation with the director for the therapist to buy into this plan – what the therapist kept calling such a silly and small issue. When she did take it to the group, however, they listened carefully and asked a few questions. Then they dove into problem-solving mode. If the situation wasn't working for the therapist, then it wasn't working for them. All angles were on the table. The therapist now realized how adept the women were at improvisation, something they did every day! The women developed a plan and by the end of the evening, it was complete. They worked through what the therapist was dealing with and came up with a solution. Several group members volunteered to reach out to people from their neighborhoods and churches asking if anyone wanted this babysitting work.

The response was heartening. Younger women without families jumped at the opportunity, even though the pay rate was low. It was better than no job at all. Two long-standing members of the group agreed to serve as liaisons with the selected new employee, offering instructions and support. Following a private conversation with the current child-care worker, another group member reported that the worker actually wanted to leave the job. She'd stayed quiet because she did not want to disappoint her friends in the group. But she had found a better job with higher pay. She did not know how to leave. Breakdowns can help us practice telling truths. Yet, the first few weeks are anxious and difficult – at least, typically. Yes, children had to adjust to the new babysitter. Of course, mothers had to step out of the group a few times to help. But within a few weeks, the program's stability was returning. The therapist felt relieved. She had more energy for the group work. Burnout, it turned out, was not fatal; though it was very difficult and time-demanding.

What We Can't Bear to Know

So, what keeps us stuck in the old model? Traditional responses come quickly; pride, self-justification, fear of failure. You know the list. The titles of each chapter in this book reflect the phrases we usually think, say, or do, to keep us linked to the old non-resilient model of service. They go by the names: all up to me, willfulness, take it all in (no healthy boundaries), keep on (no matter what), and not naming the truth. They are non-resilient, distorted principles, which keep us trapped in the old script and stuck on a linear line to service-ending pain. But it's hard to let go of these values. They run deep. I remember, for example, times when a service colleague asked me if I might be burning out. What a blow! How embarrassed I felt to be failing at what I loved doing. I could not hear it. I cut them short. But now, we must break that taboo. End the old script.

It's hard work. I remember one young professional who volunteered at a clothing thrift store. Every Saturday as we opened the shop, he arrived. When we began discussing store-related difficulties and how they stressed us, he disappeared. Usually, we could find him in the store's supply closet, which he retreated to. He must have rearranged it uncountable times. Even just talk about service tensions made him flee. We weren't honest with each other. We were just venting. No one ever thought about leaving the old model. We were just anxiously talking. But his need to hold on to the myth of service without boundaries overruled everything. So, he resorted to restacking coat hangers, reorganizing bins of mannequin body parts, folding cleaning cloths, and on. What's your strategy for avoiding service tensions and talking honestly about burnout at whatever level?

You'll find your strategies in this book. Here's some I think you'll recognize in shortened versions. More details about these strategies can be found in the upcoming chapters.

Keep Going to Avoid Self-Judgment

Keeping burnout at arms-length or tightly muzzled is full-time work. The well-worn strategy of denial works because the stigmas of failure and lack of dedication are too heavy to bear. Much of this is due to self-judging. We want to avoid that and we feel that people who give up on service deserve judgment. Believing we should keep going no matter what, we silence any thoughts of limits or recognition of mis-matched intentions and goals. Questions, alterations, doubts; these all deserve judgment. The committed do not ask such questions. To ask them is to be without dedication, to be unreliable. On the page, this feels silly. Why judge yourself? But the fear of admitting burnout at any level quickly translates into letting others down, not following through, lacking dedication. Self-judgment is powerful, enough to keep us in denial. How do you judge yourself? When do you take the blame without deserving it? How's it working?

Keep Going by Shifting Blame to Others – Kindly, of Course

Another burnout denial strategy is to point out others' burnout, and their failure to serve. We deflect our frustrations and exhaustion by focusing on their inadequacies: the way they drop the ball, their lame excuses for missing work sessions, and so on. Ever heard someone who regularly critiques other team members' commitments? They spend more time talking about "them" than about the real pushes and pulls of their service. We should perk up and notice when someone – or ourselves – talks mostly about how *they* are failing to serve. Often, we point to others when we can't face our own growing burnout. The only thing that makes this worse is blame-shifting done sweetly. Those sugar-coated words that nauseate, "You've been such a great tutor for so long with us, I know you'll keep coming despite your job change." Or that slight sweet suggestion that you've missed the mark. "Oh, leaving a little early today?" Has this been done to you? Have you done it to others, out of fear of naming burnout?

Struggling for Control

A final common strategy for denying burnout – there are many more and you'll find them later in the book – works by feeling in control. Never admitting confusion. You precisely and completely fulfill each duty. And you make sure others precisely and completely fulfill each duty. Such hyper-accounting distracts us from the uncontrollable aspects of service, which are always there. Unfortunately, it's a no-win game. Life is service and life brings ongoing unpredictability and loss of control. So, the main outcome of this strategy is driving our teammates crazy due to our rigid regulations. We all need lines of authority and expectation, policies and procedures. But this is a tight-fisted holding onto a service reality that is only an illusion. But it makes us feel temporarily safe, invulnerable to burnout. In control. We are not.

There are more denial strategies, of course. They feed off the distorted principles that are rejected and reworked in this book. They urge us into practices that only woo us into impossible corners of burnout, which eventually undo the work we love and us. Think of your own list of denial strategies, those ways you feed your narrative of unlimited, always-stable service. Post the list where you will regularly see it. It's seductive. Those assumptions only drive you away from the work you love. This book teaches new approaches for recognizing and working with failed and fulfilling service using a resilience approach.

Strategies for Failure and Fulfillment

During this time of reframing burnout in a resilience model, my husband and I took a trip with friends to Bolivia and Peru. We flew into La Paz, the capital city, around 9 p.m. Expecting to stay two days in La Paz to acclimate to the high altitudes, we looked forward to sightseeing in that amazing city after a good night's sleep. Arriving straight from the airport, our main goal was a hot shower and bed. Our group entered the lobby of our small urban hotel and several of us drifted from the check-in process toward a huddle of men and women gathered around the lobby's coffee table and couches. Professional-looking bags of climbing gear sat piled to their left. One man, later identified as their local mountaineering guide, claimed their group's full attention. He described the best routes for their Andean mountain climb, which would begin the next morning. He specifically strategized about changing weather conditions and trail options to avoid avalanches. Then, the guide turned to each climber asking for details about individuals' technical skills and weaknesses.

Going around the table, each one named a competency and a short-coming: solid with an ice axe, not great on snowshoes; able to carry extra weight, terrible at map reading in snowfall, and on. Some had experience with medical emergencies. Others felt uncomfortable when solo rappelling. The listing of skills and shortfalls mesmerized and impressed us. But we drew back in confusion when they began discussing strategies for abandoning the climb. Their approach included preparation for breakdowns – even the most radical. They *planned* for disaster. They listed people's skills and shortcomings. They seriously discussed mission abortion, playing out scenarios of failure at different altitudes and for various reasons. Their discussion addressed different levels and scales. They did not intend to abandon their goals – though they would do that if necessary – but redesigning them on the spot based on their planning now. They prepared for failures. They embraced adaptation.

The lesson hit home. Expecting failures, they prepared several choices based on their team's strengths and weakness, a household adaptive approach. They identified shared values: team first, no ego, willfulness gets in the way, think smart, go with the instability (that's reality) and name the unnamed – fear, regret, over-ambition. How different from most introductions to service programs. In our service orientations, we usually resent gift-wrapped packages of happy anticipation tied together with silly bows called something like "tips for success." These orientation sessions ignore real-world pitfalls and keep volunteers generally ignorant of typical problems. Most service orientations lean toward a fantasized map or story of the work preparing us for what "should" happen. The problem with our usual service story is that we do not know what will happen.

Real Maps of Service and Burnout: Values and Tools

Let's reimagine a service team strategizing ways to make it through service that will – like all service – fall apart or disintegrate. What would happen if each of us shared a personal inventory of strengths and weaknesses? Would that make a positive difference when breakdowns came? Stepping into my first lessons in the power of realistic team inventories came after a major fall or breakdown of a service program I directed.

A wealthy religious community interested in social action agreed to house the city's first Meals on Wheels program providing midday hot meals to registered clients. Local social service offices gave us the names and addresses. We made mistakes continually, but after four months, we were rolling along, except for one thing. Storms brewed in the kitchen. The program grew exponentially and the over-subscription of meals stretched our capacities. We responded by digging in our heels and pushing forward. Soon we needed more bodies at every level of the work from meal planning to food buying, cooking, packaging, delivering, and clean-up. The tipping point involved the clean-up. Most volunteers signed up for the earlier jobs, and we needed every one of them. By the end of the day, the religious community's kitchen staff stood alone amid a mess of pots, utensils, and general debris. Already juggling too many requests for their own institution's meals and program snack, the staff asked their boss to talk with me, the young program coordinator.

"It's over," the boss said. "Either your folks clean, or our cooperation with this program is done." I nodded and said nothing. I left the conversation with no reorganizational ideas in my head. I slithered back to my cubicle and tried to jot down a few ideas – not much luck. The next day, the Rabbi in charge of social programs came to reinforce the kitchen boss' point. I promised we'd do better. He conveyed the message to the kitchen staff; and, we kind of did better for a while. But soon, they stood alone again facing a mound of work. As the kitchen staff's good will eroded, so did our initial organization of volunteers. More people began dropping their duties. Breakdowns in communication increased. People just didn't show up. We could not plan fast enough to cover the gaps. Soon our Meals on Wheels were zigging and zagging through the day like a stone-wheel cart. Everyone began smoldering, some with anger, others with embarrassment, and still others with irritable confusion. What had been a small spark began to catch.

What else might we have done? My mind goes to the climbers. For starters, we never discussed the priorities of our work. We privileged feeding people over staffing considerations. We chose cooking as more important than cleaning. No wonder our increasing numbers, and scale, overwhelmed us. We had no agreement about our service area or constituencies. When a social service group called, we simply took down the names and addresses. We had no inventory of needed tasks. As teenagers – well, some teenagers might, but not most! – we left "clean up" off the list of tasks. We never held a serious discussion about that. So, our already thin inventory of needs and skills did not address clean up. Our future was unsustainable with no adaptive resilience.

The organizational level's lack of inventories tied to our goals and capacities mirrored a lack of personal inventories as well. Who did what well and with enjoyment? What did that same person *not* want to do or *did not* do well? Matching skills and interests to our goals went lacking. No serious climbing team would do that. Now we were stuck with an avalanche already too close to stop. In fact, we had to temporarily shut down the program while we reworked our goals and capacities from top to bottom. The kitchen staff became a core planning partner. Our better-late-than-never response helped, but the program's original misalignment continued to play out on smaller levels.

For the sake of this book, let's imagine a different story. What if every volunteer – let's start at that level – was asked to fill in a personal service inventory as a first step in matching individuals' capacities and expectations with the organization's goals, objectives, and resources. An inventory can be as narrow or as broad as an organization needs it to me. It should highlight areas where skills and temperaments are needed. This inventory tool can be used at other levels of a program, but we'll stick to those who we magically hoped would just stay longer and work harder cleaning up. I'll offer a general description and also use myself as an example of a volunteer. I'll admit how startled I feel each time I fill out a personal inventory. To honestly claim my strengths and weaknesses, interests and disinterests, highlights the power of the old either-or narrative. Resisting the barrage of oughts and shoulds takes all the energy I can muster. It's hard to tell the fuller truth about me and service. No wonder I burned out.

Making an Inventory

Anyone can draw the grid for a personal service inventory. Take a piece of paper and put your pencil about two inches to the right of the paper's left edge. Draw your pencil straight down from the top of the page to the bottom. Now draw a second line about three inches to the right of your first line, top to bottom of the page. Keep drawing these lines down until you have five columns. Give a name to each column, writing at the top of it: "tasks," "materials," "emotions," "interests," and "teamwork." "Tasks" indicates the basic and often repeated service activities most settings require: work with people, write reports, develop programs, listen, talk – you get the idea. "Materials" involves the stuff needed to serve, what materials we work with: clothing, food, healthcare materials, bus tokens or money, certificates, etc. If you're allergic to or not comfortable with certain materials, here's the place to note that. "Emotions" is the place we write down the range of feelings and responses we associate with serving in a particular setting. "Interests" signals what and/or who keeps you coming back to service. Is it people in a certain age group, particular experiences you enjoy, talents you bring, or what? And finally, with "teamwork," think narrowly and broadly. What do you enjoy about teamwork? What do you expect from team members? What makes you nuts about teamwork? Do you prefer shorter or longer projects with teams?

Now, at the mid-point of the page, draw a line from left to right, splitting the page in half. The top half is labelled "strengths." The bottom half is labelled "weaknesses."

Think of this in the way the climbers did, not as a condemnation, but as an honest assessment that can help the team step in for support and/or decide against work that puts the group in a vulnerable position.

Tables 1.1 and 1.2 show that inventory filled in – just as examples. The lists of strengths under each column signal an ideal experience; probably no one's reality. The lists of weaknesses function in a similar conversation-starting way. As examples given to volunteers or people interviewing for service positions, these two inventories can raise helpful questions and support honest discussions about limits and gaps amid expectations. Having seen this overly optimistic example of strengths, for example, volunteers and potential staff members can fill in their own inventories of strengths and weaknesses. These exercises help serving people more realistically name and assess expectations of themselves and others. Preferences and dislikes, as well as self-admitted weaknesses can be reflected upon. When teams share more of this self-reflective work over time, they can better calculate capacities for sustained involvement in the work. They benefit from noticing how their inventories shift over time and with additional experiences.

Table 1.1 Strengths

Tasks	Materials	Emotions	Interests	Team Expectations
• **Organize cleaning** • **Clean** • **Dry** • **Put away** • **Tidy up kitchen**	• Clean-up materials provided by Kitchen Staff	• Enjoy cleaning and straightening • Happy to stay at center • Fulfillment seeing team end the day's work well	• Finishing the job of this important work • Creating smooth-working team for clean-up • Develop a team that sticks, keeps coming	• Shared commitment • Ready response to problems • Share the load • Positive environment: the work matters

Table 1.2 Weaknesses

Tasks	Materials	Emotions	Interests	Team Expectations
• **Clean-Up Team**	• Labor: gone missing • Organization of work: gone missing	• Dread or resistance • Frustration or disappointment if others do not show up • Embarrassment if fail kitchen staff	• Lose energy or interest for as time goes by • Face waning interest: no glamour at this stage of process • Not interested in trying to force or shame adults into action	• If tired, team matters less • Worry about how to handle the need to miss a day – feel others' pressures: don't know how to talk about this

Meals on Wheels Program Level Inventory – Focus on Clean-Up

Pragmatically then, inventories encourage more realistic looks at volunteers' strengths and weaknesses, their capacities and limits, as they imagine doing this job. To create these examples, the staff spent time talking over the various categories and fine tuning what they could imagine going in each of them. This reflective work ought to signal edges of resilient service and seeds of burnout. Imagine what a staff would learn about their goals and objectives as well as their expectations and concrete needs if they offered "sample" inventories like these to incoming volunteers or potential staff.

To compile a personal inventory for work with this service organization would require taking the imagined strengths and weakness they expect and seeing how your personal strengths and weaknesses do or do not fit into the picture. Be honest. What would make you leave or stay? What would burn you out or help you thrive? Get into the nitty gritty. Think of real examples. Sometimes it really is the little things that do us in. It makes me crazy when I can't find something to write with! Other times, the big things get our goat. Whatever gets you going in service or pulls you up short, learn to share that honestly with members of your team and your boss or supervisor. We all have strengths and weaknesses. Own them.

As noted earlier, no inventory is permanent. If you return to an inventory in the midst of a service experience, you may discover that your attitudes or needs have changed. A skill you did not recognize may have showed up. Do you want to mature it? The more I work with inventories, the less my self-condemnation button gets pushed. I'm claiming what I need and trying to match that with what an organization needs and gives. If I'm having trouble knowing what I'm thinking or feeling in a service setting I turn back to my inventory. A key work as I ask myself about each category is "*because*." It helps me get unstuck from generalized feelings or thoughts. Keep pressing toward the very specifics: I cannot find a pen!

Of course, the headings of each column are utterly flexible. When working in a setting over time, I change the headings. It gives me additional perspectives on my work and my team. In other situations, the chart form just doesn't feel right, so I reflectively write about my experiences or draw. I always include details relevant to burnout, naming points of frustration, disappointment, or where my skills and emotions are lacking. This approach not only boosts my honesty, but also helps me realize that I can count on others in my community for skills and tools, emotions and commitments I cannot or do not want to offer.

The Personal Is Always Communal

As this inventory exercise and other aspects of this chapter make clear, this book focuses a lot on the personal. For some readers, this approach might seem at odds with the communal emphasis of service. I think this tension misses the realities of service as a web of individual and communal partnerships. The old version of service that nixes burnout tends to emphasize the communal. It leaves no room for self-reflection that identifies how, why, and when service thrives for us or not. This approach doesn't deny the communal. The household image will continue to serve as a core example of the interworkings of serving and burning out. Like any life system, service evolves through an interdependent web of resources, actors, and infrastructures that continually shift internally and externally. It takes individuals, communities, and systems to shape adaptive strategies after collapses, resilience involves all levels and scales. But this book starts with the personal, which often gets overlooked because the personal feels self-indulgent.

But learning to know yourself well enough in the ongoing cycle of service and burnout better prepares you for team work. The medieval contemplative Bernard of Clairvaux writes, "We (each) drink from our own wells." This means, know your own resources – and what's lacking. Without that, one can't do the core work of community, which is critical to contemplative life. Bernard's approach deeply influenced the contemporary Peruvian theologian-activist Gustavo Gutiérrez, whose projects of liberatory work in solidarity with the poor transformed lives in need of clean water, housing, and education. Though his writings and work rooted in community-based empowerment, Gutiérrez embraced the necessity of honest and gentle self-understanding. Without self-examination, community-generated knowledge and action goes lacking. Eventually, the household will breakdown because it has no inventory of strengths and weaknesses.

The exercises offered in each chapter for moving into and through burnout's tough times draw on contemplative insights and practices from in Christian and Buddhist contemplative traditions. As noted above, these are reworked to be accessible to all readers. This book welcomes readers with no affiliations to religious of spiritual traditions. It speaks as well to those with broad spiritual interests and those committed to a specific spiritual or religious path. Generally, contemplative traditions embrace a standpoint of interdependence. Conscious of our personal stories, emotions, and contexts, these chapters embrace the contemplative standpoint that all life is interdependent. In our interdependence, personally and in whatever size group or context, the core ethic is love. Not love as sentimentality, the core value here is ethical, rooted in questions of how we live alone and together without harming, with empathy and actions of kindness.

Dorotheos of Gaza, who led a community of Christian contemplatives during the 600s c.e., used the image of a wheel to explain how this interdependent ethic of compassion worked. Drawing on a daily image of their shared life, the wooden wheels of their simple carts, he explained how we are to live in service to others while self-aware. The wheel, like life, continually turns. It goes through phases. It moves. And as it moves, each spoke of the wheel, representing a single monk, engaged its distinctive talents, gifts, and struggles. The rim is the community's shared life based on an ethic of loving service. The wheel runs because of individuals linked in community – interdependent. But interestingly, as each member more deeply embraces the community's approach to life, each one moves closer to the center. That center signals stability, but stability as an ethic – not an expectation of life. Love holds the work together and love is honest in rougher or better times. The wheel keeps moving and changing, like life, like service.

Step by Step

So, the work keeps unfolding step by step, or round by round. What centers the work in that ongoing change is a core ethic of humility and love that treasures diversity and service. So, on that deep blue night when my connections to service shattered, I found myself out of context, out of the service wheel or household I knew. I had no place to go and an experience I could no longer deny. So, I turned to a simple meditation practice I first learned at the Episcopal monastery of The Society of St. John the Evangelist in Cambridge, Massachusetts.[7] I later also studied this practice at the Naropa Institute, a Buddhist University and Center in Boulder, Colorado. Under the canopy of Atlanta's many trees, I walked. My walking meditation headed out into the world I knew but felt disconnected from. I went step by step, just trying to breathe, to be there. I walked by children playing in the parks. Creeks ambled through their crooked paths. Volunteer baseball coaches held practice.

Though I felt empty, the walking put me back in the context of life. It did not go away. The wheel, the household kept turning. Though I felt isolating failure, I was not alone. Though I felt lonely in my pain, the world around me reminded me that suffering is part of all our lives, part of every living system. The simple movement did not erase my burnout. Passing by the homeless woman I knew well, I offered a limp wave. She still sat on her same park bench. She still ate at a local shelter. My collapse did not shift her life or our relationship and the ethic of love that brought us together. The world went on. The after-school programs sponsored by the local community garden continued. They were working in the gardens now. The ending of my work did not stop the wheel of service from turning. What went missing was the wheel of insight that retold service as also a story with burnout.

I needed this inventory into reality, one way of understanding the Buddhist monk, Thich Nhat Hahn's teachings on walking meditation. In his book, *Walking Meditation*, he suggests we head out into the confusions, the rubble, the burnout without having to fix it, shove it away, or grab it. We can be with things as they are. The inventory as it really shows up in our lives. The scorched debris *without* judging, blaming, or refusing the damage. The wheel, my feet on the pavement, kept moving. So does service after burnout when we learn to tell the truth to ourselves and others.

Time to Tell Truer Stories of Service

A few months later, I received an invitation to take part in an interracial worship service: "City-Wide: Celebrate Women of Faith." Annually organized by women of faith who worked in service centers addressing needs of women and children, the service happened in a large church in West Atlanta. As the main service, it called for action. This year's theme was a tough one, "Tell the Truth." There were many truths to tell: the volunteer and financial needs of the high-tech neonatal unit at our mammoth city hospital, Grady; the need for food and clothing to support the recently opened shelter for homeless women and their children; the need for more money to support a redesigned neighborhood after-school program that included a safe place for children to sleep the night if a home had become violent, and more. But the highlighted issue was the radical climb in rates of domestic violence and its effects on families, children, and housing. Our "guest preacher," Chief Beverly Harvard, Atlanta's new Chief of Police, left none of us out of the circle of responsibility.

That morning, the sanctuary overflowed with a wide cross-section of people from Atlanta. When Chief Harvard rose to offer her remarks, she wasted no time. Her bottom line went something like this:

The police force of the City of Atlanta will *not tolerate* violence against women in any form, in any place, or at any time, period. When women are violated, when child-support is not forthcoming, when children and mothers are threatened or abused, when women's public leadership is in jeopardy, we will come, pursue, arrest, and prosecute. The turned-away eyes, the cover-ups, lies, and collusions are finished. Neither class, nor education, nor money will deter us. We will pursue and prosecute the truth of domestic violence's destructive forces.

She verbally drew shocking pictures of blood and bruises and banishment. She provided statistics that broke our bulwarks of denial. She used scripture. She made an "altar call for action." And later that day, I could not get Chief Harvard's simple question out of my head. "Will you tell the truth"? "Will you step forward and tell what is real?" The words punched the devastation of domestic violence. But, for me, they also hit my inability to tell the truth about my burnout in service. Drawing on her clarity and courage, I found myself leaning into a new story of service, one that involves burnout, that leverages collapse for adaptive resilience. But how could that be? I determined I would find out. I would try to tell the truth. I would try to discover paths into and through that truth. I would write this book of principles and practices about service *and* burnout.

Exercises

1. Using different strategies or pathways, service partners may arrive at an agreed-upon goal. When your partner does that, how do you respond? Did your partner's approach feel like a break from your agreements? Instead of *treasuring diversity*, why do you feel burned?

    _____

    _____

    _____

    _____

    _____

    _____

    _____

2. Over the next week, use the format in Table 1.3 to start paying more attention to fissures in your service life. Use the first column to record any tell-tale signs. In the second column take some guesses: is this the start of burnout or are you noting early debris of burning in progress – even if quite small. The last column offers space for musings; maybe next steps? (See page 6)

Table 1.3

Early Signs of Burnout	Stronger Burnout Signs?	Next Steps You Can Take

3. When did you intervene to pre-empt additional service breakdown by fixing a conflict or problem, rather than investigate it trusting in the capacities of those involved? (See pages 10–11)

_____

_____

_____

_____

_____

_____

4. With a specific service team in mind, though this format can be used generally, fill in a Personal Service Inventory (Table 1.4). Read what you wrote. Honest enough? Detailed enough? Any surprises, even small ones? What would your team learn about you and your shared service?

Table 1.4

Strengths:				
Tasks	Materials	Emotions	Interests	Team Expectations
_____	_____	_____	_____	_____
_____	_____	_____	_____	_____
_____	_____	_____	_____	_____
_____	_____	_____	_____	_____
_____	_____	_____	_____	_____
_____	_____	_____	_____	_____
_____	_____	_____	_____	_____
_____	_____	_____	_____	_____

Weaknesses:				
Tasks	Materials	Emotions	Interests	Team Expectations
_____	_____	_____	_____	_____
_____	_____	_____	_____	_____
_____	_____	_____	_____	_____
_____	_____	_____	_____	_____
_____	_____	_____	_____	_____
_____	_____	_____	_____	_____
_____	_____	_____	_____	_____

Figures

From *Panarchy,* edited by Lance Gunderson and C.S. Holling, Figure 2–1, 34. Copyright 2002 Island Press. Reproduced by permission of Island Press, Washington, DC. Holling, C.S., Lance H. and Gunderson. "Resilience and Adaptive Cycles." In *Panarchy: Understanding Transformations in Human and Natural Systems*, edited by Lance H. Gunderson and C.S. Holling, 25–62. Washington, DC: Island Press, 2002.

Notes

1 See Walker and Salt, *Resilience Thinking*, 2006, Walker and Salt, *Resilience Practice*, 2012, Tidball and Krasny, *Greening in the Red Zone*, 2014, Krasny and Tidball, 2015.

2 Holling, Gunderson, and Ludwig, "In Quest of a Theory of Adaptive Change," 5.

3 Ibid, 5.

4 Holling, Gunderson, and Peterson, "Sustainability and Panarchies," 74.

5 See Walker and Salt, *Resilience Thinking*, 2006, Walker and Salt, *Resilience Practice*, 2012, Tidball and Krasny, *Greening in the Red Zone*, 2014, Krasny and Tidball, 2015, Gunderson and Holling, 2002.

6 Ricard, *Altruism.*

7 See https://www.ssje.org

References

Gunderson, Lance H. and C. S. Holling, eds. *Panarchy: Understanding Transformations in Human and Natural Systems.* Washington, DC: Island Press, 2002.

Holling, C. S., Lance H. Gunderson, and Donald Ludwig. "In Quest of a Theory of Adaptive Change." In *Panarchy: Understanding Transformations in Human and Natural Systems*, edited by Lance H. Gunderson and C. S. Holling, 3–24. Washington, DC: Island Press, 2002.

Holling, C. S., Lance H. Gunderson, and Garry D. Peterson. "Sustainability and Panarchies." In *Panarchy: Understanding Transformations in Human and Natural Systems*, edited by Lance H. Gunderson and C. S. Holling, 63–102. Washington, DC: Island Press, 2002.

Krasny, Marianne E. and Keith G. Tidball. *Civic Ecology: Adaptation and Transformation from the Ground Up.* Boston, MA: The MIT Press, 2015.

Nhat Hanh, Thich and Anh-Huong Nguyen. *Walking Meditation: Peace Is Every Step. It Turns the Endless Path to Joy.* Boulder, CO: Sounds True, 2006.

Ricard, Matthieu. *Altruism: The Power of Compassion to Change Yourself and the World.* New York: Little, Brown and Company, 2015.

Society of Saint John the Evangelist. Accessed January 21, 2019. www.ssje.org.

Tidball, Keith and Marianne E. Krasny, eds. *Greening in the Red Zone: Disaster, Resilience and Community Greening.* New York: Springer-Verlag, 2014.

Walker, Brian and David Salt. *Resilience Thinking: Sustaining Ecosystems and People in a Changing World.* Washington, DC: Island Press, 2006.

Walker, Brian and David Salt. *Resilience Practice: Building Capacity to Absorb Disturbance and Maintain Function.* Washington, DC: Island Press, 2012.

Chapter 2

Contemplative Principles and Practices

Putting Adaptive Resilience to Work

We Get Up and Fall Down and Get Up

A young man sought out a desert hermit in Africa, hoping the holy man could teach him how to live a more resilient and joyful life. Worn out by the heat and shoe-consuming sand, he quickly pitched a first question when he found the old man. "What do you *do* all day and all night out here?" The monk answered, "We fall down and get up and fall down and get up." Maybe not what the young seeker hoped to hear, but so realistic. In our daily lives, as well as in the life of service, we face tough times. To get up is not magic. It's practice guided by tested and effective values. Doris Sommer, a Harvard professor and founder of "Cultural Agents," a global pedagogical movement, quotes Samuel Beckett's maxim echoing the hermit's: "Try Again, fail again, fail better."[1] This chapter explains why and how contemplative practices help us navigate cyclic ups and downs with more ballast and benefit. Explaining the core principles guiding these tools and skills, it sets the direction for the rest of the book.

Soon after meeting the hermit, the young man left the desert. He had hoped to find a way *around* reality. The monks were learning to live in it. We've all known times when we wanted to avoid the pitfalls of life as well as service and burnout. In many service settings, this practice of avoiding reality gets more traction than it should. How many times did you hear a service partner explain that everything fell apart? Have you found yourself trying to fit the puzzle pieces back together that were left in the wake of burnout? Service breaks down *regularly*, and often painfully, but we're not engaged. If you've been coached to express your anger during a collapse, but without blaming or shaming yourself or others, you're a rare breed. We need these alternative competencies to the old models of throwing up your hands and giving up. Contemplative perspectives teach us how to leverage and lean into burnout's work. They develop strength and steps for recrafting service using empathy, practical wisdom, and caring.

We Start Where We Are

Thomas Merton, the writer and Cistercian monk, served for many years as the Novice Master in the Abbey of Gethsemani in Kentucky. The life and practices of this order are relatively severe, so these young men needed coaching and explanations as well as loving care. Digging into the big questions about life, themselves,

God, and community offered rewarding and sometimes trying work. Failure happened regularly – part of the training, part of living. One novice, who studied under Merton for seven years, remembers a pithy piece of advice about the process. Merton regularly repeated:"Start with who you already are, what you already know, attend that, go deeper with that, with candor."[2]

A good and thriving life begins with you being who you are. We build community from there, as Dorotheos explained. The point of community: service in love. We've heard this in earlier chapters, but Merton's core advice shines a stronger light on a key ingredient: the *complete (if possible) absence* of self-judging or useless self-care. Self-denigration dulls. It fosters empty preoccupations with trying to be someone you're not while giving to others. You know what comes next, that preoccupation turns to other-blaming. It's core advice for us too. And since all of us experience service burnout, don't pretend you know nothing of that experience.

This is the contemplative version of responsibility. Disinterest in vilification or denigration feeds more energy directly into the work of reorganizing and revisioning. We now know through scientific research that the focused redirection of our thoughts, intentions, and actions shapes effective decision-making. It keeps us less mired in thoughts and feelings that derail next steps. But keep working with this idea of particularity. Read these descriptors and think of a particular service burnout situation you've faced. Imagine an approach that could help you calm your racing pulse, or quiet those self-recriminations, or find a better use for that extra pulse of energy than correcting someone else. We serve in communities, but this additional lens cherishing particularity helps us zoom in on our own dynamics and responses. We can start where we are and with who we already are.

By starting with the personal or particular, we dig right into the concretes and pragmatics of service and burnout through our own experiences. Here our thoughts and feelings rub up against realities. Our expectations and histories in service drive and reign in our emotions. All of this simultaneously sweeps into broader cultural, economic, and racial or ethnic dynamics and structures. Add the impact of relationships and actions unfolding daily in our specific service household, and our service world – even at just the personal level – shows up as multi-layered and complex. Up against this thick lifeworld, sugary generalizations about being humble or caring of others must turn rock solid. To feed a stranger or assist a grouchy and sick old monk turns ideals into pragmatics, values into embodied insights and actions. We learn how and why we can make it through service burnout.

That we are evolutionarily built to work together with caring attention[3] doesn't mean we can easily do that when just left to our own devices. At all contextual levels, we do better with guideposts or blazes and a map. That's what these contemplative principles and practices – rooted in the fundamentals of life and service, tough times and joyful ones, suffering and happiness—provide. In addition to teaching us how to settle ourselves and take a closer look at our personal thoughts, emotions, and actions – with candor – these skills and tools encourage multi-layered examinations of the work, when service hums along or when it's flailing. Questions serve as conversation starters, the kind I struggled to ask myself or others, about burnout. Why is this situation the way it is? Why is this happening? Can I feel grateful while the work implodes? Have I allowed myself that kind of honesty? Can I reach out to others about the fatigue and loss of clarity? What changes in attitude or action might reset the trajectory of service?

These questions and others building from them encourage us to reset our attention toward what contributes to service rather than what's bad or good according to our solitary estimations, which can easily get overblown or denied. In these traditions, neither happiness nor suffering are permanent. Focusing on processes and contributors to processes makes the most sense, so looking at and listening to the process is crucial. We must explore, rather than react,[4] at multiple levels. Then we will have good information about ourselves, others, the service household, and the systems we work with and in.

Household Life

Eugene Odum's household model embraced a similar reliance approach reflecting contextual and multi-layered views of life systems. How, when, and why does adaptation emerge? Interestingly, in Odum's famous book, *Fundamentals of Ecology*,[5] he notes that his Russian scientific colleagues prefer the terms "biocoenosis" and "biogeocoenosis" to the term life system. In Greek, the word "bio" means life. "Coenosis," in Greek, finds roots in the word "koinonia" typically translated as community. I imagine the Russian environmental scientists used these terms because they root in the Cyrilic linguistic forms of the Russian language and science. They take inspiration from Greek and European scientific derivations from Latin. I also believe these scientists recognized the resonance of household with Russia's immense history of Christian monasticism.

The hermit-monk Pachomius, in the fourth century C.E., drew on the same Greek derivation. He began a new form of monastic life near the Nile River. The radical change involved living communally. Interdependence stood as an alternative houschold model to hermit solitude. Pachomius called his model *coenobitic* monasticism and it became *the* primary model for all Christian monasticism including those practiced in Russia. Convinced that humans thrived in empathetic and caring groups, Pachomius took this new path, training monks in resilience through the cycles of daily life from phases of stability through phases of exploiting underutilized resources. Certainly, some challenged his model. They assumed it would destroy the core values and skills of monastic life honed individually. It did not. Soon enough, hermits left their solitary caves to associate with Pachomian coenobitic monasteries.

We gain physical, spiritual, and emotional direction and support when cooperating with and supporting each other. We all fall down and getting up happens singly and together. Teams work more effectively with breakdowns. Creativity increases when several hearts and minds try to name troubles, fears, and resentments that have collapsed around our feet. Next steps also become clearer and are more effective when individuals interact. To strike out alone or only with talk brokers fantasy. Daniel Berrigan, a high-profile Roman Catholic priest-activist during the Viet Nam war era, worried about this mostly imaginary, mostly isolated service and compassion. A well-known quote of his partly inspired Adrienne Rich's poem, "The Burning of Paper Instead of Children." Referencing the devastating deaths by napalm in that war, the quote is placed between the title and the first line of the poem: "I was in danger of verbalizing my moral impulses out of existence." Talk – especially singular talk – empties reality of what's burning. The tactile pain abstracts, as do our values and impulses to act. Denying the fire of burnout happens best among individuals. When alone, we believe our verbalizing. We pretend our confusion or rage fosters action for good.

Cheap talk also speeds up a service household collapse, whether due to denial or window-dressing facades, or blaming. The opportunity to reorganize, rebuild, and exploit new or other resources disappears, goes out of existence. Opportunities for service and burnout are lost. Berrigan's quote struck a chord in me. The aim resonates with contemplative perspectives that expose our strategies of avoidance and denial, especially around pain. Father Berrigan certainly had studied contemplative principles and practices. He knew these teachings did not countenance cheap talk, especially dressed up as morality. Life-giving values occur in practice, in action, and in community. They move us through the sometimes scorching, sometimes solid, sometimes joyous work of service and daily life. Thich Nhat Hahn, who lived through Viet Nam's napalming and helped negotiate the war-ending Paris Peace Accords, enacted the potent power of contemplative approaches to destruction. He calls this action compassionate inter-being. It is communal. It acts by going through the wreckage and fire.

Contemplative Practices Today

The relatively new academic field of contemplative studies now filters through international academic and research societies such as Mind and Life and the Contemplative Mind in Higher Education. Monks and nuns from various contemplative traditions, as well as indigenous healers and shamans, contribute to these programs and global research centers. Other study centers link contemplative research with service. Applied programs such as the Cognitively-Based Compassion Training® through The Center for Contemplative Science and Compassion-Based Ethics of Emory University and the Courage of Care Coalition train physicians, teachers, foster care workers and children, social workers, and other activists in contemplative compassion-based practices and values. Their goals for community-based transformation intend to foster health, healing, and social justice. Magazine and book racks in stores across the world along with our TV and computer screens and podcasts flood us with images, teachings, and expectations. We hear many claims about contemplative principles and practices helping us lead more balanced, insightful, and compassionate lives.

With so many today talking about mindfulness and meditation practices, one wonders how much is true and where to buy in. This book focuses specifically on particular contemplative approaches relevant to service burnout. Tuned predominantly to individuals' experiences, all chapters' narratives, principles, and practices engage, at some level, with broader systemic and structural forces impacting people's lives and choices. Although welcoming the benefits of individual practice such as medical or psychological interventions using mindfulness to address physical or emotional pain, this book also works more broadly. It embraces relational and systems questions, analyses, and actions. As some athletes in the National Basketball Association believe, the work thrives best in households, meaning when individuals work as part of a team. They get it. And as is true for any team, this approach requires practice, training. The impetus, at least ideally, is love among the team and commitment to the shared work of their play. In some cases, their principled practices broaden as service in local communities. This book embraces aspects of contemporary contemplative practices, but goes deeper. It teaches how to engage the suffering of burnout and talk together about what went really wrong. It asks from that place, how can or can we go forward.

Though I gratefully applaud and learn from recent neuroimaging and psychological studies on contemplative practices at the University of Wisconsin, the University of Miami, Stanford, Harvard, the University of Virginia, Brown, Emory, and other research centers, this book takes a broader and action-driven approach. Using scientific knowledge, it infuses that data into the daily contemplative activist work of reframing burnout as part of service. Using tools and skills of contemplative awareness, inter-being or interdependence, empathy, and kindness, these chapters teach how to take next steps through burnout's hard times.

Building Resilience Through Choices

As we already discussed in the Preface and Chapter 1, contemplative approaches choose attention as the pause that orients. To orient *to* burnout instead of away from it is a big first step for most of us in service. Attending serious program disruptions or flailing and flagging emotions requires increased focus, but not the fixated kind that merely wants trouble to go away. We start by honing our skills to tune into specific, often small, moments of miscommunication or missteps without picking them apart in order to shove the trouble somewhere else. We use these tools to note negative consequences, like a lag in external funds, but do not immediately call to complain or immediately start a plan to fix. The first steps in these approaches highlights making a good choice for a next step. We keep some space from the full maelstrom, a space of awareness. We're in the burnout but not fully of it. This is a fine and important distinction in contemplative approaches. The lack of volunteers registers. We do not start calling people on the phone. A crucial board member with strong community connections ups and quits. We sit with that change and do nothing at first. Let it be what it is. Take it in. Choices will emerge *and* they'll work better for the space given to them.

That space in Buddhist tradition gives us time to identify which or which combinations of the three poisons are moving into play: aversion (pushing away), attachment (grabbing; got to have more), or delusion or ignorance (I don't understand; so, I'll fix it) — or some combination. We've pointed to these before, but it's interesting to intentionally translate our service burnout issues using these three broad categories. We start with neutrality. From what we learn, we shape decisions for action. The process radically differs from today's usual responses — dive right in and immediately fix, show strength, push pieces around to get the outcome you need. Instead, the heavy lifting happens in studying the weaknesses, the breakdowns, and the pieces as they are — not as we wish they were or could imagine they might be. Sticking with burnout without panic or controlling requires serious discipline and reflection. Best choices emerge from these spaces — less and more quickly, as possible and needed. The choices begin not with doing, but with choosing to stay with what's happening.

Sharon Salzburg offers additional angles on the power of paying attention to choices. She reframes choice-making as an act of kindness, beginning with ourselves. Even difficult choices, those that disappoint or terminate service, unfold with more resilience when empathy and interdependence infuse the work. That kindness disappears when we try to wrench choice-making to match old expectations. Of course, we're also yanked and twisted in the process. Again, she uses an image to capture this kind of compassion-driven decision-making, the flow of water through our open palm and fingers. Holding on or clenching our fist as water pours over it only deprives us of the amazing sensibility of free-flowing experience. Life comes as it comes and leaves as it leaves. The same is true for burnout and service. Kindness spreads like water. Self-understanding that nourishes our resilience informs our household's teamwork as well as partnerships in the broader community. When we simply let go of that muffed decision or our team's inadequate preparations, like so much water running through our hands, we are not pretending the breakdown doesn't matter – as if it didn't happen. We're not fixating on the fact that it happened. We're kindly moving through it to discern and discover what's next.

There's so much more to learn from a service burnout experience than meets the quick eye. When we refuse to deny or agree to a surface-level assessment, we also refuse to try to patch broken pieces back together as they were. We're encouraged by contemplative perspectives to keep asking for more information. Maybe your frustration over a teammate not following through carries signals more than just that presenting irritation. Led by kindness, you can probe a bit deeper. What's really burning you? Is your teammate facing more than you realized? The point is not to make things up, but to more rigorously inquire. Contemplative traditions have long histories in training analytic thinking. They are inquiry-driven. As ideas come to mind, test them attentively. Narrow to the ones that resonate most strongly. Is it the lack of openly-shared planning? Does his sloppiness trigger some self-recognition? From contemplative viewpoints, such a process of hypothesis creation and then testing holds us in the actual tension we usually want to avoid. To move forward from any other process bodes failure, a shallower form of burnout denial.

These themes of kindness and deeper questioning play central roles among members of a weekly suicide-attempters group I co-lead with a trained psychologist at Grady Memorial Hospital. Part of the NIA program on the Psych Floor,[6] the group is learning and practicing a compassion-based protocol emphasizing many of the key elements we've been naming, attention and awareness, interdependence, empathy and affection, and kind actions. Professor Lobsang Tenzin Negi of Emory's Religion Department with others in the The Center for Contemplative Science and Compassion-Based Ethics, developed Cognitively-Based Compassion Training®,[7] which we use. Elements of that protocol come to life through our shared experiences. Most members of our groups have a mental illness diagnoses, some also struggle with addictions, all of them daily face high demands with little resources. Finding shelter, food, trustworthy friends, and access to crucially needed healthcare fills their days and nights.

Choosing to learn this protocol is a big step in addition to their individual therapy. Practicing self and other kindness in a world that takes much more than it gives might seem either trivial or impossible. But our experience confirms the power these approaches offer for daily living when times are good and very tough. Once signed up for our six-week course, group members generally do not miss. They understand that the protocol has been developed, as the principles and practices of this book, without requiring any affiliation to a religious or philosophical tradition. Fundamentally, we are learning to make resilient choices rooted in kindness and more serious scrutiny of what goes on when we're making personal decisions or interacting with others. We fall down and get up and fall down with regularity, but our household support keeps us together and moving toward reconstructing lives we can adaptively live for the long term.

Over the last six years, research on our group shows positive results for participants, especially around issues of compassionate self-knowledge and caring as well as empathy for others, a recognition of our interdependence.[8] The participants describe why and how calming their minds helps them drop down below the chaos of their lives and a good deal of guilt and pain to choose self-understanding instead of self-blaming. In our groups, they share how these values support better decision-making. Though most groups using these approaches begin with sitting meditation, we learned to trust our own experience and needs; so, we begin with walking meditation. Members say their minds and emotions need the steadying movement to keep better focus on the present moment and remain calm. We choose to learn by walking. A choice of kindness and analysis.

Some days, it feels utterly improbable to me as we walk double-file down a long hospital corridor. The orderlies pushing beds just go around us. The custodial staff continue cleaning and gathering trash. Other patients and staff quiet their conversations as they pass by. We work on our focus, noticing the water fountains' hum or the elevators' clanking, but not letting those sounds hook our minds. We keep refocusing on the experience of walking. Even at this simple level, this practice of choice-making to refocus and reorder our attention and behaviors recalibrates and strengthens our capacities to make adaptive and resilient decisions outside the hospital. From our brokenness and burnout, we are learning to walk again at the pace of self and other care, to put the pieces back together. The Grady group calls our walking practice, "two-footed compassion." One foot, the first foot, steps – self-compassion. The second foot steps – other-compassion. Balance and stability in reflective decision-making takes both. This is true burnout and service too.

Turning Choices into Action

Professor John Dunne, a scholar of Asian Languages and Cultures at the University of Wisconsin-Madison as well as Distinguished Professor in Contemplative Humanities within the Center for Healthy Minds,[9] broadly describes the work of contemplative practices as:

> (providing) an explicit and/or implicit instruction set whose implementation is meant to induce changes in mind and/or body ... The instruction set can itself involve both mental techniques (focusing the mind on an image or phrase, for example) and physical techniques ... as well as environmental requirements (e.g., a quiet location).[10]

Research scholarship analyzing the content and impact of these instruction sets is continually broadening and deepening. This book uses insights drawn from a range of scientific experiments in cognitive psychology and neuroscience, as well as phenomenological models informed by ancient and more modern religious texts,[11] to secularized protocols and their uses in scientific studies and classes on contemplative practice and action.[12] As already noted, these chapter engage this information, but press it toward application in everyday service. What are the processes that produce an action grown in and by these principles and practices?

Let's do a thought experiment. Imagine you walk into your service center, your household. There's water in the hallway puddling near what had been a big closet and is now a reconstructed and desperately needed additional bathroom. Taking a breath instead of jumping into action, you choose to pause and pay closer attention. Questions quickly arise. Where's the water coming from? Is it still flowing? How much damage has occurred? Notice, the queries focus on information not frustration over an unknown cause or blaming. Attention shifting into awareness ups the curiosity. You notice a wet streak down the hallway from the puddle. It seems the source of water is up a wall near an air conditioning vent. Ideas start to pop.

The metal plate for airflow also looks wet. Suddenly a different thought intervenes: why didn't we sell this old house when we got that offer last year? The maintenance issues at times can overwhelm our budget. The neighborhood is rough. But instead of building that wave of irritability, you drop below it to remember that this is still the neighborhood of your clientele, immigrant families newly arrived in the United States. Many of us end up in service centers with less than ideal buildings. These add pressures and sometimes costs, but service adds pressures and costs. Finding perspective, choosing not to overblow a newly noted problem, increases the likelihood of solving it and moving on. Even as we notice irritability and blame heating up, drop down. Keep looking. Maybe the problem is mostly a matter of collecting condensation.

That's when it comes to you. Two months ago, the center put in a new air handling unit. The architectural design of this old house and its urban site required the new unit go into the attic. Maybe something's wrong – even though it is new. A next step, a choice, get a ladder and head into the attic. Investigate more before you make another move. Maybe the unit is having trouble. Of course, the ladder isn't easy to find, another catch ready to erase your growing equanimity. But these experiences can provide more empathy for others' who also face unexpected challenges amid normal work that swamps them with details. It's easy to just look the other way and hope that *someone else* will handle this. Once in the attic, discerning next steps is easy. Water is obviously leaking from the unit. Take another breath. Don't catastrophize about the whole ceiling falling in. Once down the ladder, check with the program head and make the call to your air conditioning service contractor.

Choice-making with kindness and thicker analysis looks so simple on paper, but in the push and pull of service, it's hard work. Falling down and getting up is hard work. Action, however, is where these traditions put their main emphasis. To act with intention and discernment as well as kindness is the daily, ongoing goal in community and service. But action often stymies us. It's one reason denial, quick-fixing, or blaming can take such a strong hold. We know these traditions begin processes of action by "starting where you *actually* are." To investigate from a standpoint of being fully in a situation, what's called first-person, and then from one a bit more distant with additional perspective[13] claims first priority as action. We let go of how we thought things should be happening or wanted them to. We take first steps recognizing that where we are will not last. We will move, and often that's tougher to do than we thought. We all long to find stability in service and stay there. But that devolves into stagnancy. Resilience requires attention to now for moving into a next phase.

The Personal and the Political-Structural

To make that move, to act, these traditions work from a dual standpoint, the personal and the socio-political. Both press on and impact service and burnout.

Stories across contemplative traditions mix these worlds of individuals, groups, institutions, and politics. The work of contemplative insights happens in more places than on a cushion. In Iraq during the fifth century, C.E., Daniel the Stylite offered counsel and suggested actions to local communities, people coming from far away, and political leaders. Stylite identified a specific kind of contemplative practitioner, one who stood on a pillar or "style." Of differing heights, styles also served as platforms for teaching and healing. Though to us this approach seems seriously extreme and bizarre, in Daniel's day these contemplatives used their pillar to heighten the local and structural lessons of attentive care and service to others.

People climbed a ladder to ask advice, receive loving concern, and leave with a sense of useful next steps.[14] In addition to this daily counseling, Daniel also leveraged his position for public advocacy and sometimes for political justice. He worked through disputes to bring conflicts to equitable resolution. He served as a representative on behalf of local communities to the state. On several occasions, he left his pillar; famously in one case, to debate with and change the mind of the King. Personal, social, and political aspects of life and service freely intermixed in Daniel's practice and in the actions of many other contemplatives.

In our own day people like Dorothy Day (1897–1980) took vows as a lay practitioner of contemplative traditions. Day joined the Benedictine monastic order and in 1933 with Peter Maurins, founded the Catholic Worker, an advocacy movement for the hungry, poor, unsheltered, mentally ill, and/or addicted. A longstanding activist, writer for social change causes, and visionary of a common resources society, Day went daily to pray at a nearby Roman Catholic Church. Most knew her as an energetic and internationally renowned leader with socialist leanings and an edgy demand for justice. Few knew her practice of stilling her mind, sitting alone in the back of a church to consider her work, vision, and next steps. After sitting, in part for personal restoration and insight, she went right back at it, demanding local political authorities and the church put their resources, heft, and money where their mouths were.

Catholic Worker houses opened in other major cities across the United States, including Atlanta where Murphy Davis and Ed Loring founded the Open Door with strong involvement by many including Nelia and Calvin Kimbrough. They focused on homeless rights and ministries as well as Death Row ministries and advocacy for ending the death penalty. Still, their public structural work interwove with daily personal and community meditations on sacred texts and prayer. The meditative writings and sermons of the Rev. Dr. Martin Luther King, Jr. also drew on contemplative traditions particularly those shaped by one of his Boston University mentors, Howard Thurman. Other civil rights activists including Ella Baker, whose civil rights work expanded to issues of women's rights, and the Berrigan brothers of anti-Vietnam war activism fame also drew on principles and practices of Christian prayer and contemplation.

Principles Come Alive in Practice

In addition to working on several levels, these values, tools, and skills privilege pragmatics. The point is action upon reflection. Contemplative values translate into the work of assessment, decisions, and doing. That's the point and that's the point in this book, to find ways of generously and effectively moving through burnout's suffering to next phases of service. The work is to participate with change to caringly and ethically move forward. Individuals, groups, and community stakeholders all participate in these processes. Let's use an example to better understand how these principles come to life in practice.

Suppose a city decides to close a neighborhood park in a multicultural area of town. The public reason is hung on an official sign in the park: Park Closed; Stream contains dangerous pollutants. The city's principle: protect and sustain community health. The park will be closed. But the neighborhood resists. From their perspective, two values are at stake. The first is maintaining spaces for their community life. They want their children to have a nice park to play in where parents also can gather. The second value is justice. The neighborhood knows the source of the pollution, over-building practices in upstream neighborhoods. Construction debris from chemicals to physical materials fill their stream with dangerous toxins. Who will support justice for the neighborhood if not the city?

The neighborhood's complaints get the city's attention. Officials propose building a new park near the neighborhood but away from the stream. The proposal falls flat. The new park is two miles away from the current location. To get there, the community's children would have to cross a four-lane street. No bike lanes exist. The new park's neighborhood is home to mostly new immigrant families from all over the world. The two communities have no connections though only blocks from each other. No simplistic urging for the two communities to "treasure their shared diversity" will work. Too much is at stake.

If we were city officials assigned to parks or to community relations, we're facing a breakdown on several levels, our office, two communities, and constituencies within the two communities. We'll just forget the construction companies for now. To begin reorganizing for next steps, we'll need some guiding values or principles. Obviously, closer listening to everyone involved is a first step. Had that only been done before the sign was posted! To build a conversation able to move from distress and anger into problem-solving will initially require attention to what people think, feel, and need now. That work will have to begin separately, in the two separate communities. From a contemplative standpoint, these initial listening sessions need to go deeper, to become aware of the community's view of their park not only as a socializing site, but as just one more instance of downstream pollution at the hands of their richer and more politically wired upstream neighbors. To wake up to the real issues of environmental injustice in one more poor, urban, and multicultural neighborhood demands action. This issue is bigger than a neighborhood wanting to keep its park.

Contemplative approaches expect to discover thicker political or social inequities as well as personal suffering and breakdowns. Attention and awareness as tools and skills come to fruition in more comprehensive understandings that produce active responses, which are truly relevant to the range of troubling problems and issues. One could imagine how quickly a city official, probably with almost no power, would burn out in a job like this without a set of values, tools, and skills to bring to such a situation. Contemplative approaches offer a holistic view to problem-solving, which starts with pausing rather than quick-fix action and specific techniques for shaping next steps with community partners. Those tools and skills also often reveal additional layers to situations, the kinds of layers that can exacerbate or quicken the usual phases of burnout in service.

We've all faced those times when it feels impossible to find the energy to do this transformative work of moving values and skills into actions that take us through burnout. We can convince ourselves that steps to slow down the damage are good enough. We will suffer the edges of self-blame rather than try to find the energy to strike out toward next steps. Others of us fear the possible condemnation enough that we choose to plow forward just to do something. We start working with Home Depot to get special recycled materials for the park at almost no cost. We skip the processes, the practices, and hope for the best. This approach guarantees burnout by denial, the usual suspect. We wish things could move faster. We dread the heat of those tough-to-have conversations. We duck what my graduate advisor at Harvard used to tell me, "Slow it down a bit. It takes what it takes." Contemplative approaches drive toward practical action, but they don't overlook process. This is key for working with and through burnout.

A fifth-century contemplative text addresses these issues directly:

> A man had a plot of land. And through his carelessness brambles sprang up and it became a wilderness of thistles and thorns. Then he decided to cultivate it. So he said to his son: "Go and clear that ground." So the son went to clear it, and saw that the thistles and thorns had multiplied. So his spirit weakened, and he said: "How much time will I need to clear and weed all this?" And he lay on the ground and went to sleep. He did this day after day. Later his father came to see what he had done, and found him doing nothing. And he said to him: 'Why have you done nothing till now?' And the lad said to his father: "I was just coming to work when I saw this wilderness, and I was deterred from starting; so, I lay on the ground and went to sleep." Then his father said to him: "son, if you had cleared each day the area on which you lay down, your work would have advanced slowly and you would not have lost heart." So the lad did what he was told, and in a short time the plot was cultivated.[15]

Compassionate, respectful, and focused action involves step-by-step effort. It takes time. Short-changing the process only weakens our spirits and bodies. Our creativity flags. Often in service when facing burnout, we avoid the trouble by just doing what we've always done – keep going, no matter what. We just keep going and this gets reinforced by the old model's determination to pretend burnout is only for losers. To tackle what's cornering us or collapsing around us often means challenging the routines of service we've gotten used to. The model offered in this book informed by contemplative insights claims a different strategy. Do less. Pay attention more. Aim low. Burnout and breakdowns are part of the process.

By letting go of a particular type of early American Protestant stoicism[16] that encourages us to keep going no matter the difficulty or strife, we are developing capacity for life-long service. We are capable of living through the troughs and crests of giving back with others. We let go of a distorted service story equating full commitment with never-failing sacrifice.[17]

Dispositions and Temperaments

This reorientation in attitude and approach sparks other shifts, which gain useful leverage for making it through burnout when viewed through a contemplative lens.

As we relinquish the relentless can do all of the old model, we gain more clarity about truly available resources during tough times. Teams in service, like the mountain climbers, bring their range of gifts, talents, disinterests, and incompetencies. Contemplative traditions add insight to any basic inventory of skills and inabilities by discerning individuals' and teams' temperaments and dispositions. I'll unpack their insights using myself as an example in a situation unrelated to service. Temperaments and dispositions show up in every facet of our lives.

In 2013, I trekked in Nepal with an amazing group of women friends guided by a team of skilled and caring Sherpas.[18] In the region of an old Tibetan Buddhist Kingdom named Mustang, we decided to pursue a particular meditation-retreat cave known for having more than one hundred beautiful drawings of buddhas and bodhisattvas. At 14,000 feet, the cave lay hidden, but a local caretaker agreed to lead us. Beginning at 12,000 feet, we followed a harrowing narrow trail. Turning one corner, a new challenge appeared, a short section only navigable by a hand-over-hand climbing rope. We stopped to regroup. The cave was worth it. We took our time with help and cheered as the magnificent and tucked-away cave came into sight. Devouring the images, we stalled the Sherpas for extra time. It had begun to rain. Finally, they put their foot down. We must go. As rain began to fall, we did not know what they knew. In this area when skies turn to rain, the water comes in buckets. Worse, the dirt on the trails turns to grease.

Soon, we were in it. We slipped, slid, and struggled. Each faulty move drew a Sherpa to our side – before we could ask. I watched steadying hands take the hands of my friends or place arms around their waists. The support helped us work our way down the trail. I too received a hand, but not from one of our Sherpa team. After taking my hand, my escort stepped in front of me, all five foot four inches of him. I would go down with the help of the local villager in charge of the padlocked "chicken wire" fence that "protected" the sacred cave. Now, he was protecting me. His rough brown hand surrounded mine with what felt like indomitable strength. He smiled. I said, "Thank you." And off we went, but in a very unexpected fashion. He did not follow the trail at all. It had become a buttery "slip and slide" by then. So instead, he began cutting a new path down the mountain, edging in steps for us with his flip-flops.

I followed, putting my big hiking boots in each just-made crevice without additional directions except for his strong hand. Beyond my limits, I embraced his hard-won expertise. Rarely looking up as the water washed us and the mountain-side, we worked our way down using this newly-carved path. Once everyone arrived at a small level field, we sat down as the rain dissipated. We shared juices and cookies, wild stories of our descent, and we women expressed gratitude and relief. My local guide sat next to me as calm as if we'd just taken a stroll down the main street of his small village.

During a heightened experience like that, my temperament shifts into a slightly different gear. Let me explain. Temperament in Christian contemplative perspectives and perhaps in other contemplative schools signal a way of seeing and being in the world that impacts how we relate to and work with others. We can think of temperaments like DNA. The code is there. For my kind helper, the caretaker, our weather-related descent held no special energy. His whole life, lived mostly at 2,000 feet below the cave, revolved around mountain weather and hiking. It appeared that his calm reflected his temperament. He took things as they came, used his developed skills, and simply went on. This was ordinary temperament-informed life for him, which may be one reason why he had been selected to protect this very significant cave, one the *National Geographic* had just discovered.

Dispositions, from these perspectives, differ from temperaments because they are malleable like the soil on the mountain. Temperaments remain pretty much rock solid. We respond to situations from a temperamental standpoint, but our disposition can soften or appropriately strengthen our styles of communication, relational sensitivity, and capacities to act caringly. Dispositions in these traditions reflect choice particularly in our processes of decision-making. Temperaments lean into our decision-making. In a crisis on the trek, my temperament tamped down. It didn't lean in as it usually did. Normally, my temperament puts me and anyone with me right to work. I like goals and have a kind of can-do approach. I not only enjoy work, but I like getting work done. My temperament can urge me toward impatience when others want to extend a process of discernment. When I have been in a position of leadership, in charge of teams of co-workers, I have to hire people who will slow me down.

If I'm in a familiar setting, I can leverage my dispositional gear and back off my temperamental irritability when plans unfold more slowly. That proved to be the case under the additional pressures of the rain and our retreat from the cave. But my temperament often got the best of me during the first few days of our trek. As an experienced kayaker and camper, I never *walked* nine hours a day, nor moved up and down such long-haul slopes. I don't know what I expected, but the first days of our trek proved to be a mismatch. So, my temperament grew irritable. Like a child, I whined at breaks and over lunch about how much time all this walking took. Boating would be faster, I claimed. Too bad there was no water around. You get the sense of how locked in a temperament can be. I couldn't find a way to get to the goal I had in mind – a day's walk that did not take a whole day. Each time we stopped for rest – appropriately, because of altitude and the need to drink and restore a bit – I balked. Let's get going.

The Sherpas ignored my barbed comments and questions. They took turns walking with me chatting me up about the amazing geological features around us or pointing out a far-off monastery and telling me its stories. They modeled a disposition I might embrace. They invited me into our reality rather than the one I temperamentally wished for. Using their dispositions of kindness and non-judging, they helped me grow into a better attitude, one able to notice how my thoughts shaped a useful, as they might call it, or rotten, as I might call it, approach. I began to apprentice myself to their disposition, being mindful of their words, and deeds with more generosity for us all. Amid the day's long haul, we had options, singing or sharing stories. It came slow at first. My temperamental tendencies toward reaching a goal remained, but my disposition began to flex. I even tried a new practice or two, ones that nourished less judging and more understanding. I tried to take a more interdependent approach. I chose to walk with others – even at the very back of our line – rather than always charge ahead. When someone offered me a new topic, I let go of my grousing and took it up. I learned to offer my own new topics for others to engage. Temperament intact, with their help, my disposition found a way forward.

Contemplative traditions value dispositions *and* temperaments. Dispositional shifts help us work through the realities we're facing in the present without demanding our way or the highway or demeaning someone else. Dispositions help my husband kindly ask me to leave the kitchen when he first gets up. At that hour of the morning, there's simply not enough room for two in any kitchen – no matter how large. But temperaments also play important roles. In addition to fostering diversity, they also encourage humility and empathy once we come to know our temperament. And each temperament offers gifts to a team. If we know our mountaineering team has a naturally skilled rock climber who's also trained a lot, we can count on her solid strength. If we know a team member in service has a deeply reflective problem-solving temperament, we gain skills from his temperament and more group capacity.

Of course, temperaments go both ways, which is why it takes a household. And, as contemplatives explain, it takes practices that strengthen our dispositional repertoires. Many exercises and practices in the chapters to come intend to strengthen our dispositional flexibility. They are designed to embrace your temperament while dispositionally finding opportunities and pathways of service capable of working through burnout. Perhaps you can think of examples when a service colleague seemed unable to let go of an idea or plan in the face of obvious opposition. Temperaments offer you a way to think more thickly about what's going on instead of just assuming she's resistant and obstructive. We can better strategize next steps. Dispositional thinking encourages us to team train, learning from each other specific skills for flex and creativity, for taking realistic next steps.

Knowledge of our own and others' dispositions and temperaments in service and burnout encourages us to get to know our co-volunteers and co-professionals better. To make it through tough times, especially times that really put our temperaments at edge or on fire, we need skills and tools for upping our dispositional energies. Neuroscience might describe this as practicing the plasticity of our dispositions or attitudes, exploring and using their adaptability to nourish resilience. I call it leveraging our dispositional choices in real time. From a contemplative practices standpoint, we reorient our energies, and repeat the new practice, and repeat. Like we do in yoga or lifting weights, we set our intentions and enact the change we want to live. We practice a different disposition, one that won't stymy us in dead-ending burnout.

Generative Practice: Serving and Burning Out

No contemplative principle or value fully counts or really works until it is put into action. To use these guiding values, from a contemplative understanding, we have to practice. To unpack the significance of this, let's look at a service example. Suppose there's a member of your service group that somehow never takes his required turn to work at the intake desk. Everybody else does. Many do not enjoy the front-line tasks: helping upset clients fill in intake forms, discerning priority issues, and figuring out if the client has any applicable resources. But the rule is, everyone gets a turn. That's made clear at Orientation. The policy reflects the supervisor's insight that no one could do this job all the time. It's a guaranteed source of burnout.

Suppose you're the supervisor who made this rule. What to do? How might you begin a conversation with the person who's not showing up? Where might empathy and interdependence lead in a pragmatic discussion of what appears to be irresponsible behaviour? To think this through, now's the time to drop down a bit from the surface irritabilities and unspoken accusations. Settle into more curiosity-driven next steps rather than coercive ones. You might, for example, try to learn more about what drew this person to this service work in the first place. See if you can sense temperamental leanings and ask more questions about his interests and gifts related to this work and beyond. Often, it's through the non-service focused conversations that I learn the most about someone's temperament. This approach reflects a contemplative understanding that temperaments matter, but it also assumes, as contemplative perspectives do, that there's more to a story than what initially presents as just shirking responsibilities.

I once learned in a related situation that a team member who consistently dropped the ball truly struggled with her introversion when working with strangers. Maybe your teammate becomes easily distracted with any other task and can't stay focused enough to remember this is the day he's supposed to be at the front desk. Perhaps your teammate had a really bad incident at another organization's intake desk and still feels accountable and guilty – as if the breakdown was all her fault. People in service are complex. To avoid judging or quick fixing or demanding everyone fit the same mold, we need to put empathy and interdependence into practice. Otherwise principled talk not only cheapens the power of the values but wrests the problem-solving from the practices. The integration of learning about that person's temperament, dispositions, and service experiences helps us put into practice problem-solving that doesn't fire up more tensions. To use this approach not only with individual, but to also have team conversations requires a bit of courage as well as attentive and inclusive planning. But practices of smart planning won't win the day if the core principles of humility, empathy, and interdependence, often with healthy boundary-setting, have no traction.

If Dorotheos' wheel is just a model, an abstract principle that never turns, then, who needs it? The intention and content of this book privileges application informed by contemplative principles for making it through service burnout. The approach is flexible, not binding. The emphasis falls on contextual choice-making, not formulaic regulations based on real stories. Hopefully, these values, tools, and skill will spark your own creativity to adapt and apply them to the specifics of your situation. At bottom, this book provides answers to Morton Kelsey's question: "Is there something beyond this turmoil?" Our turmoil is assuming burnout is wrong or not part of serving. The answer is, there is something more and there are practices that work that "something beyond" in the cycles of service.

Also, a Roman Catholic contemplative, Kelsey's concern resonates with Berrigan's fear that his values had devolved into talk instead of practice. That quote caught my attention in Adrienne Rich's poem because it linked back to my first experiences with these practices, in their simplest forms, in the basement of the Chapel at Smith College when I was an undergraduate there. At the weekly 8:00 a.m. communion service, we read scripture, prayed, took communion, and spent time sitting and breathing. We let our attention drop down below the pushes and pulls in our lives for insight for letting go. These were my first introductions to just being. Neither embracing a position or understanding, or sure of a way forward, I learned to ponder, to get curious. This is how I came to the conclusion that resilient service includes phases of burnout.

At these services, visitors came and went. One man appeared semi-regularly. Coming for a week or three at a time, he always wore a black shirt and black pants. We shared only first names. With his irregular attendance, his name never stuck with me. By my senior year, I counted on this practice group and began taking classes on contemplative traditions and approaches to life and justice work. I also took on the task of picking up the morning donuts and juice and making the coffee, which afforded me extra time with our wise chaplain, Dick Unsworth. He seemed to know lots of people in the valley and beyond. He claimed a fast and long-standing friendship with the man that came and went. I learned a bit more about him.

Our visitor seemed pretty involved in national movements for social justice. He was a priest with an intense and playful wit. At our breakfast times, he occasionally spoke about current events and his frustration with contemporary politics and the church. Toward the end of my senior, Reverend Unsworth and I stood washing and drying dishes. For the first time, I asked him about the man. Who was he? Why did he come? I was told he was one of the two activist Berrigan brothers, perhaps Daniel of the Adrienne Rich poem. He stayed sometimes in the valley and sometimes with Dick. I got the sense that he had been putting his values into action and living with the fruition and fallout. Service cycles. We stabilize, breakdown, reorganize, exploit, and stabilize again. It's a contemplative process we can embrace.

Hopefully, this book helps you find ways to make those same connections, to move into burnout as part of service using contemplative principles and tools.

Exercises

1. Think of a recent time when you "fell down" in service or felt your service work drop out from beneath your feet like a collapsing floor? Just sit and remember what happened. In the first column write your "this happened" descriptions – be specific. In the second column, list the sources of the collapse – who or what's to blame?

This Happened	Who or What Is to Blame?

2. Can you/how might you clear a small next step taking you further into the splintered scraps?

_____

_____

_____

_____

_____

_____

_____

3. Developing non-judging attitudes and actions takes practice. Try this practice: choose an area of your current service setting that is moving into breakdown. In the first column, write your complete honest responses. In the second column, try writing those same responses but shear away any judging or blaming tones. Invite others into honest assessment with you.

Honest Responses	Non-Judging Honesty Inviting Others
_____	_____
_____	_____
_____	_____
_____	_____
_____	_____
_____	_____
_____	_____
_____	_____

4. What do you intend for this service work once you let go of blaming and judging? How will your service household thrive?

_____

_____

_____

_____

_____

5. As you expand your household attitudes and actions through kindness, how will you work with your temperament and dispositions as your household team begins rebuilding with the resources you actually have now?

_____

_____

_____

_____

_____

_____

Notes

1   See www.culturalagents.org.
2   See Finley, *Mediation for Christians.* Merton quote remembered by his then nine-year novice, James Finley, a therapist and teacher of contemplative Christianity.
3   See De Waal, *Age of Empathy*. De Waal confirms elements of this contemplative approach though from an evolutionary lens: the strategies, especially among mammals, that link empathetic compassion to thriving.
4   Komjathy, "Approaching Contemplative Practice" in *Contemplative Literature*, 1–86. For a full range of religious communities by contemplative principles and practices including, Buddhism to Judaism, Christianity, Daoism, Islam, American Indian Religions, Hinduism, African Religions, and more.
5   Odum, *Fundamentals of Ecology*, 1971, pp. 4–5.
6   See http://psychiatry.emory.edu/niaproject/. The Grady Nia Project was founded by Dr. Nadine Kaslow. It is a long-running series of group and private psychotherapies and research studies with African-American women who have a history of domestic violence and suicidality.
7   See https://tibet.emory.edu/cognitively-based-compassion-training/index.html.
8   See Zhang et al., "Shame and Depressive Symptoms," and Johnson et al., "Compassion-Based Meditation Among African Americans."
9   See https://centerhealthyminds.org/.
10 See Lutz et al., "Attention Regulation and Monitoring in Meditation."
11 See Lutz et al., "Investigating the Phenomenological Matrix of Mindfulness-Related Practices from a Neurocognitive Perspective."
12 See references for additional sources.
13 Hal Brown, founder of Brown University's Concentration in Contemplative Studies uses these three perspectives to describe one aspect of how the major approaches these principles and practices. For more information on the Contemplative Studies Program at Brown, see www.brown.edu/academics/contemplative-studies/. For specific discussion of the first and third person approach, see www.brown.edu/academics/contemplative-studies/about. These perspectives have also served as foundational pedagogical frameworks for classes and majors at Naropa University. See www.naropa.edu/the-naropa-experience/contemplative-education/index.php. Judith Simmer-Brown, a professor at Naropa, has written and publicly presented on this. See her edited volume, *Meditation and the Classroom: Contemplative Pedagogies and the Classroom.*
14 From the Greek word "*stylos.*"
15 Chadwick, Western Asceticism, 93–94.
16 Wuthnow, "A Reasonable Role for Religion," 116, 123.

17 See Hefner's *Democratic Civility*, 1998 to learn more about America's cultural myths and
    assumptions about giving back.
18 The company name at that time: *White Himalayas.*

Supplemental Reading

Keating, Thomas. *The Foundations of Centering Prayer and the Christian Contemplative Life: Open
    Mind, Open Heart; Invitation to Love; The Mystery of Christ.* New York: The Continuum Inter-
    national Publishing Group. 2002.

References

Brown University. "Contemplative Studies." Accessed March 2, 2019. www.brown.edu/academ-
    ics/contemplative-studies/
Brown University. "About: Contemplative Studies." Accessed March 2, 2019. www.brown.edu/
    academics/contemplative-studies/about
Chadwick, Owen. *Western Asceticism.* Philadelphia, PA: The Westminster Press, 1958
Cultural Agents. Accessed March 3, 2019. www.culturalagents.org/
De Waal, Frans. *Age of Empathy: Nature's Lessons for a Kinder Society.* New York: Three Rivers Press, 2009.
Emory University School of Medicine. "Grady Nia Project." Accessed March 2, 2019.
    http://psychiatry.emory.edu/niaproject/
Emory-Tibet Partnership. "CBCT Compassion Training." Accessed May 31, 2017. https://tibet.
    emory.edu/cognitively-based-compassion-training/index.html
Finley, James. *Meditation for Christians: Entering the Mind of Christ.* Boulder, CO: Sounds True, 2003.
Hefner, Robert W., ed. *Democratic Civility: The History and Cross-Cultural Possibility of a Modern
    Political Ideal.* New Brunswick, NJ: Transaction Publishers, 1998.
Johnson, Suzanne, Bradley L. Goodnight, Huaiyu Zhang, Irene Daboin, and Nadine J. Kaslow Bar-
    bara Patterson. "Compassion-Based Meditation among African Americans: Self-Criticism Mediates
    Changes in Depression." *Suicide and Life-Threatening Behavior* 48: 160–168. doi:10.1111/sltb.12347
Komjathy, Louis, "Approaching Contemplative Practice." In *Contemplative Literature: A Comparative
    Sourcebook on Meditation and Contemplative Prayer,* edited by Louis Komjathy, 3–52. Albany, NY:
    State University of New York Press, 2015.
Lutz, Antoine, Heleen A. Slagter, John D. Dunne Slagter, and Richard J. Davidson. "Attention
    Regulation and Monitoring in Meditation." *Trends in Cognitive Sciences* 12, no. 4, (April 2008):
    163–169.
Lutz, Antoine, John D. Amishi Jha, and Clifford Saron Dunne. "Investigating the Phenomenologi-
    cal Matrix of Mindfulness-Related Practices from a Neurocognitive Perspective." *The American
    Psychologist* 70, no. 7, (2015): 632–658.
Naropa University. "The Naropa Experience: Contemplative Education." Accessed March 2, 2019.
    www.naropa.edu/the-naropa-experience/contemplative-education/index.php.
Odum, Eugene P. and Gary W. Barrett. *Fundamentals of Ecology.* 3rd ed. Philadelphia, PA: Saunders, 1971.
Simmer-Brown, Judith, and Fran Grace, eds. *Meditation and the Classroom: Contemplative Pedagogy
    for Religious Studies.* Albany, NY: State University of New York Press, 2011.
University of Wisconsin-Madison. "Center for Healthy Minds." Accessed March 3, 2019.
    https://centerhealthyminds.org/
Wuthnow, Robert. "A Reasonable Role for Religion? Moral Practices, Civic Participation, and
    Market Behavior." In *Democratic Civility: The History and Cross-Cultural Possibility of a Modern
    Political Ideal,* edited by Robert W. Hefne, 113–130. New York: Routledge, 1998.
Zhang, Huaiyu, Erika R. Carr, Amanda Garcia-Williams, Asher Evan Siegelman, Larisa V. Niles-
    Carnes, Danielle Berke, Bobbi Patterson, Natalie N. Watson-Singleton, and Nadine J. Kaslow.
    "Shame and Depressive Symptoms: Self-Compassion and Contingent Self-Worth as Mediators?"
    Journal of Clinical Psychology in Medical Settings 25, no. 3, (February 2018): 408–419.

Chapter 3

Willingness/Not Willfulness

Hating Mornings

I waved goodbye to my husband as he drove away in our yellow Volkswagen bug. 8:15 a.m. and the heat already pulsed from the pavement of this mid-sized southern city. I walked south toward the back door of St. Stephen's Episcopal Church. An imposing structure, classic stone gothic, the church leveraged substantial religious and civic authority in this city. Generations of members held local political and community leadership positions. Recently, a wealthy member of the parish gave three years of funding for a full-time urban minister. The position signaled refocused dedication to social services and activism. I got the job, to partner with people living without housing, enough resources, and/or healthcare and provide support and shared activism, an asset-based approach. We also hoped church members would strongly participate.

With my Masters of Divinity degree focusing on urban ministries, I had moved to this city a year earlier taking a job in public social services. In this position, I could use my divinity school training including my classes and internships in urban community development. My boss, the dean or head minister of the Cathedral also wanted a woman in this position. Those were contentious days when Episcopalians argued over supporting women's ordination to the priesthood. The staff adjusted offering support and guidance to their first woman minister. I relished the learning and work, and sometimes felt overwhelmed. Beginning several programs from scratch takes a toll. We started with a more robust ministry with the homeless. Then, I added the city's first Meals on Wheels program. Parishioners asked for some Sunday School curriculum on faith, service, and social justice. I developed that class every Sunday. Members of the class developed a youth mentoring program within the Juvenile Court system. We matched parishioners with particular expertise and skills to youth interested in those areas. I offered the mentors resources and support. These were typical activities of an urban minister. But most of my days involved talking with people who turned to the Cathedral for help with bills, housing, travel needs, and more. Early morning was like a quiet low tide before the waves shifted into high gear. I felt the calm even as the humidity mixed with exhaust fumes covering my skin like a sticky goo.

Sleeping on the streets in southern summers makes a mess of your clothes, hair, and whatever bedding you've put together. I've slept on the street only a few times and only as an exercise. I vividly remember the way *everything* stuck to me. People living without housing know how to create a kind of dressing room out of their bedding. In that smallest corner of privacy, they somehow change clothes for a blessed minute or three of freshness. I thought about this as I arrived at the

Cathedral's fence enclosing a small courtyard near the entrance. Charlie and Alma would likely be there. They became a couple about a year ago and asked to sleep inside our courtyard. Alma preferred to avoid what she called the "riff-raff" of shelters. We let anyone sleep there who asked. Most found the grass suffocating, but Alma and Charlie had strategies for minimizing the humidity.

That morning, only Alma raised her head. Charlie must have already left to hawk morning papers on W. Danmouth Street. I had come to count on their greeting as I opened the gate. They provided stability before each of my hectic days; I enjoyed learning the stories of the people I met. They did too, so we usually chatted a bit. Lately, I noticed the drag in my feet as I walked to work. The days grew increasingly like a relentless pinball machine, and I felt jilted this way and that. I needed to muster a new kind of will just to get by. Partly the gaps in our community delivery systems caused frustration, even anger. But my recent grinding fatigue seemed to grow from something else. I could not name it.

Serena, a regular guest, would be coming to my office this morning. She and her children faced losing their apartment. Trying to put the pieces of her life back together after suicidal depression caused a collapse, but she found part-time work and self-respect. Now she was being told that she made *too much* money. To be eligible for her current housing, she could not make above a certain amount. Her new job paid more than that. Devastated and confused she wanted to talk. I wanted to scream. The prospect of returning to the low-level shared apartments provided by the Salvation Army (though these were wonderful emergency resources) pushed her back toward despair. Should she quit the job? But how to have money for school supplies, clothes for the kids, food? A return to a life dependent on canned goods from our food closet spelled defeat – for all of us. We would talk it through; maybe working just a few less hours to get below the cut-off line. Typically, I could refocus my energy and find an upbeat attitude when anticipating such a meeting. But that will seemed not as reliable lately. Something in me was sinking. I blamed the heat.

Many of the homeless we worked with rode trains in summer. Poorer families grew gardens and heat bills disappeared. Organized shelters saw less use. As a result, I actually had time to pull together data and use it to shape next year's programming. I also hoped I could leverage this information to put a fire under other service and activism groups in the city to form a coalition of advocacy. This administrative work offered some satisfaction, but I missed seeing our guests and sharing chats. The lines between us were thin. One regular guest had managed a large custodial staff in New York, but the job was terminated because the building group signed a new contract. He came home to this city thinking he'd find family support and employment. So far, neither proved true. Another guest worked as a research tech at the famous marine biology station, Woods Hole, but lost his way in addiction. He struggled until the Salvation Army offered him work within their homeless shelter. A woman guest, a few years older than me, finished college but couldn't afford her bi-polar medication. The state's public healthcare did not cover it.

It's impossible to predict who will fall into life's sinkholes. The tales of our guests' courage and brokenness seeped deeper into my own fissures and pain, inflaming my impatience and judgment of other service staffs and programs. We all seemed stuck in old models and afraid to join together for advocacy. Having trained for this work,

I knew how to walk the tight-rope of working for the present while building for future change. But I couldn't get their attention; and lately, my own focus seemed wobbly. I understood the insidiousness of labeling others who, like me, struggled to keep serving. But blame came easily these days – on others and myself. Patching and pasting "next steps" exhausted me. These thoughts rambled through my mind as I walked through the gate, but Alma pulled me back into the present.

She mumbled while cradling a cup of coffee that Sara, our Cathedral administrator, handed her through the back door earlier that morning. Now back in her bedding, her fashionable pink robe wrapped around her body over her regular clothes, she struggled to bear the morning light, fumes, and heat. Alma grew up in an upper-middle-class family and was well educated. She preferred breakfast in bed. No one understood how she did not melt with all those clothes on, but this morning as she surveyed the world, she stated to no one in particular, "I'm trying. I'm trying to get used to the idea of morning. Shall I say it? 'Good Morning'!" She paused. Drank coffee. Then added, "Hell! I hate mornings!" By now, I'm inside the gate on the sidewalk next to the grass and her "home." "Hi, Alma!" I chimed in.

No one quite knew the reasons behind Alma's choices, but we did know that her family cared about her, but had run out of next steps. We all reach limits. Roger, the police officer on this beat, checked most nights on Alma and Charlie and any other guests in the Cathedral courtyard. A committed Baptist with theology considerably more conservative than mine, he cared and felt responsible for the welfare of this inter-racial couple. Enough mornings to count, he delivered a small McDonald's breakfast to them as he went off shift. All these stories surged through my mind as I walked up the steps and heard myself joining Alma, "Hell, Alma, I hate mornings too!"

Willing My Way

My body tightened as I stepped through the back door. Lately, I'd noticed this con-vergence: arrive – tighten. Two weeks ago, I committed to a small mental practice, which I hoped would be a deterrent to the wrenching: as I walked up the sidewalk and through the door, I tried to see the day in a positive light – piece by piece: guests, my Cathedral co-workers, that I had resources to offer, committed volun-teers, and so on. But the items fell out of my head with a dull clank on our granite floors. Just a list – maybe a game. The realities. If I juggled a housing voucher's dates just right, the family would get extra days over a weekend. I could extend school lunch vouchers to include breakfasts if I filled out the forms a certain way. These thoughts provided solace. But of late, I felt crankier as I slipped and slid through regulations. I got in more arguments, like the one two days ago with my friend who ran one of the largest overnight shelters. He banned a guest I was trying to support. I couldn't talk it out. I just wanted our guest to get what she needed. As my skills eroded, so too did my confidence. Somewhere, I knew, lurked a truth I struggled to avoid. I stood at the tipping point. *That* tipping point. Service burnout.

My inspiringly smart and wise professor of Urban Ministries at Harvard told us to expect these times. Meet them head-on, he encouraged. Write! Keep a journal – always, but especially when the heat is high. Talk to your trusted friends! I bought the journal, black faux leather with grid-lined pages, which always helped me feel orderly. Now it lay in the right drawer of my desk. I struggled to write in it. Not enough time. The pages couldn't contain all I needed to convey. I kept hoping our nascent advocacy-activism group would get going and offer me support – maybe even shared journal writing time. Not yet. Two weeks ago, a local mentor with over twenty years of professional service experience surprised me with a suggestion. "When I'm feeling stuck, that's when I turn to art. I never could do that journaling stuff," she said, "but I can put color on a page and move it as I think and feel my way through my work at that point." I loved the idea. I did not do it. Instead, I turned for insight and consolation to the local bakery around the corner. Their apple fritters: the best! A lousy strategy, I knew but felt too cornered to do much of anything else. How do you respond when your willingness in service deteriorates into willfulness fed by something empty?

Willing myself through each day, I still helped others strategize and develop skills for next steps. Only the week before, a father and I created an Excel sheet schedule for his bill-paying. He created choices, options to pay enough and be able to buy food. The determination of a seventeen-year-old to find daycare so she could continue classes at the local Junior College made me work harder. We found a scholarship. A woman in recovery told me she'd walk to a job if we could find one. We did. She did. They practiced self-care while I grew more negative and willful. As I opened my office door that morning and turned on the lights, I soured over the fact that my "office" actually was a large storage closet. I put my lunch in the ever-humming, second-hand mini-fridge, sat down and stared at the list of the day's work on my calendar. Then I heard Sara's distinct footfall coming down the hall toward my door.

The Front Porch

Her tone is exasperated. "Bobbi," she sighs, "you're needed at the front of the church." I know this look, and I am familiar with the distancing grammar. We are now not on the same team. I am "you," not "us." I understand; Sara's job makes her the gateway to everything that comes into the Cathedral. She tires of the daily dramas brought to her desk by all of us on the staff. But my dramas often bring sharper edges. "What's up?" I ask in a friendly voice. I get up from my desk to approach her. The vague sense of potential maelstrom raises my pulse rate. She does not answer me, but turns around and walks down the hall toward her office. I follow. As she recedes to her desk, she sighs again. "Honestly, I don't know how to describe it." Drawing the sweater of her light blue twin sweater and skirt set tighter across her chest, she adds. "You'll have to see for yourself." Isn't that a Biblical phrase, I think? "O.K.," I respond, trying to sound chirpy but feeling my lower back tighten.

Having no sweater, I wrap myself in willfulness. Unable to create distance from the anxiety caused by my work, I have resorted to emotional bulwarking. I start down the hall toward the back of the sanctuary, which leads to the doors to the Cathedral's porch. Pushing one of the massive doors open, I step into bright light and the hum of busy downtown traffic. The porch is huge, forty by fifteen feet. As my eyes accustomed to the light, I can make out James, a homeless man I know well. He is leaning over a small table busily at work. About five feet, seven inches tall, he is thin with grayer hair than a forty-eight-year-old should have. James approaches problems intellectually. He talks about his homelessness in the third person, and he laces pragmatic concerns with debates about the effects of economic downturns and paltry governmental policies for homeless populations. Almost never does he directly ask for a place to sleep or something to eat. Last Wednesday he dropped by, and we chatted for thirty minutes before he said that someone's left eye was not working quite right. His eye. We made an appointment for the once-a-week eye clinic.

I stand on the porch and look around. My mind tightens its grip trying to take in what's before me. James has created and furnished a home on the Cathedral's front porch. In the far-right corner lay his familiar sleeping gear, an old blanket and a plastic bag containing all his earthly possessions, which serves as his pillow. Next to this stands a small night table with an unplugged reading light on it. Centered between the first and second pillars of the porch sits a dining table topped by Sleeping Beauty purple linoleum, flecked with silver. Four chairs surround the table. They have matching purple plastic seats. Behind this, are simple wooden bookcases filled with books of fiction, history, and art. A large dictionary holds one row up along with a "Z" World Book Encyclopedia. Now my jaw is locking. I move into his "home."

As if in another room, to the right of the dining room stands a small end table with chipped white paint. Placed next to that is a brown cloth-covered love seat. Missing two legs, it has seen better days. He has china! A teapot and a few plates, all in a multi-floral pattern, stacked on the floor near the love seat. A five-by-five-foot piece of material hangs between the second and third arches, a sign of privacy, I assume. A dressing room? Looking back, I notice two small rugs by the couch and James' bed. They look like the "irregular bathmats" that the Salvation Army called me about two days ago. They had a truckload of them. I'd missed the large metal bowl with kitchen utensils sitting at the end of Sleeping Beauty's world. I do not want to know where the bathroom is.

All items have the familiar look of local giveaways to homeless folks. Perhaps an eviction happened yesterday nearby. James is inventive and loves a good joke. This one, for me, had a wicked hook. We care and we back that up pretty well with our actions. But he has actually moved in. By setting up house in our space, James exposed certain contradictions in our service. Care for our neighbors and our guests cannot put additional pressures on our space. Our money, yes. Out good intentions, yes. But not our space, though James knows we have more space than most downtown. He has occupied us. Is he challenging our hypocrisy? Chastising us? Neither? My mind is racing. Or is this just one of his whims? One thing I know. I do not like this joke – if it's a joke. I start shouting.

In part, what moved up my throat was rage about the lack of affordable housing for James and others. For those wishing stable shelter – and not every homeless person does – the stability of a place to stay provides a crucial first step toward livelihood. We do not offer them that step, nor do we plan to. James stepped directly into this debate by claiming a home – even if his was an act mostly of art or humor. James was testing my ability to hold it together, to serve in the face of continued setbacks and empty talk. As my thoughts raced, my jaw locked tighter. I tried to take my willfulness down another notch. Could I hold it back? If it released, would that rage swell like a blazing fire consuming all, including me? Trying to quell the force rising from my heart, I lost control of the fire inside.

"James! James! Bottom line: You have thirty minutes – THIRTY MINUTES!" It was my voice, but I felt disconnected from it. "You know very well that Wednesday noon Eucharist is now. You know people are coming! You and all this crap must be gone before they get here! James! Have you lost your mind! The Cathedral's front porch is not your home!"

He looked up from his project, unperturbed. His square jaw and smaller torso framed the brown T-shirt he wore with the logo, 5-K Run for Food. He said nothing. I continued. "And – No, I will not help. No, I do not know where you can take all this damn stuff! No, I will not provide my car. No, I do not know anyone else who wants these things. No. No. No. Just get it all gone!"

The words tumbled out somewhere between a rant and a confession. I burned with the heat of a double-edged rage, fury over his situation and fury over our lack of response. My will to serve melting, I shook. "Fix this now, James! No discussions. No negotiating. No working together. No nothing. Just fix it!"

As the words poured out, the burning grew stronger, scorching the core of my service commitment and exposing deep layers of self-condemnation camouflaged by willfulness. But it wasn't all about me. The stored-up rage and panic began to roll like credits at the end of a movie, but they were about so many things. Now they derailed to focus solely on James, who walked toward me smiling, revealing his few upper and even fewer lower teeth. I knew this smile, his response to distress. When frictions sparked, he smiled, I stuffed. Now I seemed to embrace a new strategy; I screamed one more "NO"! as our eyes met. Then, he looked away lingering on the details of his home.

Drawn to him while my inside bulwark began collapsing, I felt duped. My visions of shared work with people living without homes slammed against this scene, this unbelievable scene. I could not breathe. I could not even begin to appreciate his joke. I stood captive to my own intractable willfulness. Solitary. I could not will this away, and so the firestorm fueled faster. I was burning – out.

As James turned back toward me and smiled, I began to cry. Seeing my tears, James walked over to his "china cabinet." "This lovely violet-laden piece came from the Vincent DePaul store," he said. "Can you imagine they wanted a nickel for this?" He began gathering up the china and stacked it neatly on the Sleeping Beauty table. Salad plates on top of dinner plates. A gravy bowl next to those and then the cups and saucers. He had moved before; he knew how to pack his things. At first, I stood watching. His human act of turning to do the next thing, anything, somewhat released the choke collar I had kept on myself. How choked life becomes when reliable housing for those needing it goes missing. How choked public and private service groups become when resource-sharing defies homeless realities, especially the ability to make a living wage.

After organizing the china into piles, James turned to create other orderly piles. Small furniture here. Books and bookshelves there. Next thing I knew, I was helping. We moved the biggest piece, the three-legged couch, down the Cathedral's front granite stairs and hid it behind the large yew bushes to the right of the porch. We would deal with it later. As James, my personal Samson, broke down the two willful columns propping up my current service life, I let him be my guide. He took over the porch-home removal. He suggested we use large heavy-duty garbage bags as portable containers to move the rest of his home somewhere out of sight. Several times, he received bags like these with clothes and/or canned food. I nodded, good idea; and went through the same giant Cathedral door to the kitchen to get them and quickly return.

We were madly putting things into the bags as early arrivals to the noon service came up the steps. Several began helping us, probably thinking we had used the porch to sort donated items to be shared with our guests. Others walked around us wondering, perhaps, if we had lost our minds. But they said nice things. "It's so important that the Cathedral does this ministry." One elderly woman, a regular noon worshipper, quietly whispered, "Thank you." James cut his eyes toward me. If only she knew! They were outside the joke while at the same time in the heart of it. Something in me began to feel willing – to laugh, to shake my head at the irony of service, to not take myself and our work so seriously.

Retrieving his usual form of transportation for his worldly possessions, a local grocery's cart, James loaded in the last few things, a small end table, a lamp, and he tossed in a few of the plastic bags. We tied several of the lighter weight bags to the sides of the cart. Standing together, we looked back at the porch, now empty and clean. I managed to say, "It was a good joke, James. Just had such a wicked hook; I couldn't handle it. My own stuff." "Yeah," he quipped, "A really fun joke to pull off." We pushed the cart further down the sidewalk. At the corner, I turned to walk back to the Cathedral but first asked James to come by later in the afternoon. He assured me he would. I knew the odds were low, maybe in a few days. For now, he had more pressing work, figuring out what to do with all that stuff. As I hurriedly walked back to my office, I felt wobbly, burned.

Exposing Willfulness

Have you turned to grinding determination when service lags? Has someone or something fallen apart so thoroughly that the grip of your will to succeed in a service venture just up and let go? Did that feel like failure, specifically a failure of will? Did you, let's say, send extra emails the next time to remind the volunteer English-language tutors to show up on time? But they didn't show at all; and somehow, you turned that reality into a test of your will to keep things going? Or maybe you flipped the tables of willfulness and labeled the tutors laggards. They didn't have the true will to serve. Driven willfulness wags its finger during planning meetings that devolve into bickering about who's giving more. What's more disturbing is that these examples only reveal the nastier surface of willfulness. The deeper levels of distorted will even corral our thoughts and behaviors into narrow chutes called good or bad. This mostly interior wrangling of our wills to never give up or always press harder distorts service's life-giving principles. Soon, service demands we ignore our anger by rerouting that extra energy into "getting the work done" or "trying another strategy – and another – and another." We will our way through while our creative energies disappear.

Willfulness breeds in the choking constraints of driven, emotionless solitude. As I quickly closed the door behind me and fell into the cradling arms of my 1950s wooden office chair, I believed my will had failed. When willfulness fails, burnout is not far behind. Double failure. The antidote, find some way to squeeze out any bits of willpower left or face the downturn I could not stop. Our work, my work, at the Cathedral did not make the cut. My will did not suffice. I lacked something I called *real* determination and ardency. But alternate approaches to willful service registered limp and undirected. I would keep to my boot camp fortitude: stay the course, get the work done. The warning signals went unheeded.

Blind willfulness specializes in blaming and judging, which begins with self, but turns public when we focus on others. Willfulness still brings enough positive affirmation that we stick with it. Most of us turn to it at some point as a strategy for keeping on. When we turn to it consistently, it becomes lethal.

Making the Shift to Willingness: Another Angle on an Inventory Practice

Making the shift back to willingness as a fuel for service will not erase tough times or serious despair. Nor can a willingness approach keep us out of conflictive situations. Service involves questions of fairness and justice in every context. Sometimes, we willingly grind through tough times. Willingness, despite common reports, is not a push-over. It fuels agency, the capacity to do what's required. Thomas Merton, the contemplative monk, viewed willfulness as a playmate of reactivity – that blaming and judging. Such reactions are a form of slavery, a succumbing to domination,[1] he wrote. But genuine, life-giving agency acts more like adaptation, a bending of will to fuel what's necessary for building resilience.

How does willingness work? If you've ever been swept up in the strong directional flow of an ocean rip-tide, you know getting free from its radical pull does *not* happen by resisting the rip-tide. Fighting is futile. We wear ourselves out. You can, however, work with a rip-tide. How? By willingly going with it. As you move with it, you maneuver its power just enough to keep your body parallel to the beach, the direction most rip-tides run. As you willingly move with it, the drowning energy of the tide fades. As that pull weakens, you can literally swim out of it. Willful fighting of a rip-tide only brings a world of hurt, sometimes death. But chosen realignment with that seemingly destructive energy offers us leverage for next steps. How do we begin to notice our willful patterns? There's no retraining what we don't acknowledge.

In Chapter 1, we learned how to better match our talents and temperaments with the programs and skills needed by a service organization. In that chapter, we worked at the group level using an inventory that helped us better identify and match our skills and needs with the group's. To recognize how willfulness bends our service on a personal level, a variation of the inventory practice is needed. Start by listing experiences, interactions, issues, and people that push your willfulness buttons. When you feel that willful gear engaging – learn to feel the willfulness gear – jot down what it feels like and what triggers it. I call this my working inventory list: no return calls from tutoring center – pissed off; client rejected by another job training program – running out of gas/options; scout troop denied additional funding by sponsoring religious organization – stuck.

It's perfectly OK if you don't write anything down for a day or three – even a week. When items on the list come more frequently, willfulness is gaining energy. When you see two or three items going on the list practically *every* day, willfulness has become your go-to strategy for continuing to serve. All it can offer is more lumber for the fires of burnout. Willingness has the adaptive vision to rethink and reorganize. Inventories help us notice how our emotions bend us toward strategies of holding and controlling – feeding the fire – rather than letting go to gain a fresh perspective. Devote a small notebook or writing pad to your willfulness inventory. Include your emotions whenever you can. Count that jaw-tightening as feelings trying to grab for control. Record that low-level panic trying to force outcomes you believe will save you. From what?

This inventory relies on a non-judging attitude toward ourselves. Avoid labeling things on the list as good or bad. When I can't find words, I draw, and often this simple act of creativity shifts my mood. I feel more ready to ask myself questions I've been avoiding. Once I drew a wolf – well, I knew it was a wolf – with bared teeth. Until that moment, I hadn't realized how defensive I felt, like a mother wolf defending her turf, which faced cut funding due to a partner's pulling out. My charged feelings eluded me until my wolf appeared. So, again – don't control what shows up on the list. It's just for you.

Belden Lane wrote about his inventory process. He mapped his way back into life after his mother's death by describing the gaps, holes, and bridges he had to build to regain stability. He had to tap resources formerly left untapped. The book of this inventorying, *The Solace of Fierce Landscapes* describes modes of self-protection, clever forms of denying death, and serious struggles with anger and grief. They sometimes felt endless, he writes. Drawing on Christian contemplative principles and practices, he describes the work of getting through and getting back as "ardent," willingly staying with the pain or burn of death. He shares no easy fixes, but lots of assumptions about life that needed revising. Amid his documentation of slippages into and out of denial or self or other blaming are lists of attempted rebuilding, new awarenesses, and sometimes painful realizations. These bridge-points in the midst of grief marked moments of courage. Count these, he says. They signal small, even hesitant, moments of rebuilding. These begin, when we note them, in the midst of our grief and rage at death or burnout. So like Lane, notice it all when inventorying. With honestly and kindness stay with reality – willfully or willingly. Be and document where you truly are.

Growing Curious: Attention and Awareness

We've talked about pausing to pay attention. But attention has a deeper phase, awareness. Many metaphors speak to the distinction between the two. Attention rides on the surface of the ocean's wave. It stays afloat by continually adjusting with each swell and trough. Awareness drops down below the surface into the deeper quieter sea below the surface's ebb and flow. Another way to think of the distinction is to imagine an eagle in flight continual correction and adjustment to the wind's dips and surges. This is attention. Awareness is that same eagle soaring with only periodic adjustments on the moving airstreams above earth. Both offer help for living. Attention is a gift of evolution, always scanning our environments for safety and support.[2] You're here because an ancestor of yours caught a glimpse of the tiger's bright eye before trouble hit. But attention can be tricked by camouflage, fear, or desire. We experience this when the sound of our email or a text on our phone pings or plays like harp music. Our attention is grabbed, and a whole network of neural and biochemical processes go off.

Awareness works below surface attention. It offers a meta-perspective, meaning a richer and broader capacity to pause and wait before launching into biochemical or physical action. Awareness provides that moment needed to take in as much information as available before striking out at that semi-hidden form that is your sister or neighbor. Awareness fosters emotional regulation because the pausing allows us to monitor our responses. We have enough time to notice we're edging toward panic or anger or resentment. That monitoring can bring us back to equanimity or calmer balance. We can keep thinking when emotions rise. We tune into relationships rather than fixate on isolation. This is serious work and requires practice. It can be cultivated the way athletes mentally vision a swimming stroke and then put that image into action over and over until it becomes second nature. We can learn to observe our resistances to burnout but not buy into them, not go down that path. Instead, we wait, to see what else might arise, like a small realization that mornings have become a time I too hate.

Willfulness depends on attention. It drives to respond to what's immediately happening. No waiting. Just get that problem gone. At times in service, this approach is very helpful. Get the child in an urban playground away from the cornered rat that he thinks is a kitty. But more often than not, awareness helps us step back from the spin cycles of churning minds, hearts, and bodies, in the midst of service's ongoing energies. If we only ride those waves of surface energy, we'll soon be worn out. Dropping down settles our minds for decision-making choices less driven by judging, fixing, or grabbing to control. We recognize those push-pull waves above us as our experiences, thoughts, and feelings,[3] but without becoming entangled. This leverages our freedom to choose. In service, this stepping back awareness helps us take in and process the consequences of our thoughts and feelings. We can choose to move into and through burnout. We develop *willingness* to change.

Here's a practice that fosters awareness. Find a comfortable position in a chair with your back straight but not tense and take a couple of deep breaths – all the way in and all the way out. Focusing on one breath at a time draws our mind, body, and heart to the moment, the breath. Once your mind is generally settled, riding those waves, remember a time when you got through each day by sheer will. Remember the details, how everything seemed a struggle, like waves buffeting you all day long. If useful, you can imagine each wave carrying a specific message of worry and pressure: budget not met, staff person not working out, launch of new program causing more chaos, you name it.

Now imagine going below those waves of willfulness and their turbulence. Drop down and embrace the more settled, calmer flow of the currents around you. Able to see the waves above you, those problems and worrisome thoughts, feelings, and memories, notice them but try to avoid getting caught up in them. Settle. Notice. Let them move by. Still, without getting engaged, you may be aware of certain patterns, noting those emotions that pull more strongly on your attention? Their waves may be higher creating more turbulence below. But notice that they do flow on moving out of your immediate experience and dissipates. This is what waves do, even the strongest, the most willful. For me, these buffeting waves included lack of support for learning and problem-solving with my professional service peers, struggles within our own staff, and my own unrealistic expectations for the speed of positive change.

What are your buffeting waves, their sources, and directions? Just notice them while in the practice. This is not the time to begin problem-solving or debating fault. If you find yourself going there – into those buffeting waves, settle down again into your body and refocus on your breathing. Perhaps take a few deeper breaths. Then return to the process of noting the waves as they pass over, including the ones that impact you more. But let them all move on. After a period of time, ten to twenty minutes is typical, close this practice by refocusing your attention solely on the breath. Acknowledge that the practice is ending and offer gratitude for the chance to acknowledge those waves of chaos that redirect your work with and without your involvement. It's useful to get a deeper sense of how those tides impact our immediate responses. This practice also reveals growing currents of discontent, which we may deny or try to control. Both strategies only up the level of destructive collapse. When the practice is finished, you may want to jot down words describing those buffeting waves. If some questions come to mind, write them down too. But now's not the time to move into problem-solving. Just be with the ride for now.

On the next day or in a few days, return to what you've written. Do other thoughts or links among the words and phrases arise? What emotions come up in relation to what you've written? Is there a quick solution that comes to mind? Don't reject whatever shows up. Frustrated with my social service peers' lack of response, I intended to go forward with homeless advocacy alone! Not a great or realistic strategy, but one I needed to admit. Notice whatever comes up. Which aspects of the work conjure more frustration and worry? Where are the moments of settled calm? Can these increase? It was from those calmer spaces that I could more honestly recognize and analyze how many forms my willfulness took. More than I realized. This practice, a kind of inventory, invites you to discover the forms your willfulness is taking and how it encourages a sense of stuck burnout, that feeling of being cornered with no way out. Unless we know more about those corners, we cannot begin to discern they are illusions. Turn around and go with the tide that's taking you in new and sometimes uncomfortable directions.

This practice of deepened awareness born of what's changes also introduces new yet related questions to our willful strategies of service: Does my will have enough fuel to get me through each day? If not, what sources of energy for service can I tap into? How might I pursue those? What would sustain them willingly? We can't work with all these questions at once, but being mindful of their general trajectory toward rebuilding our service on willingness, they begin to map, as Belden Lane discovered, steps to be taken through the burning. Whether on smaller levels or larger ones, the journey moves forward with more openness to questions, alliances, and next steps we did not see or imagine while in the grip of willfulness. We need not stay stuck in assumptions that drive us into locked-jaw service. We can reorient our skills and emotions to move into and through changed direction and reconstructed serving with others.

Learning to Let Go

I served as a member of a design team tasked with developing a new volunteer program for college students at a large university. Like everyone on the team, I felt pressure to push through the planning and get the program started. So, we hurried into a testing phase with two community partners eager to participate. Each site hoped to have five students working with them for one semester. The student sign-ups went easily. But the required community-engagement training did not. To make sure things went well on the first day, I came with the first student group to their site. Only one of them had done our community-engagement training. But even he had no sense of service as partnership. Like the other students, he did not listen but brushed off questions the supervisor asked about his knowledge of this local community and its issues. Twice he responded, "I'm here to work! Put me to work – whatever is needed!"

The predictable happened. The students' energy to serve overwhelmed their ability to listen to details of their tasks. They had no ear for nuances about the community members they would be helping to fill out government forms in just a few minutes. Their plan was to drop into the site, do good, and leave. Our trade-off to get going as soon as possible sent the whole project into a tailspin. We made it through that afternoon, but our partners expressed serious concerns about the model the next day. We talked to our supervisor asking if we could slow down and put more requirements in place. We tried to talk about the impossibility of adding this on top of our other work especially with no access to training space or program funds. His only response was to plow on through. The dream of this program would be worth it!

So, we tried, willing our way forward. Each of us committed to a rotating schedule of going with the students. We hoped to do on-site training with them. But this only put extra pressures on our other jobs, and the students felt bounced from our training tips to the community supervisor's instructions. The knots of miscommunication and logjams of work done wrong grew. Students were not required to attend post-service reflection sessions; so, opportunities to work through these problems did not happen. Student frustrations grew. Some quit. Disappointed community partners began to question putting time into the program. Increasingly empty-handed, we felt cornered between anger and despair at the impossibilities we faced from the start. But we kept willing our way forward as long as we could.

After six months, everyone realized the program in its current state would not make it. Facing pressures from his boss, our boss blamed the students, calling them irresponsible and immature. He implied their privilege contributed to their failure. Now the tensions of our predominantly suburban campus failing to responsibly participate with local African-American communities sat like a lump in our throats. We willed our way forward by not talking more about it. The complexities, including his uninformed assumptions that we might have unpacked, went untouched. But two of us did suggest a conversation with the students might bring more information to light. And so, we with about half of them and learned more about the fall-out of student willfulness in service hitting staff willfulness in service. Bottom line, student and staff goals shared very little in common. They needed easy access and tasks. Community partners needed collaborative commitment as much as tasks. Without time to engage with each other, our willed service dead-ended.

So be it, we concluded, and as soon as the decision happened, the relentless tension in my shoulders and heart began to ease. The pummeling I took trying to keep going while my other responsibilities wavered took a higher toll than I admitted. Always in the waves of willfulness, I never found a way to get beyond their crashing, to drop down to pause and discern the sources of the pummeling. Willfulness, I believed, served me and service. But this dead-end hit hard enough that I let myself feel the failure and sink below the fight. This worn out principle had worn me out enough. I began to test its polar opposite, willingness as a principle for serving with others. Not a silly letting go, but a serious decision to willing relinquish determined inflexibility. To slow down. To ponder more and listen to others better. All tough asks for most of us in service, these shifts came slowly – they're still coming. It takes practice to embrace a deeper, more contemplative flow of not-always-so-programmed service, to settle into reality as it is and work from there.

Finding Thicker Questions

This distinction between service unfolding through willful attention and service fueled by willing awareness shifts our preoccupation with "right" answers toward staying longer with the questions. Willing awareness, it turns out, moves us through burnout more effectively than driven attention. Willingness avoids willfulness' rigid arguments and quick-fixes that keep things static. What can we bring to this open awareness? Our inventory practices! Once when more aware of my responses to struggle (perhaps pre-burnout) and burnout in service, I turned to my inventory list and took note of a recurring phrase arising during my practice. Like a strong current driving through my mind, I named it, "I want to be home – anywhere but here!" In later reflection, I wrote a series of questions in response to that pressing current. What's at home that I can't find in this work? What counts as "home"? Specifically, where is "anywhere but here"? As I thought about and jotted down some ideas in response to these questions,

Over the next few weeks, I continued tracking down more information about my history with this current of thought. I reconnected with some feelings I'd been ignoring. The work helped me move into the resistances and breaking apart of this phrase, this current. I could move into those to discern what might be next steps rather than remaining stuck and angry. There were other similar phrases I had overlooked, but once I engaged this one, they rose to my attention. One phrase was "total frustration today." We've all thought or said that but what if we let that riptide take us into deeper insight? Using this practice helps us not only acknowledge the surface reality that service brings frustration, but we can dive deeper into how that's actually showing up and what's our response. When I heard my head or voice thinking or saying this, I now had more of an inventory of insight to bring to the present situation. That inventory offered possible ways forward into the fray. Did I need to reorganize the work? Did I need to let something go? Was this a resource-need matching problem? Do I need a break or do I need a bigger change?

By dropping down into our questions, we not only become more awake and aware of our responses in service without suddenly getting swept by a tide of willfulness, but we also discover unexplored angles on a service struggle. If this inventorying work spurs useful questions, other changes also may arise. We might uncharacteristically explore a really different angle on our service work – more activities or truly different activities. We might turn our energies back toward education about certain issues for our sponsoring organizations. We better recognize leadership or commitments that are and are not working without resorting to blaming or self-blaming. These newer angles, of course, emerge over time. They are not the work of quick revelations once a riptide of willfulness hits. But if that tide takes you to a truly new beach, it might be just the beach you've really needed. Willingness might just flourish there.

By retraining our reactivity to move below the chaotic waves of initial attention, we settle into awareness and can discover more about our service, our burnout, our community, and ourselves. Here's another awareness-building practice.

Practice Walking It Through

When we're caught up in willfulness, can't ask questions using our inventory, and certainly can't explore other angles, try this variation of Chapter 1's walking meditation. This version pays closer attention to every step. To begin, start walking. As the rhythm of your steps settles into your awareness, focus more specifically on the details of your basic body movements while walking. Tuning into the particulars of each step hones attention to the finer grain world of awareness. Sink into that sharper focus. Notice the experience of your toes touching the ground, how your weight shifts across the mid-foot, and then releases as your toes leave the ground. Feel how the weight of your hips change and your legs surge and release as your footfalls continue. Notice the touching and leaving, the moving and releasing movements as never precisely the same. The wobbling, the unevenness, the tilting of our bodies this way and that, all of this is heightened by awareness' finer-tuned attention. The experience of now, of the present, complicates in awareness.

Service able to move with and through burnout is like awareness of walking, each step feels more impermanent as we tune in more closely to our experience of movement as flow or a trip or a wobble. Even in a wheelchair, no movement is completely predictable. Surfaces below the wheels alter the roll. The angles of hands on wheels or joysticks bring slight variations in angle or speed. Some changes require counter movements or patience to wait until the altered movement stops. Similarly, in service and burnout, the subtleties of growing willfulness can escape our attention. But with regular focus on the level of awareness, we begin noticing the sources of our wobble or trip. We may or may not fall, but we will key into the feelings, thoughts, and experiences we're trying to erase from our view and what's actually happening.

Awareness tips us off to the angles of fall. We may get a bit more preparatory time – a pause – because we're more tuned in and less buffeted by each experience. This deeper walking meditation practice sharpens our noticing skills first in walking, but by extension in service. In contemplative traditions, awareness builds impartiality, that capacity to release our preferences to be with what comes up. We let go of each step to take another as it comes. Impartiality in service and burnout means learning to release our tight grasp on what *must* happen in good service, to directive willingness. We practice equanimity, sometimes called impartiality, by going with the heart, mind, and body (and their capacities to) be with things as they are.[4] And how they always involve others; it's communal. In awareness, we have time to notice we're not on our own. We don't have to will service, or it will collapse. Things change. Willingly move into them.

These ideas came alive for me during a ten-day trek in the Sinai Desert in Egypt. Moving into the desert near Alexandria, Egypt, we walked through the cross-roads country of Jewish, Egyptian, and African religions as well as Christian and Muslim traditions. This is the home of early Christian contemplative life; the landscape is dotted with monasteries, retreat caves in the high hills, Bedouin communities, and searing landscapes. We spent one night in the guest house of St. Catherine's Monastery, the most ancient and continuously functioning monastery in Christendom. To get there, we negotiated days and nights of hiking across high sand dunes. We periodically lost our footing and the sheath of stability we counted on flowed away like water.

Often entranced by this magical landscape, I found myself careening downhill. The experience marked the difference between attention and awareness. Willfully trying to make my way back to my feet, I dug into the sand around me – only to bog down more. Getting back to the top of our current high dune might never have happened without the help of our guides. Their advice began with "pause and regroup," become aware of where you are and what's happening. That reset of my awareness helped me discern the angles of approach I needed to slowly make my way back to the group at the top. But each step brought its own tipsiness. The guides and my buddies made helpful suggestions about the angle of my ascent. Like riding a rip-tide, I learned to go with the line of fall on the dune rather than fight it. I increased my awareness, including reaching out for help. Once back at the top, I continued to try to keep my awareness higher, to watch my footing more carefully. We move forward willingly with awareness.

Communal Flow: Shared Stories

Macarius, a famous teacher from the Egyptian desert, taught about the importance of community awareness and interdependence. In the collection of his "50 Spiritual Homilies" or short sermons, he described the four keys to loving community-based service. To start, let willfulness go. He especially emphasized releasing willfulness that condemns self and others. These are useless, he advises. As the leader of desert-bound people trying to live together in love, Macarius heard it all: anxieties, bickering, angry feelings, and blaming – all human interactions. Willful determination to move beyond these all-too-human and understandable problems repeatedly failed. Though well-intentioned, this tact distorted how change works. When we expend energy in hand-wringing resistance to mistakes, to life's jumble, to real pain or genuine human selfishness, we only get more stuck – like me in the sand.

Do not engage in blame-filled willfulness, wrote Macarius. That response only fosters "trouble or pains or sweat . . . "[5] Shift to willingness, which is the experience of letting go to the fullness of where we actually are and what is truly happening. To do this, Macarius encouraged reflection, activities like our inventory listing and more focused walking meditation. These fuel willingness when times are tough. In reflection, we can honestly ponder which attitudes and expectations drive our decision-making, and how assumptions about "our responsibility" calcify into willful acts to go forward or fail. So, when we hear a throw-away line from a colleague about frustration or despondency, let's pay more attention to their story, the deeper story born of awareness. Self-reflection nourishes awareness of others. It's not a one-way path.

I felt too caught up in my own willfulness to approach James and his home as anything but my problem. It had to change – now! Pausing, listening, reflecting fell so low on my list of skills I never considered turning to them. I already knew the story, and it was a disaster. I must fix it. Because my will dominated, I had no willing flexibility, no subtle insight. But after that very painful – and funny – day, I tried to build my awareness and willingness muscles. As an example, I shifted my approach to starting a city-wide advocacy group for our homeless and poor guests. Instead of demanding meetings I willfully called, I got to know my colleagues better over coffee and lunch. I tried to let go of my agenda to become part of the team, a caring, willing team. It took more time, but it wasn't wasted. We shaped a looser consortium than I originally imagined. But the willingness we bred helped to hold it together for several years, which in service and burnout was pretty remarkable.

Four Antidotes to Willfulness

When I feel my teeth gritting or my eyes narrowing – which comes with service – I try to turn to the four antidotes, as I call them, to willfulness: laughter, gratefulness, imagination, and pace. Using my experience with James on the porch, let me explain how they work.

Laughter

That moment when I first opened the Cathedral's doors to the porch, what if I'd been willing to go with the joke? To take in James' new home as the joke it clearly, artistically, and dramatically was. A challenge, no doubt, but James knew there'd be no living full-time on that porch. Knowing him as well as I did, I knew he wouldn't choose to live there anyway. Stable housing signaled confinement to James. But being confined to my never-burnout, willfulness-fueled vision of outreach ministry, my creativity also went bankrupt. Joking had no place in my life and work; it never crossed my mind to laugh as I took in the porch. What a loss. The magic of the purple linoleum, silver-flecked table – lost on me. The privacy curtain – out of my ken. I missed the play on the church's rather patched-together advocacy for people living without homes. I stood willfully stymied.

Laughter loosens our grip on willfulness. It teases our sensibility that service is always life or death. Holding for dear life onto a narrow version of justice work, I had no hand free to grab some humor. Thinking I stood tall for commitment and dedication, I, in fact, stood off balance and collapsing under the weight of my own misdirected will and rigidity. Self-blame, anger, and loss of self-care held me on the surface. I was only able to pay attention. No wonder I felt constantly buffeted and unaware. Hating mornings wasn't a wry insight. I marched forward without laughter, falling subject to what Thomas Merton called "precious self-respect."[6] It sounds harsh, but it's also wry with humor. I lost out on the laughing. I was burning out and stymied.

Gratefulness

Laughter is a strong ingredient of self-care. Consistent shunning of self-care feeds self-blame, which erases gratefulness, a second antidote to willfulness. David Steindl-Rast, the Benedictine contemplative says it this way, "It's not happiness that makes us grateful, but gratefulness that makes us happy." By substituting gratitude for whatever we think *counts* as happiness, we draw attention to what's *actually* happening now. The porch scene did not make me happy. But had I tuned into gratitude, I might have noted James' art and wit. What amazing innovation to be grateful for. But my gratitude had narrowed to a very small subset of program successes with overdrawn and rigid lines. James colored outside the line, inviting my gratitude to run broader, to be delighted by things out of control as well as in control. That's still a hard balance for me to get today. But service and burnout outcomes rarely come wrapped up in pretty bows. We can gratefully count on times of flourishing stability as well as collapse, which press us to rethink and reorganize. Service is so much more than happiness. Gratitude helps us see that and go with it willingly.

Imagination

By clinging to distorted versions of control, which fostered denial, I lost the art of imagining anything else. Imagination softens and releases overly rigid, willful expectations. Caught in that will-driven grip of reactivity, we harden, feed our self-defenses and deny burnout. We choose not to work with it, but to survive – a bad choice with no energy and creativity. Without an inventory of burning issues and no awareness, I believed I could not afford to get curious about my frustration and pain. I had no idea I could approach service while experiencing burnout. So, I spent all my imaginative energy defending and resisting – never softening.

My lack of imagination also limited my capacities to pause and find creative space for thinking through next steps. I could not imagine an alternative to my constant drive to make things go as I thought they must each day. But what feels intractable need not be constantly pushed against. I could go with the breakdown, dig into and through the rubble. I could reimagine a walk-through collapsed programs or burned relationships without trying to control despair. Teresa of Avila, the medieval contemplative, believed that imagination includes despair, "I have been to the bottom of the pit, and it is firm." Imagine that! Imagination helps us step outside that box or that corner of defensiveness against burnout. But burnout is only a phase, a necessary one. Resilience requires imagination – a great antidote to willfulness.

Pace

Softening to open up to imagination will not avoid burnout. It takes us into it – willingly. So, what to do then? Become aware, think, and take a human pace, the fourth antidote to willfulness. Willing our way through service and burnout keeps us jacked up. If runners in training drew only on willfulness, they would only do sprints. Willingness reorients us by using a variety of paces, some slower, some at race pace, and even faster. Willingness helps us kick it up when needed because we're not all out, all the time. Pace is another form of space where gratefulness and imagination appear. With pacing, we have enough space to actually feel the panic or distress of burnout without having to deny it or completely fall into it and get stuck. Pace encourages reflection and insights born of awareness. Pace encourages us to walk mindfully through burnout paying deeper attention because there's learning to be gained.

In my case, willfulness meant my surface panic never let up. I remained on lock into the drowning waves of trying to keep the rest of the fire out of my view. Smelling the smoke, my pace demanded full tilt. I gave more than I had, ignoring the community and our stories of service thriving and failing. My pace meant feelings flew wildly in all directions, as James experienced. Never sitting with them, mostly spewing them out – I hate mornings – I never willingly attended to them. That colleague who might have been ready to willingly listen, I ignored. Pressed beyond my capacity, I flung my will in a panic at James. And my emotions. I ran relentlessly on fire.

Your Porch, My Home

In every collapse, choices exist. Willfulness never even sees them. The doors of insight and imagination remain closed. On many days, I felt, "If *only* I could breathe." By this, I actually meant if only I could release, soften, open, become aware of service as it was, of me and others in it. Scientific research continues to confirm that there's resilience and healing in breathing. When we mindfully attend or be with, collapses as they are rather than bulling our way through them, we do better.[7] We find sources for recombining and moving forward.

Thomas Keating is a contemporary Christian contemplative who created principles and practices called Centering Prayer. Leveraging therapeutic insights with contemplative knowledge, his practices always begin with deeper awareness of the breath moving in and out. Keating describes this process, and we can translate it to leveraging awareness as a willing step for moving through burnout:

> (as one breathes the) less conscious (the deeper awareness) parts of one's being, say . . . "Simmer down and listen, there is something beyond this turmoil. (This) is communication in action that often works when words merely go in one ear and out the other, not even changing the cognitive mind. In essence, the effect is to turn all the elements of one's will toward stillness and waiting . . . Learning how to use our lungs is one way of opening our spirits to (the) new . . ."[8]

Patanjali's foundational text, the yoga sutras, share a similar sentiment: "Yoga (body and breath) stops the whirlings of the mind."[9] The breath's constant, present-moment rhythm serves as an easy first signal reminding us to pay attention, drop down into awareness, and willingly begin to shift our motivations and choices. Here we foster readiness to choose next steps (Kadloubovsky and Palmer: 33) But be patient. The transition from willfulness to willingness takes time.

Eventually, James came by for a visit. Not too interested in the details of our reorganized advocacy group, he, Charlie, Alma, and others went on with their lives. I kept learning to let go to see if next steps might emerge and willingly take them. I tried to remember that I could not precisely control their direction – and laugh in gratitude. But these next steps proved good enough. I kept my inventory going. I worked with it and walking meditation and stronger listening to the stories of all of us. I upped my self-care, which fostered more capacity to listen to others. Of course, some days, I still ground my teeth, but willingly.

Exercises

1. When did your vision for urban service begin to narrow into a checklist of tasks to be done with? Who in your circle – think broadly – could understand these feelings? What would it take to share them with that person or group?

    _____

    _____

    _____

    _____

    _____

    _____

2. As you tipped from willingness to willfulness, what parts of yourself disappeared? Consider as well, your self-care, your creativity, and your capacities to be fully present with others.

    _____

    _____

    _____

    _____

    _____

    _____

3. When unexpected tides of burnout took your service in new directions with less sense of control, how did you or how might you map your way forward as Belden Lane did?

    _____

    _____

    _____

    _____

    _____

    _____

4. Choose one of the four "antidotes to willfulness" and apply it to some area of willfulness active in your service now.

_____

_____

_____

_____

_____

_____

Notes

1 Pennington, *On Retreat with Thomas Merton*. 42–43, 64–65.
2 See Goleman, *The Hidden Driver of Excellence*.
3 Professor Hal Brown of Brown University clearly defines and describes the usefulness of integrative work with attention and understanding. See www.brown.edu/academics/contemplative-studies/about.
4 See Noah Levine at www.dharmapunx.com/.
5 Mason, *Fifty Spiritual Homilies*, 50.
6 Merton, *New Seeds of Contemplation*, 187.
7 For an example of this approach, see Susan Bauer-Wu's book, *Leaves Falling Gently*, a guide to living with illness using mindfulness and compassion practices.
8 Kelsey, *The Other Side of Silence*, 112.
9 Bouanchaud, *The Essence of Yoga*, 5; Desikachar, *The Heart of Yoga*, 149. Second Sutra taught to me by Desikachar, Mombai, India.

References

Bauer-Wu, Susan. *Leaves Falling Gently: Living Fully with Serious and Life-Limiting Illness through Mindfulness, Compassion, and Connectedness*. Oakland, CA: New Harbinger Publications, Inc, 2011.
Bouanchaud, Bernard. *The Essence of Yoga: Reflections on the Yoga Sutras of Patanjali*. Portland, OR: Rudra Press, 1997.
Brown University. "About: Contemplative Studies." Accessed April 26, 2017. www.brown.edu/academics/contemplative-studies/about
Desikachar, T.K.V. *The Heart of Yoga: Developing a Personal Practice*. Rochester, NY: Inner Traditions International, 1995.
Dharma Punx. Accessed October 8, 2017. www.dharmapunx.com.
Goleman, Daniel. *Focus: The Hidden Driver of Excellence*. New York: Harper Collins, 2013.
Kelsey, Morton. *The Other Side of Silence: Meditation for the Twenty-First Century*. Revised edition. New York: Paulist Press, 1997.
Mason, Arthur James. *Fifty Spiritual Homilies of St. Macarius the Egyptian*. Society for Promoting Christian Knowledge, New York: Macmillan, 1921.
Merton, Thomas. *New Seeds of Contemplation*. Boston, MA: Shambhala Publications, Inc., 1961.
Pennington, M. Basil. *On Retreat with Thomas Merton*. New York: Continuum, 1995.

Chapter 4

Not Taking In/Taking In

The *Newbie*

My first full day in the Bethlehem Center washed over me and then took me like a rapid. The experiences blurred. Kindergarteners finger-painted in one corner, pre-teens sat on a rug in the middle of The Center's Rec Room reading books, and a third set of raucous girls and boys played Four Square in the back corner. On the wall of that same back corner hung a large-lettered sign: NO FOUR SQUARE INSIDE! Obviously, today's game was regular as were the pods of children coming every day to The Center to read, color, and do homework. I was on a tour led by my new boss. The Four Square game got louder until she sharply called them out, "Rashid, Jennifer, all of you – Quiet Down! We're inside!" She knew these children, and they obviously knew her as the roar down-shifted slightly. Approximately one hundred kids flowed in and out of the center on any given day. "Sometimes we stick to the rules; sometimes we break the rules," she explained. "Bottom line: kids at The Center need to know when enough is enough. When interactions among them or with one of us crosses our limits!" Jesse Clipper, my new boss, often used verbal bullet points to explain her actions. She demanded The Center be a safe and reliable space for all who came to it, including us, the staff. I wanted to learn as much from Jesse as I could.

She took me to my office area, an open space with three metal desks, the "Social Services office." My desk sat in the back-left corner. The front of this fifteen by fifteen-foot room was swamped with file cabinets. Without a door, the space opened into a hallway lit by the same fluorescent lights as the office. All day long, they hummed in accompaniment to our work. Sarah's desk sat on the left side of the room. An insightful African-American woman a few years over thirty, she took great pride in her social work degree. From a working-class home, Sarah dressed formally with stylishly coiffed hair and matching jewelry. Though she did not grow up in this neighborhood, she knew people from it, their struggles to find work, access to healthcare, and protection from violence. This all-Black neighborhood retained histories of a city split starkly across racial lines.

Shirley, my other office mate, sat at her desk on the right side of the room. She had worked for fifteen years at The Center. Supervising Sarah and me, she spent most of her days interfacing with county social services offices and making visits to families or people in jail, or filling out forms. An African-American in her 40s, she would be my direct supervisor, assigning me tasks as she also did to Sarah. Her gift for making the wheels of service-provision turn drew on the power of her faith, though she rarely talked about it. Both women had been part of my interviewing process. They asked pragmatic questions, in congenial tones. Did I know how to help neighbors apply for social security? Had I worked with the Veterans Association, the Salvation Army? Their questions gave me a glimpse of the daily tasks of service in this place and their approach. Both claimed my attention, especially being new and the only white person on the staff. Most of the time, I was the only white person in the building. Still, in the early years of my work as a paid employee in service settings, I listened more than talked. Perhaps that's why Jesse suddenly suggested we all to go to lunch. Maybe she hoped I would tell them more about myself and my experiences in that social setting. Enjoying the food and camaraderie, I remained basically quiet.

Back and organizing my desk, I noticed a man passing back and forth in front of the opening to our office. He did this two or three times, slightly slowing down, but never completely stopping. Sarah and Shirley didn't look up, but the last time he crossed, they each said, while still not looking, "Afternoon, Sam." "Hi, Sam," I chimed in, getting up from my desk and moving toward to the front of our space to put a few files into my assigned filing cabinet drawers. When I turned to go back to my desk, Sam was pulling up a metal folding chair in front of it. He sat. Getting back to my seat, I said, "Afternoon, my name is Bobbi – what's yours?" He didn't answer. He looked down at the floor. I smiled, sat down, tried to look busy organizing things in my desk and tried a few more times to engage him in conversation. He didn't respond; and I tried to brush off my anxieties. Had he come to check out the newbie? Was I doing OK?

How This Chapter Works

This chapter examines how different people in service settings establish and hold healthy boundaries or not. Using interactions at The Bethlehem Center, stories demonstrate how people in service relationships negotiate interactions, some through compliance, others through surface compliance without follow-through, and still others through resistance, from asking more questions to disagreeing on next steps. These examples highlight skills for open conversations and tools that contribute to honest relationship-building amid issues of diversity and inclusion. Interactions in this chapter range from misunderstanding, to empathetic listening, to shared discoveries of realistic expectations in provider-client service relationships. An experience of communication breakdown explains other dynamics that contribute to healthy relational boundaries. Highlighting the principle, "Not Taking In," the stories clarify why surface pleasantries though seeming effective in service actually fire up more intense burnout than honest sharing.

The interactions in the chapter reveal the dangers of machine-like service interactions that produce a service product but with the feel of plastic. For all involved, these non-relational interactions eventually become intolerable and lead to acting out or attempts at boundary-breaking. Establishing healthy boundaries early on not only energizes relationships but produces more trust for moving into and through the inevitable tough times to come. Explaining the sense of being dispensed with as client or service provider rather than engaged as a person, the chapter rebukes such caricatures and the damage of their non-relational approach. To *not take in* the humanity of another, to refuse to engage as if service were a commodity exchange, the interactions in this chapter teach skills for long-term resilience.

I would learn these lessons over the next six months, but in the first month, they left me baffled. I felt Sam's pensive turbulence and my anxious desire to calm him and me. But I had no ideas for next steps other than to take in whatever he offered. I thought that demonstrated my willingness to establish a service relationship. But my approach was not working. Even that first day that he pulled a chair up to my desk, he said nothing. I kept offering empty pleasantries, trying to take him as he was – or at least that's how I explained it to myself. He did not respond. Eventually, he pushed back the chair he sat in. Stood up. folded it, and carried it to the nearest wall. He leaned it there and then left the room.

Learning the Boundaries

It's tough to be the new person in a service setting, whether you've had former service experience in a professional role or not. Still learning about tasks, relationships, when to take charge or back off, we dance between listening and engaging. Humility helps us ground ourselves to listen longer and learn more. But in time, our own good sense about service content and relationship-building will come into play. Many of us, especially in unfamiliar settings, are given opportunities to shift our usual styles of serving and interacting. The early stages of pleasing and stepping back from tensions are typical for many of us in new settings. But over time, our resilience benefits from learning to honestly yet humbly (meaning grounded) relate with those we serve and serve with. The work of calibrating healthy boundaries in each service setting plays a crucial role in maintaining strong personal interactions, communication, and emotional sharing. It makes service better, more resilient.

The chapter provides two key skill sets which help service givers in new settings learn how to develop skills for healthy relationship-building. That first period of listening with humility grounds us in the setting's style of interactions. We learn to hear colleagues and clients more fully before we dive in to correct or fix. Humility also roots us strongly enough in our new setting to encourage new growth in our approaches to relationships and boundary-setting. We establish enough stability in those relationships to consider actions we'd never considered before or were too afraid to try. Often it is only a new setting or its new challenges that push us into new growth or changed behaviors. But this growth goes missing when we resist carefully observing and thinking about the way people relate in our new setting. How does the energy flow among them and between individuals? When and why does this energy create resilient, shared service? Skills for recognizing local patterns of relating to get work done must develop over time. This chapter explains how to pay attention and grow with the local style, including offering our own relational contributions.

The second skill involves letting go of styles we've used to protect either an image of ourselves in service or fears we keep, which weaken our abilities to shape productive and meaningful service relationships. This second skill develops over time, like the first; but more than time, it requires risking new ways of relating. The second skill must be practiced. Yet as the chapter makes clear, that risk can be hard to take. We avoid learning experiences; keeping ourselves at a safe distance from our staff colleagues and/or clients. We patch old assumptions and patterns on top of new information and hope for the best. To practice new forms of boundary-setting and holding, we must take in new information, including the histories of relationship-building in our setting. Leveraging this information, we take risks to develop our own styles within the service community.

This chapter offers insights about discovering how people communicate and work in service settings. It explores lines between more formal and informal interactions, including how management styles in a service setting impact ways client and staff relate. Scenes in the chapter demonstrate how quickly false assumptions develop about a client, often one with complex needs, and the damage done. When interactions hit a tipping point, more honest and real understanding emerges born of honest interactions and healthy boundaries.

Relationships Energize Service: Where Does the Energy Go?

My new boss, Jesse, met weekly with me for the first two months. Initially, these thirty-minute sessions were presented as opportunities for me to ask questions as I moved into my responsibilities. In reality, they were opportunities for me to learn from Jesse's many years of service experience. She laughed a lot as she pointed out the past week's foibles and problems. Once the breakdown was noted, however, she moved into the deeper issues. How did relationships break down, meaning where did communications glitch, when did trust go missing, why wasn't anyone talking honestly about the obvious problems? She talked a lot about building the kinds of relationships that supported different styles of service. Each staff person was encouraged to discover their strengths and styles of case management and goal-setting with clients. Sure, she expected tasks to get done, but she welcomed tension as much as "smooth sailing." She didn't trust quiet, viewing it as avoidance of real relationship-building. Nothing much seemed to rattle her except people's unwillingness to honestly and caringly relate. I heard all this, but I shied away, especially as a newcomer, from tensions. I wasn't yet prepared to claim my stakes in our work or our relationships.

About a month in at one of these sessions, she directly asked what I noticed about the way people interacted at The Center. I stumbled through some generic sentences and ended my non-answer by reminding her that I was new, still learning. She nodded but pressed on. "How's it going with Sam? What's it like relating to him?" Inwardly, I pulled back. Had she seen my anxious fumblings when I tried to coax a conversation with him? Did one of my co-workers say something? Had Sam told her something? Trying to stall, I asked her what she meant. She looked irritated as if I were ducking something important. So, I jumped back in and tried to *nicely* describe his "somewhat odd patterns of relating." She pulled me up short. "We won't tolerate angry outbursts from Sam, explaining it away as 'he's having a bad day.'" She went on noting his behaviors: rambling through the halls of the building, looking into offices, etc. I nodded, saying nothing. "Does he make you uneasy?" Before I could stop myself, I answered yes. Then, I added, "I don't know why."

She popped back, "Why don't you find out?" I felt flummoxed. How do you find out why a service relationship is uneasy? Where do you begin? "Most folks don't spend serious time with Sam," she went on, "so they don't get to know who he is." She then informed me that relationship-building was the heart of The Center's work and I'd best get good at it. Again, I nodded and sat mute. She continued, "Don't you have something to say to me." Only later would I understand this as an invitation to grow in my relationships with her, to push back, to have my say.

I wasn't there yet, so, after a small time of quiet, she went on. "Let me make this plain: It's a mistake to try to avoid him, or placate him; that's trouble. Figure out what he's about, then get to know him."

A double whammy. I now felt wobbly in my relationships with Sam and with Jesse. How do healthy service relationships get formed? What kinds of interactions build shared energy and interest? I didn't need to think long about these questions because Jesse was already pulling out a sheet of typing paper and giving me an assignment. "Here's what I want you to do. I call it an 'Energy Map.'" She then explained an exercise I vaguely remembered learning about in a graduate school class on city planning from the perspective of community partnerships. Later in my service teaching, I used it in a college-level internship class. Each student-intern created maps of the flows of energy in their placements, flows that also revealed relationship strength and resistance. Now many years later than that class, I was the student.

Making Maps

Using Energy Maps to track where energy goes, moves through, revs up, and revs down offers a concrete way to take the pulse of a service organization's activities and relationships. How you define energy may change the flow of your map. Perhaps you're interested in the energy flows that meet your management goals, numbers of cases resolved well or semi-well or stuck. Perhaps you're more interested in who on the staff seems to generate energy, meaning lines of energy flow to that person and gain strength. Does their energy then spark energy among others and make it flow for good work in many directions. Or maybe you want to see where it gets stuck. Jesse wanted me to track relational energy, where energies between people flowed well between them and then through them to acts of serving. She hoped I would discover which people on the staff and among our clients generated connectivity that kept the flow of service moving forward. Maybe they related or connected to the tasks or maybe to other people, which helped them leverage the tasks better. Charting that would be my practice.

To develop the basic skills for drawing an Energy Map, decide which type of energy you want to focus on. If you're not sure, just begin tracking the flows of energy, ask some questions at key points of the people most involved: What are you working on? Do the relationships help you get tasks done better or are they bogging you down? Where do you put most of your energy, etc.? To start, draw a map of the floor plan of your service organization. Include spaces like the kitchen or breakroom, the coat closet (if you have one), the mail room, spaces where money is handled, areas where forms like intake sheets are filled out. Bathrooms also count; how many conflicts or resolutions get worked out because you finally ran into the person you needed to talk with in the bathroom. For some service sites, the building's back steps draw people who work out issues while standing outside together. As you draw the basic layout, stop and think of areas where energy gathers, stagnates or disappears. Note doors and if they are open. Note if people gather near windows. Discover literal places in which people seem to gain or lose energy. Of course, the drawing need not be to scale. It needs to work for you.

Now add the people to your map. Start by noting people's desks, but if they often are found in other places, use some symbol – perhaps their initials – to typically show where you can find them. Give their initials a color and use that color to track their movements throughout the office. Again, make choices. You can't track every place, every staff person, or every client. What's the main question driving your map? Then, begin by observing. Where's the flow of energy? Where and with whom does it move, move more slowly, not move at all. Is there one office or desk that everyone goes to at least once, if not multiple times, a day? Once in an internship setting where several students in my class were working, their energy map indicated a very high energy spot at one person's desk. Turned out that this secretary had the only keys to the bathroom. Good to notice!

Are there places where the energy turns into conflict, whether silent – a kind of dead-end energy, or verbal? Do you notice a place where energy seems to quietly rebuild itself as if this site on your map were a kind of refueling station? Is a person involved or nature? Or is it something about the place that draws people together and they listen better to each other there – humility happens there. Do some settings encourage boundary-setting? Is it the set-up of the furniture, or who comes into that space, or how the space is used?

Whether for staff or clients, the more closely you observe and draw on your map's flows, gaps, and absences of energy, the more you will know about how your organization is working now and for whom. In some cases, the map confirms what you already suspect. In others, it challenges certain assumptions. For me, it introduced me to the broad process of how relationships worked at The Center. I recognized at a much deeper level how often Jesse was behind the scenes advising people as they went in and out of her office every day. I also noted that Sarah checked in with Shirley more than I knew. I assumed Sarah needed no advice, having worked there so many years. But the map gave me better data.

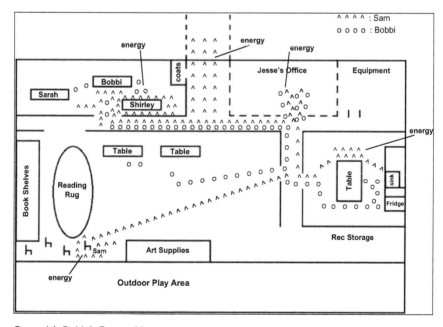

Figure 4.1 Bobbi's Energy Map

I also became aware, for the first time, of how many people came into the service office and then left the building. Only a few adult clients stayed in The Center as much as Sam. Why was that? I found myself adding little notes in text-bubbles on my map. Sometimes they were questions like the one I just asked. Other times they were initial insights I wanted to test further through conversations and more observation. Of course, we can only give so much time to our maps; there's service to be done!

Figure 4.1 shows my energy map tracking Sam's and my whereabouts and interactions at The Center.

Others Maps and Knowledge

Beginning to grasp my patterns with Sam, I asked Sarah to tell me more about him and her experiences of relation to him. She shared what she knew of his history. He grew up in the neighborhood, and when he was young, he participated in almost every program The Center offered. Returning from the Army, which he joined at eighteen, he chose to live in his mother's house. This did not fit his pre-Army persona of utter independence; so his decision sparked gossip. Something in him had changed. He seemed less focused and assured of himself. When he came to The Center, he wandered. People struggled more than before to connect with him. His anger came in sudden outbursts. Some felt threatened. I could relate to that. Yet most of us couldn't exactly say why we felt uncomfortable. After only a very short time at The Center, I already knew more about Sam than any other member of The Center's community.

Imagining myself as a social worker at The Center felt energizing. Then, I would think about Sam and sense my energy dropping. I felt hesitant. Could I be open to his requests and suggestions while explaining what services we could and could not render? Could I keep my personal boundaries strong enough to disagree with him when I thought a service intervention did not fit his situation or would offer no real support? I began noticing that my anxieties went up a bit when I knew he was in The Center. If I heard him arguing with someone, I hoped he would not turn to us to mediate. I knew, of course, that all these feelings and dynamics regularly showed up in community-based service settings. Some clients and service professionals bring such high energy that it sparks relationships and positive outcomes before the organization can publicly buy in. Others, in the same setting, bring energies that smooth out and stabilize service interactions. Still others seem to heighten any interaction to the level of controversy if not conflict, and often without direction or specific intention.

Probably all of us identity with aspects of all these styles of service engagement and response. Learning to pay attention and reflect together on them enriches understandings of how a staff and clients do and do not work well, less well, or not well at all on any levels and/or scales. To understand and usefully engage in life and service together, staff and participants or clients need reflection. We need to take time to get to know each other and our stories, to identify interests and limits. Probably all of us recognize these varied styles of energy and engagement as well as their levels and scales. But are we ready to accept an invitation to pay closer attention to these dynamics in our interactions. What are our intentions and how do they shape our conscious decision-making and interactions?

Figuring out why, how, and when we respond the way we do, however, is not simple. So much comes at us and our energies flow so quickly to others, that it's easy to lose track of our values and plans. Energy Maps help us keep track – maybe for the first time – of the particular situations, personalities, and/or relationships that redirect our service interactions. Mapping our energies also clarifies how complex service interactions are. So, it's worth our time to develop a keener eye for how those energies flow and collide. It takes practice to perceive our patterns over time, but building these skills offers substantive insight into patterns of service and burnout. Here's some questions to guide that skill-building. Are there members of your service community that rarely interact or only interact with each other? Do some people bring life and laughter on certain days, but on other days are more brooding. What makes energy levels in your setting go up or down? How about in meetings? Do people claim their limits or do they covertly undermine forward progress when they feel overwhelmed? What draws them into conversation and what seems to push them away? Developing sensitivities to the flows of energies in our service community increases our capacities to partner for effective outcomes. At the end of the chapter is an exercise space where you to make an energy map of your social service setting or some portion of it. Try it!

Mapping Energies with Sam

When I was with Sam, for instance, I struggled to sense his commitment to his own needs and to getting to know me. It felt as if the energy between us stalled or bounced off of a plastic sheath of pleasantries. But I was not willing to test the edges of his willingness to connect in a service relationship. It felt unfamiliar, and I was not willing to give up my service act. Well-meaning as it was with Sam, I often I felt like we were acting out a script, not actually being and working together. To shift this confusion, I could have begun mapping my interactions with Sam, where they happened and noting if the energy between us got stuck, opened up, or just stalled. Did place have something to do with it? Time of day? Where others present and offering a catalyst for us to connect or for our communication to flame into silence of Sam stomping out of the room. Energy maps when used intentionally and well can reveal quite a bit about our relationships in service and burnout.

I learned that I could literally mark where tempers flared and how often. Which spaces seem to raise people's ire in relation to Sam or not. I also noted that often nothing more ever came from these arguments. I tried to notice if he found certain areas of The Center to be cooling chambers for himself. Where there offices or doorway spaces where he went to calm down? Or were people the factor, and how were they? I tried to map his staff interactions, his patterns of movement before and after meetings. As I described earlier, by mapping my own movements in as much detail as his, I gave our different and intersecting pathways alternate colors. This mapping work tuned my understanding of how energies flowed and jammed during our work days.

Over time, I've found mapping the energy flows in my service settings a concrete way to sharpen my knowledge of our community, our patterns of interactions, conflicts, and compromises. I think this will be the case for you as well. Remember, note more than just the movements of the people. Pay attention to whose office seems to be the generator of much of the whole place's energy flow? Write some notes for yourself about the characteristics of that person's work-style, communication skills, and capacities for handling conflict. How do these invigorate the work and people of the organization? What do you learn about how energies move and interact in your service setting.

Finally, you may want to map areas of your service neighborhood. Where are the flows of resources and relationships around your site? How do those histories surge and slump with your organization's history and current plans, including the staff? Could you note areas of political activism? Which sources feed that, local religious groups, neighborhood organizations, clubs? Mapping the flows of energy in service and burnout settings can take a myriad of useful directions.

The Bethlehem Center: A Place of Respect

My first Energy Map didn't show me much. My observations skidded across the surface of relationships. To notice more details in the interactions, I had to pay closer attention to facial and body movements, to language choices (if I could hear them), and to how quickly the energy moved on, got stuck, or dissipated into nothing. The interactions raised the energy that I began to grasp. Some harsher exchanges between Sarah and the clients she worked with startled me, but those confrontations did not empty the energy. In fact, the tensions brought sharper focus to the interactions. The client stayed longer at Sarah's desk. Often, they found a way forward together. Sometimes amid the shouting, a client stormed out. But over the week, they always came back. Other clients arrived at Sarah or Shirley's desk but said little. They sat and brooded as the energy grew smaller until they just up and left.

Slowly, amid the demands of my own work, this mapping taught me how to literally track the dance that is service relationships. This was the point of Jesse's assignment. I observed how limit-opening and limit-setting established patterns of energy that demanded serious interactions between client and provider. Sometimes as named above, the energy took an edge. Sometimes not; instead, it slipped away without any hint of resolution. In one case, the client never returned. These observations began to help me notice patterns in my relationship with Sam. I felt off balance each time we talked. Every exchange felt plastic, slippery, and nondescript. Without traction, conversation drifted without direction. Only half-alive, then, our conversations periodically turned toward odd, even scary, topics.

With Sam and me, words disappeared into nowhere as our emotional tone drifted until it also disappeared down the same endless well. Exchanges taken in, but without human resonance. Sounds, handshakes, greetings felt obligatory, taken in, and then immediately vacated. No wonder I generally felt uneasy with Sam, the energy flow in our relationship offered no alignment, no traction. Any anxious attempts on my part to play some role of service kindness or provision only made it worse. Silly pleasantries about the weather or a new program, quickly emptied into no response from Sam, except for the few times he said something threatening. I tried not to take that personally. What was I doing in this relationship? Why did I have so much trouble being me so that he could be him?

From Jesse's perspective and for many service settings, relationships are central to the work. The original dream of Methodist women in the late nineteenth century to create centers of local commitment to social service and advocacy for the poor poured from relational concern. Bethlehem Centers today still do this work though no longer led almost exclusively by richer white women. Now, Centers partner in leadership and program design with local urban communities, which are usually African-American and/or Hispanic. Many Center directors are Methodist Deaconesses, an established order within the church that ministers with and to communities systematically isolated from economic, housing, and healthcare resources. Jesse Clipper was an ordained Deaconess, having graduated from Fisk University. In my interview for the job, she kept returning to one point: the work at The Center was local and relational. "Every employee offers the finest care and service available to anyone who arrives at our doors. We serve with respect, and we *expect* everyone to treat us respectfully." Relationships and respect, her words guided my first months as I worked to adjust to the high volume of regularly returning clients. Respecting clients claimed my priority. In time, I supposed – as I had in the past and many serving people do, I would worry about being respected. For now, I focused on the joys of learning a range of new skills and coping.

In those early months, Sam arrived at my desk at least once a day. Several weeks after my conversation with Jesse, he began meeting me when I arrived at the building. As I stepped on the sidewalk to the Center's front door, his red baseball cap caught my eye, along with his well-known lope, which the children mimicked. I walked ahead as he skulked behind with his shoulders rounded forward, not threatening but not welcoming either. Once inside, I turned down the hall to go to my desk. Passing Jesse's office, I chirped good morning. She responded. Turning into our area, I heard Jesse say good morning to Sam. He did not answer. She said it louder and got up from her desk screeching her chair. "Sam, I spoke. How are you?" "Fine, Jesse," he paused. "'preciate your asking" While putting away my purse in a desk drawer, I heard another screech, metal being dragged across the floor as he sat at the front of my desk. When he leaned forward, he took the first third of the desk's surface area.

"What's one thing you really enjoy about the neighborhood," I queried. He looked around the room as if distracted. "I understand you've lived in the neighborhood most of your life," I tried to keep going. "'cept for my time in the Army," he responded. I waited wondering if he would say more. When he didn't, I asked him what being in the Army was like for him. Many younger African-American men I knew joined the Army for benefits and training. For some, it became a community. I also understood from their stories that Army life demanded serious adjustments amid the added value. "You ever been in the Army," he finally responded. "Nope," I replied. "Well," he sighed as he got out of his chair and starting folding it together, "uh-huh," he finished. As he walked back to the wall with the chair, I threw out a line. "I'd like to get to know more of your story." "Maybe tomorrow ... *If* I'm around," he replied with emphasis. His back now to me, he left our space. I could not make heads or tails of the interaction.

Belonging and Boundaries

The Bethlehem Center, a single-story, 2,200-foot block square of cement, stood two blocks behind or east of the vibrant and historic main street of this African-American neighborhood. Walking down this street immersed you in a cacophony of buzz from Black-owned beauty and barber shops, a wooden-floor hardware store, and a locally-owned grocery stocked with chitlins, cornmeal, and collards. Beyond the exclusions of the city's white economy, only blocks away, Pleyson Street boasted its own economy as well as fall, spring, and summer events. A bi-yearly highlight, the health-and-family-services-fair, drew big crowds. Sponsored by the neighborhood's largest historic church, The Center had a table staffed by white and black volunteer nurses and physicians in training from nearby universities.

At the end of a fair day, many of those providing services packed up and headed down to the other end of this main street where the two community restaurant-bars would be overflowing. They met people's appetites for socializing, dancing, and music with a Louisiana-Mississippi blues edge. Pride in self-resourcing and principles of fairness activated the neighborhood's identity. Everybody knew everybody. On these days, our service team joined in the fun. My first time at the fair, Shirley and Jesse introduced me to lots of local community leaders and neighbors. I sensed the power of their relationships and felt happy to be included.

Biannual events, this fair happened in the summer. Generally, in summer, our schedules shifted. Less clients came in, and the large summer recreation, tutoring, and crafts programs needed plenty of help. Often, I was assigned to help with the equipment room, handing out baseball bats, gloves, and more. From that vantage point, I could see the Rec Room in full use and through the open doors the playing fields full of kids. Sarah sat in the Reading Corner with the pre-K children. As she read a story, two young girls were pulling one book after another off the shelves. Jesse came through the room with a local mother and asked me if we had any extra swimsuits for young boys in the equipment room. We tried to respect any request, but I knew all the suits had been taken.

I watched this relatively bucolic scene in the Reading Corner; then, Shirley stood up and raised her voice. A neighborhood client had come up to her while she was reading. She began demanding Shirley help her get access to some service. I couldn't quite hear the content. She continued raising her voice, repeating to Shirley what she "had to have now." At that point, Shirley, obviously irritated, directly responded, "Seritha, I know you're frustrated. I am too. But no more nagging, please. And after four years of working together – tone down the volume! Or choose to leave. I'm working on it – you know that." Embedded in the neighborhood and the people living there, the work of The Center redefined service relationships as I had known them. Commitment rooted in relationships over time. No one doubted that, because relationships unfolded on a two-way street called respect. It took time to understand and respect other people's stories and boundaries, what they could or would relate to/take in or not relate to/not take in. Chatting with Sarah about this a few days after hearing Shirley's response to Seritha, she added another angle. In her first year in the job, she started a small pilot program held in her home in the evenings. She was helping teen women graduates from the local high school learn about local public colleges and how to apply to them. Not expecting high levels of interest, she delighted at how many came. Soon, however, these young women requested private meetings with her to discuss their personal situations. Eventually, she found herself driving women to local and some not-so-local campuses to talk with Admissions Officers. A few of the young women were able to find resources and begin classes, but many could not. Some woke up to fact that they were not ready for the commitment. Of the few who went, over half requested ongoing conversations with Sarah about college adjustments and failures. "The next thing I knew," she told me, "I had a full-time job focused on college access and retention." She went on to detail how the work grew even more until she found herself overwhelmed to the point that Jesse asked why her other work at The Center was falling behind.

The demands exceeded Sarah's time and energy. She wanted to belong to the community, but she could not continue to serve at her current pace. She was running out of personal and institutional resources. Stretched beyond her limits, she had to take action. She finally spoke up and explained her limits, what she could and could not take in as her responsibility. "Then," she continued telling me, "the really hard part happened. If I backed off, the initiative disappeared, and that felt really hard to face." She went on to share that even months after she quit running the pilot program, teens kept pressing her to start it up again. The need was real and serious, but she had to respect her own capacities and limits. She kept saying no, which never felt good. I listened but marveled at how she could do that, especially when the idea proved so successful.

I never said anything to Sarah, but I could not imagine doing what she did. My limits did not matter as much as the teens' hopes. I would work diligently to take in their requests and keep the program going – somehow. I remained lost to the necessity of taking a realistic self-assessment in service work, of saying no in order to avoid depletion. I thought I was living the good service life, but, in fact, I was avoiding it. Sam understood this. He could see beyond my mechanical yes to every request. He knew that machine-like "yes" would eventually separate me from real relationships with clients. I would be too busy for that. I would fixate on fixes and avoid the failures. He knew life nor service worked like that. Having survived his own losses, he would not pretend. He would not settle for plastic service relationships that produced cookie-cutter outcomes for stick figure people.

I believed I was living into the legacy of my family tree of service. My duty to them remained strong. I wanted to be like all those in my family who served and never thought about themselves, never lost their cool. I assumed good service like theirs meant staying in control to prioritize others. Many of us share these unrealistic assumptions and one way of breaking up that fantasy is to find out the histories of your "family tree of service." Who were the people in your families who provided service and what happened in their service relationships? If your family didn't participate much in service, pick out a teacher or someone else you respect and find out what you can about their service story, their family tree.

Remembering Family Trees of Service

Whether through a family member of an admired teacher, recreation or spiritual leader, or community activist, we've all taken in patterns of service with others. These patterns draw from past, present, and future activities and expectations including a range of emotions and ethics. They carry assumptions about what keeps serving people connected and what keeps us separate. Some of these styles or patterns are old. Others are still emerging, like the shoot of a new branch. Think back on the people, places, or creatures that shaped how and why you serve? What in their eyes counted as "good" service? When tensions rose, how did they respond? Begin asking family members and friends for stories that will help you create your family tree, your lineage not only of service done but also of the way service got done.

I developed this exercise or practice by tweaking a reflective activity created by Mitchell Thomashow in his book *Ecological Identity: Becoming a Reflective Environmentalist*. He invited readers to create their own "ecological family tree." In addition to that drawing exercise, I've added some writing ideas influenced by Peter Elbow and his co-author Pat Schneider's book, *Writing Without Teachers*.[1] Begin by drawing your family tree of service. The act of drawing activates neural pathways different from our daily or default processing. Drawing may invite assumptions, sources, and/or values that inform our service but remain below our surface awareness. If a word comes to mind as you draw your Service Family Tree, jot it down. Other writing prompts are given below but do not lose these prompts that just offer themselves for further investigation. The drawing and writing often help us discover expected and unexpected storylines within our lives of service. You may discover unconsidered sources of growth. Resources for times of transition may come to mind. You may discover that you've already known collapse and/or moved into resilience without giving it a name.

This exercise is designed to invite you to spend more time thinking about your service story: it's twists and turns, the branches of people that taught or inspired you, and specific activities or ideas that drew, trained, and kept you engaged. You need not finish your Service Family Tree in one sitting. Take as much time as you need. Keep it in your office; so you can remember the sources of your service story and perhaps add new branches here and there that reflect your current work. Working with this practice also helps you notice where service flourished and/or floundered? It can suggest why by contextualizing your story in the midst of other stories and factors. Did you cut off some branch or area of service work that impacted your roots or other branches – positively or negatively? How did you make that decision or was it made for you? Have you graphed altered forms of service onto some branches of your Service Family Tree? Use these questions as prompts for your drawing and writing, but welcome your own ideas and angles on this practice.

I invite you to take a first attempt at drawing your Service Family Tree by using the space provided in the "Exercises" section at the chapter (see page 80). As you work with these drawing and writing activities, you may want to transfer your Service Family Tree to a larger format where you can add more details. Here are the fuller instructions:

Begin drawing your Service Family Tree by thinking about the ground that nurtured the original roots. Draw those roots, those deeply-rooted values that feed and grounded your service as it grew throughout your life. Add categories of people or specific names of people who nourished your decisions to serve and continue to feed and inspire your service work and how you approach it. Their names will likely interweave with your core values even up through the trunk of your tree. Pause a moment to consider how and why these people and their and others' values contributed to the sturdy health of your Service Family Tree? Perhaps you'll want to do some reflective writing about them and their impacts or inspirations for your own later decisions.

Now move to the trunk of the tree. Which experiences and partners or mentors helped you develop a useful set of core practices and values? Continue drawing your growing tree of service noting important influences on your service's further development. When did the first branches appear and what in your experience or whose direction or influence brought them to life? Perhaps from a particular branch or section of the trunk, you'll attach a list of key names related to that evolution in your service. Show any smaller branches that never fully developed or grew in a new or unexpected direction. Don't be afraid to draw in death, the ending or stagnation of a service experience. These are points in your reflective process where you'd like to pause and write about those experiences, the sources of change, your feelings, what emerged after these experiences. Notice if certain issues or patterns kept repeating, marking your tree's growth and/or direction. Did you try some new things? Work and play with this practice as you find most useful.

This reflective work can awaken memories and connections that reveal deep sources, influences, and patterns in your service life over time. By drawing our experiences, those painful memories of a branch collapsing can receive attention – and maybe the artistic angle softens our self or other-judging. We suddenly notice a surge in growth nourished by new interest or reorganization spurred our interest and commitment. Drawing and writing reflectively also help us include and connect service experience with other events happening in our lives. We can see the linkage between a child's extended illness or a parent's death and the impact on our service, often an impact we did not imagine when we were going through the experience. Did you graft something new onto your tree? Spending time noticing and reflection on what our service has taken in and not taken in and how those dynamics impacted our work shapes a thicker and more complex story of our service lives. This story impacts our service relationships and when we know more about it, helps us choose wisely how we claim our boundaries and interact with others when serving.

Figure 4.2   Bobbi's Service Family Tree

This practice can be done with a team using a poster-size piece of paper and many of the questions above. Encourage team members to share details of their perspectives and experiences. These trees, obviously, will show more branches and diversity reflecting the input of many members. Encourage group creativity to make room for these multiple perspectives. In this case as in the individual drawing above, remember to include guiding values, the assumptions that shaped the tree's growth and decline in service and burnout. Don't forget the smaller roots that may have larger impacts on the tree's growth, positively or negatively, than normally noticed. Welcome ideas from the group.

Figure 4.2 shows what my initial drawing looks like for my Service Family Tree.

Now you try it! Go to the Exercises section at the end of the chapter and make a first attempt at filling in some details of your own Service Family Tree.

Going to Pieces

I developed strategies for keeping Sam at arms' length because I believed the stories. People said he liked to test staff members. He wanted to find their edge of willingness to work with him. I had no idea what that meant, but I bought into the swirls of rumors and determined I would serve him well no matter what. The next time Sam came to my desk, he sat down – uninvited – and placed his arms on the table. Then he leaned forward and said, "I need money." Most of our clients requested cash to pay bills or rent by filling out a required form. Sam did not do that. Instead, he raised the volume on his challenging tone and repeated his statement. "I need money." For emphasis after he spoke, he put his hands on my desk. Determined to remain on his side, I realized I had a professional loophole. I affirmed his need but reminded him that I was still in my probationary year. Although I wanted to respond to his request, I could not provide cash to any clients.

Oddly, my out also worried me because I assumed that Sam already knew these rules. Did he know I couldn't help but asked anyway? Was this a test? The more my mind whirred, the more anxious I became that Sam would get angry. I felt a need to do something, so I stood up. As I did, he suddenly looked down at the floor and then just as suddenly, he stood up too. With a smirking tone, he mumbled, "Yeh, sorry – I need to be talking with Shirley." "Good!" I responded promptly like a perfect girl scout. Then, I shot out of the office heading toward the bathroom. The next day, Sam again showed up at my desk. I made the first move, getting up and heading out of the office. But this time as I walked out, I called back, "It's lunchtime. I'm hungry, Sam. I heard the leftovers from last night's meeting are delicious. Let's eat." I kept going without looking behind me. Later he told me that he signaled he would come but said nothing. He believed I had left him behind. His bad knee slowed him down, so by the time we spoke again in the kitchen, he felt slighted. Ignorant of that, I relished in meeting my first goal, to be in the kitchen before him. As I waited, I played out an internal conversation with Sam. I would try to affirm him. I would get along with him. I considered this a client-centered approach, but watching my peers made me doubt its effectiveness with people like Sam. Nevertheless, that's what I would do. I would work around any tensions and avoid them.

With my plan firmly in mind, I thought back on what I'd heard about Sam's life. He'd grown up on a tough street and had a reputation for fighting. Many felt his mind was "not right" once he'd returned from military service in Viet Nam. They didn't trust how he spent money. Some accused him of using drugs. He struggled financially, so, he lived with his mother in the same house in which he grew up. I'd walked by that house during my first months at The Center. Colorful curtains behind an open window moved with the breeze. The two windows to the right were covered in cardboard; the glass was broken out. The house next door harbored neat piles of oil cans, mufflers, and hub caps, perhaps for sale. The next house boasted a white-washed fence enclosing a well-tended garden. From this world, Sam first arrived at The Center Rec Room as a five-year-old, quickly becoming an unbeatable ping-pong champion. Everyone said he could still win today if he wanted to play. He didn't.

These days he seemed to come to have a place to go and be. Usually, he read or drifted from office to office, chatting with staff now and then. Shirley said he read voraciously. Others characterized him in more sinister tones. They said he came to The Center when a neighborhood drug bust was about to happen. Rumors implicated him in drug-dealing. One repeated story claimed he knew a police raid was about to happen but told no one, which made locals say he now worked for the police. They didn't trust him. But they left him alone because after Viet Nam his temper raged unpredictably. I never saw that, but always heard it was true.

The one police officer on the beat who grew up with Sam still considered him a friend. Some said Sam would snitch to that officer to keep himself out of trouble. Others thought his grandmother, Miss Ernestine, a pillar in the community, had convinced the police to go easy on him. She would be responsible. Shirley, Sarah, and Jesse believed he suffered from mental illness once he left the Army. But mostly, he suffered from a lack of relationships. The wariness others felt around Sam, to them, reflected misunderstanding. All this confused me, but I wasn't willing to get in enough of a relationship with him to find out. I wouldn't risk being honest, setting limits.

I heard his limping walk approaching the kitchen, which reminded me of the sound of his walking around The Center every day. He had a real aversion to games, especially between people. He walked all around the place, it seemed, to find some real contact. I snapped out of these thoughts as he entered the room, dismissing them as my own drama. As soon as he arrived, I began telling him my memories of leftovers in my grandmother's refrigerator, which looked just like the one in the kitchen. As I rambled on, he did not respond.

When I opened the refrigerator door, I smiled – a large platter of fried chicken and potato salad had been left by the Mount Athos Baptist Church Ladies Bible Study Group. Having used The Center for their meeting the night before, they also brought tomatoes from Essie's garden. Next to those sat a few pieces of "her famous caramel cake." Mrs. Fitzgerald's delicious egg salad sat in a bowl next to the cake. I spied other goodies brought in over the past week: ripe peaches and homemade pimento cheese, and homemade rolls. We had a feast. I called out the list of possibilities, but Sam did not respond. My anxiety grew, but I just kept rummaging around the refrigerator. What about his temper and mental instability? Why doesn't he say something? I wish someone else would come in. What would interest him?

By now I assumed Sam was mentally ill and a bit dangerous. Those assumptions were based on little fact, but I'd become convinced. That conviction grew from never really interacting with him. I avoided the natural tensions that come with relationship-building. I didn't want to set limits as would be required. I thought I was playing it safe, but now I felt vulnerable. To distract myself, I pulled out the potato salad, put the bowl on the kitchen table and began slicing the tomatoes. Mentally,

I stitched together my next sentences as Sam still said nothing. Then, with a variety of foods on the table, I turned toward him and said, "What's your choice, Sam?"

He sat down on the other side of the table from me but did not answer. "Got a choice, Sam?" He raised his hand and slammed it down on the table. Now he spoke loudly and in a scolding voice, "The only decent thing in that whole damn refrigerator would be the coconut cake. I wouldn't eat any of the rest of it!" Now we were in it. There was no coconut cake. What was he talking about? I felt my anger and my worry rising at the same time. His voice was louder now, and he was moving to my side of the table. "I will only eat coconut cake!" He was unreasonable. Irrational. Now he stood two feet from me and kept shouting. "Are you getting me some lunch or not!" Could no one else in the building hear him?

I tried to placate. I tried to soothe his sharp confrontational edge by answering, "I am not sure, but I don't think there's any coconut cake in there." He took a step closer and loudly commanded me, "Find some!" That flipped a switch. The gates of no limits shut down. "Do you usually *shout* your food preferences?," I asked him. "Do you scream your wishes at people? Do you think I will tolerate this?" Now standing right next to me, he stared straight ahead. I was mad; I would not be ignored. So, I went back to the refrigerator and threw open the door. The plates and containers jangled inside as I tapped into a pent-up fury. "You know what, Sam – I don't give a damn if you want something to eat. I don't care if you *never* eat. There's no coconut cake, and you know it! So, I'm sick of the games. I'm sick of you! You can get your own caramel cake, but I won't help. I won't tolerate your acting like a jerk. I don't give a damn how hard your life's been. Here's the bottom line: Forget it. Let me repeat: FORGET IT!"

I moved away from the refrigerator as a first step to leaving, but I caught a glimpse of his face. I expected it to have that half-crazy look he could put on. But something else showed through his eyes. He moved back to his side of the table and sat down. We were quiet for a couple of minutes as I remained standing wondering if I had just done what I did. Nothing to do now, but stare straight ahead and hope he would leave.

Then, he turned his head toward me. Again, I saw that different look as if he were sharing a joke with me. The put-off, simmering anger face disappeared. He offered in its place an insider's joke face as if we were sharing some recognition of a trick that had been played but now was over. I felt him telegraph a message that went something like this, "I wait to see if anyone will really relate, will call my bluff. You did. I like that." It was as if he had said this to me, But I could not trust it, and I still shook with anger, so I went on with my tirade. "Sam, game over. I'm over the games. Get out." That insider-understanding face shifted to a softer look as if he wanted to be on the same page, not in a game of threats and anger. Again, a short minute of silence until he said, "Sometimes I get confused about which cake is which. We don't have any coconut cake, only caramel cake. I got it now." Then he pushed his chair back and walked toward the refrigerator. "Want a piece to go along with the rest of your lunch?"

I stared straight ahead and tried to remember that insider look acknowledging that he wasn't crazy but all this while – as he did to everyone – he had been testing me. Finally, I stood up enough to begin to crack the code. But now that old threatening look was gone. The test seemed to be over. I had chosen to resist him. He seemed to view that as offering him a real connection with me, even if it was based in my anger. I seemed to have convinced him that I would give up "handling" him like some special case, like someone I didn't care to get to know.

Now, I responded to his question, "I prefer caramel cake. I'd like a piece." In that blink of a moment, the hard work of trying to be with Sam cracked and collapsed, not in neat piles but in shattered fatigue. It would take a while to figure out next steps, but something between us *finally* collapsed enough to break up the game. All I knew to do was finish eating. After that, I got up, went to the sink, and started washing my dishes. Disconcertingly to me, Sam joined me at the sink, putting his dishes by my arm and then grabbing a towel so he could dry what I washed. We said nothing but went on with our work. Together we put away our few dishes and placed the remainders of our lunch in the refrigerator. It seemed the labels we kept pasted on each other were fading. We were starting some next phase of respect and relationship in The Center. Hanging up the towel, Sam suggested we go see what's happening in the Rec Room. I agreed. Once there, we chatted with kids finger-painting on one of the aluminum tables. Then, we talked shop with a few of the afternoon teen staffers. I left him there talking to some of his neighbors and returned to my desk.

Welcoming Going to Pieces and Not Taking In

Psychiatrist Mark Epstein explains the power of learning to stay with the experience of things falling apart. Whether the things are planned activities, relationships, or emotions, their collapse breaks open parts of our lives we hope to keep tidy and in place. Sometimes, the source is unexpected, being hit with sudden news or unexpected illness that affects our service. Other times, we've worked hard to stave off the explosion whose rumblings we ignored or tried to control day after day. Epstein calls this process, "going to pieces without falling apart," also the title of his book. He assures us life will regularly deliver the phase of things bursting apart. Remember that long-anticipated program, which left everyone disappointed? We've all been asked to give more than we can deliver – regularly! So work falls apart, and in that rumble, our healthier boundaries often break down as well. We begin to blame or fall subject to our fears and withdraw, which is another form of collapse. Like the lessons of resilience, Epstein's counsel is to move into whatever it is that's breaking up. Next steps will emerge, though perhaps not as we'd wish or expect, but they will. Everything about that project, daily relationship, or future hope has *not* fallen apart.

For this chapter, the breakdown I and many of us avoid impacts the safe haven we've devised to avoid trouble. As each chapter's principles and practices make clear, resilience in service and burnout is all about getting into trouble. My attempt to stay safe by placating my colleagues and clients is fantasy. Taking in whatever comes my way only heighten the surge of collapse energy, thinking, and feelings going in all directions. Practicing not taking in, appropriately standing one's ground in an argument or continuing to advocate for a particular person or policy, and more, will not cure service burnout. But healthy boundaries do create steadiness in the process of things going to pieces. That steadiness allows us to remember that not everything is broken down. That steadiness helps us move through the rubble mindful of opportunities that will emerge. We bring resources, principles, and practices that remain comfortably present and useful amid other elements that have gone to pieces.

Epstein's advice echoes the core insights of this book. In that breakdown phase, take a breather, step back and inventory the debris around you. What will it take to move into the wreckage and see what you can learn? Maybe you'll notice what can be changed or leveraged. As a psychiatrist and practitioner of contemplative practices from his Buddhist training, he encourages honest listening to our own reactions. I had blocked out all my normal reactions in an attempt to keep taking in whatever came my way. Epstein's counsel to practice listening, which does not mean reactively acting, would have offered me insight about myself, my needs for boundaries and a healthy sense of control. Instead, I judged any thought or feeling that went in that direction in an attempt to keep breakdown from happening. But, of course, that did not and cannot work.

The book's tools of pausing, patiently observing, and treasuring diversity, including diverse feelings and needs in ourselves, went unused. Then I exploded. Not a strategy advantageous for everyday use, but, for me and others, a first step toward learning more about the role of healthy boundaries or not taking in while serving and burning out with others. That step to say stop to Sam also gave him an opportunity to move out of his role-playing. Instead of protecting his fear and anger over being dispensed with as one more service problem to solve, he broke open his despair and refusal. Going to pieces together, we took first steps toward a new and different service and burnout relationship. We would fight again, but with normal tensions, more useful limit-setting.

Not taking in, as a principle of serving and burning out, helps us see relationships as always evolving. Their health grows through phases of stability, which will then again go to pieces. In that breaking down, we can learn new things about ourselves and others, which fosters restorative work to rebuild the relationships and includes some unexpected, unexploited resources. Going through the motions and taking whatever comes in service and burnout relationships cannot sustain us or the work we do. To different degrees at different times, all service and burnout relationships require clear signals. Don't press me beyond this point. Understand the needs I bring to this service problem. Allow me to speak as well as listen. These requests highlight the difficult and necessary role relationships play in service thriving. Perhaps more often triggering burnout or aspects of the work falling apart, not taking in as a principle of service fosters stronger communication and better work. Not taking in highlights our ongoing responsibility in service to honor each other's limits and needs.

The morning after Sam and I hit our breakdown point in the kitchen, Jesse called me into her office. "What was all that shouting about between you and Sam yesterday?" "Did you hear us?" I asked. "Who didn't?" she replied. "He rattled me, and somehow I finally told him to stop hassling me." I paused. What had come over me? I never talked this honestly to my boss. "OK," answered Jesse. "And . . . I'm not taking any of it back, Jesse." Again, I surprised myself. "I mean, I think Sam and I are on better footing now. We went on from that outburst." "Good." She interrupted me. "Don't take flack you don't deserve – from anybody." She paused before adding, "OK, I'm busy. Out." I went back to my desk.

Amid the pushes and pulls of everyday service relationships, healthy boundaries prove tough to discern. When I find myself unclear about publicly setting a limit, I turn to the practice, "Waiting in the Heart." The practice encourages me to settle and listen to my inner debates. Is the task itself the problem or do I have questions about the work being my responsibility? Do I think my opinion is being overlooked or manipulated? Have I reached a point of frustration with this colleague or client and what do I sense I need? Without judging or getting caught up in disputing facts, I try to listen to whatever keeps coming up in me. Then I intentionally welcome these frictions. Are they rooted in mistrust? Do I advocate a position others reject? Does some aspect of my work strain me too much? Do I need to claim that I will not take in this unsettledness, this alternate position, this overworking? "Waiting in the Heart" invites me into some stage of service breaking apart and encourages me to openly be there.

As the questions arise, before I work to answer them, I try to wait and welcome them. Typically, I begin by calming my breath, reconnecting with it by focusing on the experience of breathing in – noting the breath through the nose, or expanding the stomach area, or filling the chest. Once settled into the breath, continue to pay closer attention to it. Then, begin to imagine your breath moving through your interior body. The inhale beginning in your lower spine and traveling up your spine to the top of your back and neck. As you exhale, imagine the air traveling internally down your chest wall until it completes the ellipsis resting at the bottom of your spine. Spend several minutes of focused breathing using this pattern. Once comfortable with this pattern, add this small additional practice.

As you exhale, pause your attention at the area of the chest wall next to your heart. Imagine the breath resting in the heart. Feel free to breathe in and out as your focus remains resting in the heart. Think of the heart, feel the heart, as a place of openness. Here nothing needs to grab, push away, or fix. Whatever thoughts, emotions, or memories show up can simply be. The kindling of your need to not take in, for example, can exist as it is, on the edge of breaking apart or sparking into flame. Rest here a few seconds or more until your attention moves back into the exhale ending again at the base of your spine. Continue to breathe and rest in your heart as long as it takes to sense some letting go or welcoming of the tensions you're debating. Perhaps the practice will help you discern your response to that tension from taking in to not taking in – or some other set of questions.

The Philokalia, a Christian contemplative text teaches this practice and explains how difficult it is to hold our attention on issues that trouble our hearts, or we feel trouble our hearts. Doing the practice helps us learn that the heart, meaning our ability to love self and others, has more capacity than we knew. By capacity, I mean space to welcome tensions and conflicts. The space of the heart can accommodate our need for healthy limits, saying no. The space of the heart offers a calm place to play out the different scenarios we imagine when we take in a service request and when we don't take it in. Fundamentally, this Waiting in the Heart practice is a discernment practice. It helps us examine our options in a settled, thoughtful way by offering calm space to examine our options, including feelings and thoughts.

From here we can discern next steps supported by the rhythm of the breath pausing at the heart as a space of insight that welcomes us "not to come out of the heart too soon. Here, at first, it (can) feel very lonely in that (space of) inner seclusion . . ."(Kadloubovsky and Palmer: 33).[2] The honesty we encounter in this practice may urge us to look at needs we've ignored, including but also more than claiming our limits or boundaries. This practice encourages choices relevant to our principle, not taking in. When we lose our sense of separateness or can't find a space for discerning how we really feel about an interaction or tasks, this practice offers settling and insight. It helps us know for ourselves the balance of taking in/ not taking in that we require in this particular situation.

Service is relational, but relationships require tension and healthy boundaries. Learning our limits in service and burnout supports more resilient choices through disagreements and tensions. To miss out on these experiences of falling apart is to miss crucial lessons in the cycles of service that build resilience. Or as Luce Irigaray puts it, we need to start the places of our "human becoming," where we cultivate and "educat(e) breathing."[3] In this recognition, we embrace our differences while safeguarding our individualities.[4] This is the grounding that implies humility, to receive others in relationship including listening and letting be while respecting our differences. Two different subjects constructing bridges of relationships. Humility often goes by the name of taking in, but the richest soil for growing service requires taking in and not taking in. Responsible, respectful relationships are born of healthy limits, another definition of humility as cultivated self-understanding, which opens us to understand and love others more authentically or fully.[5]

Exercises

1. **Service Family Tree**

    Some reflective writing questions to begin the process:

    a. Who in my family encouraged me to serve and for what reasons? OR Who in my life encouraged me to serve and for what reasons?

    _____

    _____

    _____

    _____

    _____

    _____

    b. When did I branch out to service settings of my own choosing? What or who drew me to those (consider relationships, your life situation, etc.)?

    _____

    _____

    _____

    _____

    _____

    _____

    c. Did your service skills and person insights grow more in some settings? Why/why not?

    _____

    _____

_____

_____

_____

_____

_____

Draw a First Version of your Service Family Tree

2. **Reflective writing** – Consider the questions below:

    a.   Over time, did you develop a service style of your own? Did your principles
         and practices involve you in a new setting? As you gained experience, did
         your service relationships change? Did you draw on new resources? Did your
         style branch in new activities within existent settings or new settings – or not?

    _____

    _____

    _____

    _____

_____

_____

_____

b. What values changed over time? Did self-care and limits become an issue for you? Did those issues shift your service? What happened during phases of burnout? Where did you find strength during burnout?

_____

_____

_____

_____

_____

_____

_____

Notes

1 See Elbow and Schneider, *Writing Without Teachers*, 1998, 2003.
2 Kadloubovsky and Palmer, *Writings from the Philokalia*, 33.
3 Irigaray, *Between East and West*, viii.
4 Ibid, x.
5 Bondi, *To Love as God Loves*, 41–56.

Supplemental Reading

Zajonc, Arthur. *When Knowing becomes Love: Meditation as Contemplative Inquiry*. Great Barrington, MA: Lindisfarne Books, 2009.

References

Bondi, Roberta. *To Love as God Loves: Conversations with the Early Church*. Minneapolis, MN: Fortress Press, 1987.
Elbow, Peter and Pat Schneider. *Writing without Teachers*. 2nd edition. New York: Oxford University Press, 1998.
Epstein, Mark. *Going to Pieces without Falling Apart: A Buddhist Perspective on Wholeness*. New York: Broadway Books, 1998.
Irigaray, Luce. *Between East and West: From Singularity to Community*. Translated by Stephen Pluhá ek. New York: Columbia University Press, 2002.
Kadloubovsky, E. and G. E. H. Palmer, translators. *Writings from the Philokalia on Prayer of the Heart*. London: Faber & Faber Limited, 1951.
Thomashow, Mitchell. *Ecological Identity: Becoming a Reflective Environmentalist*. Boston, MA: The MIT Press, 1996.

Chapter 5

Moving Stability

Short-Term Service and Short Fuses

Randy panted as we clung to the edge of the pool. The coach of our Masters Swimming Team blew his whistle on each timed interval. So far, Randy and I only made our first interval. After that, consistent failure. Gasping for air, we watched the clock move forward, but something else stole Randy's breath that morning. Before our workout, he complained of a rotten service experience from the past weekend:

> I've always volunteered – the experiences matter to me. Mostly short-term service. That one-day format works best for me. I'm not so swamped at the law firm like during the week. But this past weekend! Rotten! Miserable failure! I'm still on a short fuse about it.

The coach shouted us back into the present. The whistle blew and we pushed off the wall. One last interval to go. But my focus kept returning to Randy. What bothered him so much?

Drying off after practice, I started counting how many Habitat for Humanity weekend builds Randy participated in. Add to those the number of outdoor playground sets he'd helped construct. I followed up and asked him what happened over the weekend. He reminded me that he regularly volunteered with his synagogue and went on,

> We had a terrible day. What kind of community service day segregates volunteers from community members? The point is working together. Otherwise, we're just volunteer robots and they become robot hosts. Our leaders left the community out. Or something happened. We met no one from the community!

For Randy and many of us, service offers opportunities to connect a bit more with people who have other life experiences including those from different races, classes, and cultures. Well-designed community-based service links groups that ordinarily do not overlap. He deeply valued the growth and insights these experiences gave him. Through the several Sundays of building and after the work was finished, Randy often stayed in touch with people he served with. But this recent project was coordinated by a different leadership team. Supposedly partnered with a community organization, the only things at the site were tools, tasks, and people from the synagogue. Randy felt betrayed. It burned him that the usual model appeared ignored. Clearly today, he still smoldered. Having grown up in a poorer, mid-western family himself, he shared some sense of the struggle to pay for school supplies, fees, and later, college tuition. He worked several jobs to pay for groceries. He chose to forego healthcare because he couldn't afford it. In part, he served to remain connected to parts of his history as well as offer support to others. Service included performing civic tasks; but for Randy, it also provided ways of making meaning.

Many of us can relate, especially in short-term service settings. In these contexts, the pressures of time jumble the goals and short-term expectations. From a task finished to meeting community members, our hopes often miss the mark. These mismatches in expectations feed our frustrations. We arrive hoping to connect with a community. The community's priorities are different. They need help to complete a task they cannot do alone with their limited resources and time. Realistically, they cannot offer us additional personal energy. Their priorities lie elsewhere. They hope we will do the job and not ask more.

Ours is a privileged position to assume they can or will do otherwise. In longer-term relationships, community-building becomes more possible as energies wax and wane. But as schedules today only get tighter; it's no surprise that over the last forty years, we've developed a host of short-term service opportunities from Alternative Spring Break programs, to local park or river clean up days, weekend Scouting projects, single-day sorority and fraternity fund-raisers, company-sponsored one-day service work, and more. From sports teams, to civic clubs, to VFW posts, short term effectively meets our needs. And for many communities, these bursts accomplish important goals.

Clean up a baseball field. Sort out and throw out broken sports and educational equipment of a Boys and Girls Club. Sing with the Seniors at a Long-Term Care Residence. Such efforts bring positive benefits, but not necessarily relationships. Repetition creates those *or* well-designed smaller projects that make a point of creating community between outsiders coming in and those living in a neighborhood. But nothing beats extended partnerships for shared understanding and care. Roger's synagogue had perfected the short-term-relationship service experience. Truth be told, they often returned to the same communities on a yearly or bi-yearly cycle, which fosters some sense of connection. But that did not happen this past weekend and Roger struggled with his dashed expectations.

We do too, which is why this chapter focuses on the kinds of burnout sparked by short-term service. How do we adjust to what feels like the burn of disappointment? How do we find our balance when we feel tricked, our expectations exploded? When the pieces of the service experience keep changing, how do we maintain stability? Or in faltering, can we keep some sense of direction and intention rather than begin to blame "them" – whoever they are – for the failures. At least it feels like failure to us – short-term service breakdown, a busted plan, a mucked-up activity.

The stories, insights, and practices in this chapter engage these questions. Humility and non-judgment are guiding principles for practices that help us admit our struggle and find a way through them. The chapter builds answers for the unstable ground and constantly shifting goals that come with most short-term experiences. These stories examine how the principle of humility, which means groundedness in the original Greek, relaxes our quick judging of situations and others. We step into situations understanding that our expectations may give way, things won't work as we planned or anyone planned. To go forward demands we not waste energy on blaming, but find ways to recoup the energies we have and construct next steps. We exploit what's possible by moving through our searing disappointment or pissed off anger.

Mismatched Expectations Burn

Short-term service shifts the pace of a service cycle to warp speed. Each phase moves into the next one very quickly. The shift from stability to burn or collapse usually catches us off guard. We feel like stability suddenly and inexplicitly disappears. Regrouping transforms into utilizing everything we can get our hands on and minds around. What irritates in small ways when doing long-range service balloons into major issues in short-term work. Ordinary frustrations flip into accusations. Why won't our service coordinator let us stay late so we can finish stocking the thrift store shelves? The fact that the shop supervisor must go home singes our need to complete the job *we* set out to do – *today!* Without long-term relationships, and certainly without community contact, negotiations cannot occur. Service is what it is right now. Period. Randy, like many of us, chafed in these situations.

Short-term settings demand their own rhythms and outcomes. In response, we do well to slow our expectations down, to pause and check out the factors that seem to be shaping our service right now. To return to our household metaphor, short-term work is like the phone call from your in-laws saying they are on their way to your home – your untidied home! And you're just finishing a day of work and have no time to clean before they get there. Short-term service easily pressurizes service partnerships toward "done" or "not done." We receive little input about how to adjust because community members, who know how to adjust in their settings, go mostly missing when we show up for short-term work. Shifting our experience requires internal change more than external. Personal and service group insight and sharing help us adjust and readjust. Often, we readjust several more times. But accepting and enacting this approach takes practice and skill.

First, we do well to tap into humility, the chapter's guiding principle that keeps us grounded or in the moment as it is. Humility does not mean self-effacement or groveling. It stays low and close to the situation as it unfolds "on the ground." In this posture, our energy focuses on noticing possible next steps within our shared work or interdependence with others. We have to work to empathize with their situations, rather than judging or blaming others for what did not happen, meaning for what *we* wanted or expected. When your short-term service expectations fall flat, what helps you stay agile and tuned in? When you feel the urge to finger point or to press for your preferred plans to stick, what do you begin to think about the person or group organizing your service? When the heat is up, what becomes your bottom line? What happens to your empathy? Where's your hope that increases your suppleness? I'm aware of a kind of ambition that gets going in me when I show up for short-term service. Knowing the time is short and tight, I want to squeeze out every goal I can. I'm actually up in the clouds with my ideas, not grounded. Humility's present-centered work primarily attends to the levels of heat and breakdown while reshaping our expectations and goals.

Moving through a Muskeg

The first time I stepped onto a muskeg, my foot disappeared. No local Alaskan expects otherwise. But newcomers like me feel betrayed by the earth and I felt a bit betrayed by my host. In Algonquian language, muskeg means "grassy bog." A terrain of marshy land composed of rotting plants and random debris from trees and shrubs, muskegs muck up any pretense to steady walking. They retain so much water that movement dissolves into their spongy, unstable ground. The result is constant negotiation. Muskeg stability conjures contradiction. My upright body lurched forward. I started to reel and threw my right arm out to grab a handful of a three-foot high bush by the trail. Stretched out and dangling, my shoulder strained as my foot sank deeper. I started to fall and found myself getting mad. I glared at my host. It was too late for help.

As he turned his back to camouflage his laughter over my body-flight in all directions, I wondered if he had turned a clever trick on us outsiders. Communication with him felt a bit like a game. Questions unanswered. Possible plans never taking precise shape. My adrenalin, already on tilt through months of unclear planning, spiked. How could I make this short-term service trip add up to something useful, especially to the local Tlingit community? The Tlingit Head Start Center was located in the basement of the church hosting our three week service trip. Feeling my foot sinking deeper, I spied a 2 x 4 plank of wood almost within reach of my un-swallowed foot. I jabbed at it and caught an edge. Then, I juked and jived my other foot free from the goop.

Steadying myself, I panted, "In Georgia, we call this swamp muck and we warn our guests! Why the heck didn't you warn me!" The pastor laughed as I moved back onto more solid ground. No rescuing. He said nothing. Our host never acted hostile, just detached; and one plus of my misadventure was the laughter rising from the 22 college students that came on this service trip. My co-leader and one other adult stayed back at the church, our "home base" Things had not been going as we'd planned – and here it was again! As the laughter died down, I tried to resist my urge to take this prank too seriously. More important questions still loomed. The whole trip kept shape-shifting like this land, like a trickster. My doubts fueled, I worried about the next trick.

Muskegs make good metaphors for short-term service. Looking at a muskeg, you make false assumptions. It only appears to be ground. The "ground" of every community-based partnership also rests on layers of accumulated histories and relationships, some decomposed and some still taking shape. In his book, *This Side of Paradise,* F. Scott Fitzgerald describes two students taking a walk across campus the night before graduation: "The grass is full of ghosts, tonight." So too is the ground of service, a layering of hopes, expectations, negotiations, materials and money, successes and failures, and lives. The ground of our confident plans may not hold. Until you step onto it, you don't know the full experience ahead. If the ground gives, the next step also wobbles. Short-term service breakdown happens like this, creating an unreliable yet still possible service experience. We need skills, and tools for navigating that unstable ground. It may be mushy, but it's often all we've got in short-term service.

First Steps

As the plane wheels screeched upon touchdown, images of the last months flew through my mind: planning, making site arrangements through the national Methodist Church, and training our student-volunteers. We were finally here, a small fishing town in the Inside Passage of Alaska. Sponsored by our college and other funders, we hung a map of this place on the wall of our regular meeting room on campus. We knew the major economy flowed from fishing with three 24-hour a day fish processing plants in town. The oversized Emergency Unit of the local small hospital reflected the ongoing cases of major injuries at the plant and on the fishing boats. The streets wound through the rising topography like ribbons attached to wooden ginger-bread houses. Waves of newcomers poured in during the high fishing seasons from literally all over the world. Many military retirees found home here. We hoped we would too.

Our host community sat high on the town's upper ridgeline with most of the Methodist Church members coming to the building twice a week for Wednesday night supper and choir or an occasional program and Sunday morning services. Involvement appeared minimal from afar and the minister came out of retirement to be their pastor. The church's energy for our proposed service trip felt iffy from our first proposal. Nevertheless, the pastor said yes: we could come. He confirmed that we could work with the Tlingit Head Start program and he'd see what else we might do when we got there. This open-ended style proved consistent as we landed and no one from the church arrived to pick us up. At first, the small airline staff stared as we gathered in front of the very simple concrete building to wait. Then, a woman approached and asked if we needed taxis. Johnny, my co-leader, and I waived them off with platitudes about someone from the church coming soon.

The students spread out across the front of the small terminal. Some listened to their music, others chatted in small groups, and a few leaned back on their bags and fell asleep. The weather was foggy with light rain, but warm enough that we could stay outside and try to take in this complex terrain. Most of the students were juniors and seniors along with a few sophomores – twenty-three in all, and three team leaders. Though we envisioned this short-term service trip as a community-partnered opportunity, we never found the bridge to connect. That pattern repeated now. No one answered the church phone, the only number we had been given.

Thirty minutes after the airline staff person questioned us, a man appeared in a pick-up truck with a home-made cover over its extended truck bed. This would be our carriage to the church. The wet air had begun to chill us as Stewart, the driver, standing over six feet tall, explained to Johnny and me that he'd take us to the church. Johnny complimented him on his cowboy hat and boots and pointed to all our gear. Who Stewart was or how he knew to come get us only felt like another sinkhole; we asked no questions. We wanted warmth and food. Explaining that it would take several trips to get us all to the church, Stewart added that he had no idea this many folks were coming. Sigh.

With the flip of an arm, Johnny signaled to the students to fill the back of the truck with gear, sleeping bags, duffels with clothes, and plastic bags with school supplies for the Head Start program, as well as toothbrushes and toothpaste for the homeless closet run by a consortium of local churches. A student discovered that fact on line; so we added that work to our agenda of service. Only three students and Johnny went with Stewart on the first trip. By the time I got in the back of the truck, it was taking its third trip. We were packed in like the late summer salmon being shipped "fresh" to the U.S.

More questions spun in my head as we moved along two-lane roads. Where would we sleep? Were the promised showers really there? We drove past the town's main grocery store, which seemed a long walking distance away from the church. So much for easy meal planning. Finally, we arrived to our two-and-a-half-week home: the "Good Shepherd Methodist Church." Helping us get out and quickly putting the last of our gear to the ground, Stewart swung back into his seat, "Late for dinner – got to go!" We waved as he pulled away. I called out after him, "Should we lock the church?" I knew Johnny and our other co-leader, Robert, were already inside. Leaning his head out the window, he called back, "Never has been." Increasingly, short-term service felt like a bad idea.

Inside the front lobby, I turned left and found the kitchen and a hall of church offices with two additional small Sunday School rooms. Straight ahead from the lobby, the sanctuary opened up. In there, Johnny helped the students unpack and settle in. The kitchen claimed my immediate attention. Its industrial-sized eight-burner stove relieved my worries. A hefty two-door refrigerator and a sizable pantry further calmed my smoldering fears. I quickly dismissed the internal question; can we eat the food in the refrigerator and pantry? With no one around and twenty plus students unfed, the answer did not call for a rocket scientist.

The pilot light on the stove burned. We were in business for tonight. When we first met Stewart, he remarked in passing that he thought some of the church ladies had left boxes of donuts, cereal, and milk in the kitchen for breakfast tomorrow. We found them. Next, I wanted to check out the two showers downstairs. Found them. They worked. Meanwhile, Johnny had a better idea for dinner and had already ordered pizza calling the local delivery number he found on an advertisement taped next to the kitchen phone. Maybe we could craft a bit of short-term heaven, after all.

We ate pizza in the small fellowship hall next to the kitchen then headed into the sanctuary to share a conversation about the day. The sanctuary was a modern, A-frame room centered on a huge beam, which rose higher as it approached the altar area. All other beams flowed out at ninety-degree angles from this one, creating a spine and rib cage of beautiful cedar above. Its pews could hold about 300 people. The windows glimmered with a light blue tint and light from the outside still lit the room until well after 10 p.m. Most students slept in this room in their sleeping bags while a few settled in one of the small Sunday School rooms. Three men from the soccer team receded into the basement, sleeping in a small room with shelves full of games and supplies.

The other larger room downstairs housed the Head Start Center behind a locked door. Two women students found a hand-written note on one of the kitchen counters: "Head Start Expects Volunteers (2) at 8:30 a.m. in the morning." They cheerily offered their services and I spontaneously said, "OK!" and wondered what in the world the rest of us would do tomorrow.

So around 8 a.m., the next morning, I roused and fed those two young women cereal and let everyone else sleep in. We walked down the stairs to the Head Start Center eager to make connections. Through the open door, we watched children sitting on the carpeted floor playing with toys and drawing. Chatting in one corner stood two older women. They were not speaking English. Before I knew it, the two students had joined the children in their play. By 8:45 a.m., a third staff woman arrived, half-nodded in my direction as she walked past me and began talking to the other women. By 9:15 a.m., one student had placed crayons, paper, and scissors on a table and the other gathered a group of children to begin building a tower with Lego.

I tried to begin a conversation with the staff women. "How did these two communities – yours and the church – come together?" They turned toward me but did not respond. I tried asking in a different way and the woman with long grey-ing and braided hair, who had arrived later, walked toward me smiling, revealing her worn yet soft face. "We needed a space. They needed the Federal rent check." That's all she said. I felt a growing internal confirmation that this short-term service trip would offer only the most basic opportunities for partnered service. Over the next weeks, my intuitions proved true. Our visions of multi-cultural interactions continually dissolved – often at the last moment. As our hopes sunk, we oddly felt our internal need to serve rise higher along with our disappointment and anger. What we came half-way around our world to do apparently did not need doing.

I thanked the staff women and started up the stairs but stopped when I saw straight-legged grey wool pants coming down. The church member who left the note wanted to be sure two volunteers came to the Center. Neither she nor the Tlingit women acknowledged one another, but I quickly explained that two of our girls arrived on time and were eagerly at work with the Center and the children. Before I could say more, her grey slacks disappeared up the stairs as she noncha-lantly called back, "OK – you both figure it out from here. Oh, and Lorraine, I've been meaning to ask, why are the children not coming to the program on time. They seem to drift in. Isn't being on time part of the Head Start model?" I felt embarrassed. Her tone scolded the women and the tension in the Head Start Center grew palpable. No one responded. Our students determinedly focused on the children. I let the church woman leave and said nothing as I walked upstairs.

When I picked up the two students at the end of the day, I asked Lorraine what the program needed from us the next day. She responded by explaining that the families using the Center juggled many responsibilities, from work, to elder obligations, tribal community business, jobs, and more. I heard this as her response to the church member who questioned her earlier that morning. The structural pressures on these families to financially and pragmatically survive in this place demanded a lot. The history of unfair treatment to the Tlingits fostered renewed determination to make their own decisions despite complicated challenges and opportunities. She went on to plainly state that The Center only needed two students a day; some days only one and added that they appreciated our help. I replied that we would happily bring two students each morning and she could let us know at that time what was needed. More shaky ground. What would the other twenty-one students do all day?

But by day three, we had shaped a makeshift routine, which serves as the back-bone of short-term service. Make a schedule and then flex in response to your hosts' requests. The students decided to "super clean" the church as we waited for other assignments. We bought and cooked our own food, which we had not expected to do. Every evening, we built in time for reflection on the day's activi-ties, how they were feeling, and what they were thinking. Most of their comments focused on confusions over why we came.

Late afternoon of day four, while the cooking team for the day prepared our meal and the rest of us hung around, the pastor suddenly showed up. He offered words we'd been waiting to hear, "There's a project you might do – it involves repair work on a church-related building and some painting." Despite the lack of details, the students responded with ecstatic enthusiasm. Later that evening, Johnny, Robert, and I wondered, as we made our bed palettes in the pastor's office, what slippery step we now headed toward. I tried to dismiss that sinking feeling.

Regrounding: Working the Principles of Humility and Interdependence

How do we keep our emotional feet steady, our attitudes open, and our hearts willing to do what is asked of us? Pressures intensify when service timelines shrink as they do in short-term service. Every day without specific tasks fires up a semi-panic that easily collapses more balanced perspectives. We feel bad when we ask why we bothered to come and we feel bad that we are not able to help. The old model – service or no service – jerks us up and down like a see-saw. That all-or-nothing/either-or mindset lurks and distracts us from the possible. As empathy for our hosts and their situations breaks down, we lurch into anger or despair. This was the challenge Randy faced during his short-term service burnout. The attitudes and expectations we bring with us often trip us up. Preoccupied, we do not adjust, but sink deeper in our preoccupations with what *should* be happening, even when it is not or cannot.

Teresa of Avila, the medieval theologian and contemplative, faced similar struggles as she founded a contemplative order that broke away from certain traditional forms of monastic life. Certainly *not* a short-term venture, her project faced countless unknowns or pitfalls and problems. One major source of this instability, she believed, came with the people trying to participate. She referred to these distracting and sometimes destructive expectations and assumptions as the "reptiles we bring in with us." Not repulsive, but cunning companions, reptiles stood as her metaphor for ways we lose track of our big goals by giving our major time and energy to the smaller details that plague us. Now we sat in our Alaskan short-term service household completely preoccupied with the small reptiles we brought with us. These reptiles represented our expectations that *they* would provide food, serious and meaningful work for us – preferably with the Tlingits, and some small sense of community partnership with them. All of us in short-term service can follow our reptiles into these bogs. We trick *ourselves* by focusing on the less significant.

Teresa's suggestion to repeatedly pause and take stock of these expectations or reptiles helps us realize that in every new situation we bring in one or several of these with us.[1] Some of them are long-time friends, the reptiles we tend to keep. They are our habitual patterns of snap judgments toward ourselves and others, or other forms of self-criticisms and blaming. They scurry around spreading fear. If we can learn to shine a light on these free-wheeling anxieties or attempts to control, we keep ourselves more balanced. We don't increase the chances of swamping any stability we may still have as everything we expected changes. We also open to the newly emerging possibilities of shared work with others, even if the service does not match our expectations.

Longer-term partnerships increase the chances for embracing the unexpected because we believe we can count on our interdependent relationship. We can talk later about disappointments and dislikes. Short-term service can never leverage that level of shared trust and interdependence. Pausing becomes more important, since our snap judgments born of mismatched expectations – our reptiles – will quickly surface. Teresa understood her and our interest in these patterned expectations or reptiles is not about capturing or imprisoning them. They are part of us. Our work is to pay attention to them without getting all wrapped up in them. When we can take note of them but let the thoughts and feelings go on by, we just may avoid taking another sinkhole step. We gain some breathing room too, which adds to that space for them to pass on by. In time, that space becomes an incubator of change. We can let them go.

Let's play some tricks on these reptilian emotions and responses (see space for this work at the end of the chapter). To begin, either write down or draw the reptiles that accompanied you the last time you stepped into a service setting without knowing the tasks or context. The reptiles might represent your expectations for instructions and support in doing the work. They might represent the unknown work that had to be done, or who would be partnering with you to do it? Give each reptile a name and think about how they drew you in and then took all your energies, how you began to sink everything into their agenda.

I've come to know my reptiles pretty well. Conflict makes me anxious. So, in every new service setting, I bring with me the snakes of conflict avoidance. Soon, I'm slithering this way and that to duck tensions of any kind. And if I can, I get my way by slithering my agenda forward. No conflict there! What about you? Maybe your amazing Komodo dragons, those giants of the iguana family, represent how powerfully you can argue for things being done the way you need them or expect them to get done. One swipe of your know-it-all dragon tail and resistant community service partners fall to your wishes. Or at least you believe that. Have some fun. What reptiles come along with you demanding their due when service as you planned for it disappears or sinks?

How do our reptiles keep us sunk into the muck of missed expectations? How do they limit our creative capacities to leverage new options? The principle of humility helps us welcome them. They are factors in the way we've grounded ourselves in the past. But to step into the new ground of these partnerships, we must reorient. We need to shift our focus to the interdependence we're building with our service partners. How do they go about creating service? What helps them leverage their desired next steps? As one Buddhist teacher of mine described it, to shift into a different way of being in the world or partnering in service, I'll need to kindly ask my reptiles to move to their corner of my service life and rest. Not banished, but welcomed, they remain part of me. But I'm busy now with others, interdependent with their goals and hopes.

In service partnerships, we often get preoccupied with our expectations and plans, our reptiles, and resist putting them aside. It feels like service collapse. But in these settings, the putting aside frees us to join our partners in building solid planks for next steps that matter to them. We're interdependently supporting their versions of service in the short term, which is about all that short-term service can do. This work teaches us to ground ourselves and our reptiles in the present with humility. Pay attention to the situation as it is. Keep pausing and you'll see next steps able to bear the weight of the work your partner has offered – not very often the work we wished for. Moving stability grounds us in humility, flexibility and balance for steps in the middle of change. Interdependence, not judging, helps us discover next steps on ground where seemingly there was none.

Taking Next Steps: Practicing Humility

Mid-morning, the day after the pastor announced the next service opportunity, repairing and painting, we met with him for details. He asked us to scrape old paint, do minor carpentry repairs, and then repaint the pastor's home – that would be his home, which the church maintained. Johnny, Robert and my spirits sunk inside – our reptiles ran loose. We did not come for this. Nor did our students. But what else to do? We had nothing. So, we said yes, and asked him to come again after lunch to take us to the site. He agreed and left. Immediately in the privacy of the pastor's office, we released every reptile we had vainly tried to contain. The irony that we came thousands of miles to paint the church's parsonage sunk us into outrage. That work did not count. Finally, silence emerged. We ran out of complaints, gripes, and rage. And that gave us space to breathe and step back a bit. A service need presented itself. Our service partner asked us to do it. We had the labor and would figure out whatever expertise might be needed. As the ground of our plans disappeared beneath us, we would try to go forward. Take a next step.

Of course, those next steps proved to be full of tricks, another muskeg. The students adjusted better than we did. They wanted to do something – *anything useful*. Arriving at the site, we discovered numbers of missing pieces: no ladders high enough to reach the second floor, no ropes to create safety lines, not enough paint – by a long shot, no rollers and not enough brushes, no cover cloths. The list went on. But the pastor did give us the keys to his other car and the local stores had already been contacted: charge it to the church. One reptile slithered back to her corner. One more bit of steady footing. We began moving forward, creating teams and assigning tasks: scrape the exterior, buy supplies, work with Stewart – yep, he showed up again bringing serious carpentry skills. Each team elected a captain and the work began.

By day three, we sometimes forgot that we had not come to do this. We felt more grounded and the reptiles of oughts and blaming stayed more in their corners. Johnny, Robert, and I fell more in love with our students. They adjusted better than us. Even when one or a group of us got lost in frustration over some lacking tool or truly challenging task like painting the high eaves, others stepped in. They put the work on pause to talk us through whatever problem threatened to call out our reptiles. They leveraged humility, you might say, and resisted diving back into the anger and disappointment of shattered short-term service plans. During our evening reflection times, which – yes – Stewart starting attending because the students invited him, the students rehearsed the day's experiences. They named irritations. Sometimes they argued among themselves. But little by little, we let the actual difficulties of our service tasks take center stage. They offered enough real troubles to test our capacities to stay upright in our service muskeg. Maybe even move forward. Nothing felt simple and sometimes it was shouting-level tense. But we always agreed at the end of the conversation: show up the next day. The meaning of collapse transformed toward something else, something like next steps.

Practice Realigning

We adopted the practice of realignment, taking the cracked pieces of a plan now gooped in our own muck, and realigning them as semi-stable steps to the next area of more solid ground. If possible! We repeatedly lost the pieces in the mire of this misaligned short-term service, but we tried to forego our old ways of responding. Jon Kabat-Zinn describes the practice of disrupting stuck patterns as finding a new way through them. To "foster a decentered relationship to mental contents … take a wider perspective … observe (your) thinking rather than view and act upon (situations) as 'you' or 'reality.'"[2] This is fancy language for, when you're sinking, open your attention to the broader situation.

Practice holding your panic or rage – one kind of thinking – at arm's length. Observe it without feeding it, and in time its energy calms. At this point, you can choose another response. You can put a different kind of thinking into gear. You've realigned in order to move forward with your situation. By distancing ourselves from fixating on the sinking, we can notice what else is available. Part of this practice involves what Kabat-Zinn calls relinquishing the notion that "I" can change "reality."[3] Humility fosters realignment. Interdependence helps us encourage one another to re-ground in the current reality. We learn to practice what's real and possible.

Especially in short-term situations, we trick ourselves into thinking we can control service. We buy into our own reptilian tricksters who shape-shift reality until it looks like what we want. These tricksters realign our perception and activities from the realities of the world we serve in to another worldview we prefer.[4] From what's real and possible to what we wish. Unlike most of the American Indian stories of tricksters who reveal reality, service tricksters tend to urge us to ignore reality, to stick with the goals and expectations we brought. This is a dead end. We will completely fall and eventually get buried in the muck of that. Look at Exercise 4 at the end of this chapter to discover more about the maps or service realities you and your tricksters prefer.

Exercise 4 offers tools for relinquishing service we (and our reptiles) wished we were doing and getting into service we actually are doing. I call this exercise "reflective realignment." Reflective realignment begins by asking us to begin reimagining our service work to align with the intentions of our hosts. Before any insight or work toward actual next steps can occur, we need to know more about what in us will need to shift. We are beginning the work of recognizing that our assumptions are only that, assumptions. They are not permanent nor the only possible assumptions. Each time we question our assumptions, without judging ourselves, and expand our imagination to make room for other tasks and relationships, we are stepping into service reality as it is. We are leaving our reptiles behind to figure out what we actually can do in this service setting as it is.

As insight grows and willingness to try being with the service offered us, we gain additional steadiness in how we respond to requests and strategize getting the work done. As our openness to the presentation situation grows, we may discover creative interests and possibilities in the work itself or within our group. These surprises can energize the work going forward.

Sinkholes of communication may invite new attempts to talk through earlier decision-making. Reflection times within your service group realign from complaints to queries about next steps, keeping some balance as each day brings expected and unexpected work. Take some time in these reflection sessions to explore how and why certain expectations remain hard to release. Why? Getting to know these hardy and longest-living reptiles keeps us alert to the power of expectations' impacts on any form of service. All our expectations and reactions can be realigned at least to some extent, which invites us into a bit more stability, enough to keep moving with reality as it is.

Practices of Breaking Ground

A contemporary Christian monk, Curtis Almquist, SSJE, calls breaking points the breakthrough points of compassion and connection. Gregory of Nyssa, an early Christian theologian and bishop, puts it this way, "to be a human being one has to change . . . creation is changing; so we become more human through the freedom of shifting our desires and emotions . . . to move toward love."[5] Change becomes the broken ground of creative possibility, but it's natural that our first instinct is to try to avoid falling into those cracks and ditches. We resist getting "re-grounded" by losing ground. I wanted to flee from the muskeg, fight it, rather than discover how to get with it – on its terms. This, to repeat, is the work of the principle humility. But to change our emotional response, thinking, and behaviors, we have to find ways to craft new life from the decomposing mess all around us. The burnout is the invitation to rebuild and rediscover another version of service. This is the work of resilience and it begins by breaking through what we thought was solid ground.

Breaking ground is a metaphor for releasing without judgment or blaming our treasured and trusted ways of thinking through a service problem. St John of the Cross, a medieval monk, in his book, *The Ascent of Mount Carmel,* bores into this emotional and rational uprooting. It's difficult work to begin again, sometimes anew. It's like moving into a "dark night," he says – and one we did not choose. When service experiences and relationships put us "in the dark" or sink us into fear and anger, to break new ground takes practice. To not only recognize the change and agree to go with it, but actually move into, broken ground takes courage. Barbara Brown Taylor, my dear friend, describes how hard we will work to learn to walk in the dark, or what I'm calling walk on broken, unreliable ground:

> I had no way of knowing that the darkness was as much inside me as it was outside me, or that I had any power to affect its hold on me. No one ever taught me to talk back to the dark or even to breathe into it.[6]

Talking back or breathing into the broken, sinking failure of our plans and perceptions stretches us in uncomfortable ways. Widening our perspectives helps. Knowing the power of our reptiles clarifies. But eventually, the practice is to do it. To take steps. To paint and repair the house. To shift our weight from our self-styled goals and become curious about what else is possible. We claim a kind of "active indifference" as Ignatius of Loyola, another medieval contemplative, calls it. We practice going forward with full knowledge that the ground is broken all around us and see what happens. This is talking back. This is breathing with each step, as Thich Nhat Hahn invites us to do. This is making our peace with impermanence.

But don't confuse this with pretended self-denial or faked indifference. Those are ego-driven and brooding. They only sink us deeper into despair and foster undisciplined sullenness and self-preoccupation.[7] The early Christian desert traditions describe this as falling subject to the energy-sapping heat of the desert's noon-time sun.[8] Faked practices of moving into broken ground will destroy any possibility for moving stability. Realigned resilience builds from the choice to work in and with the sunken ground forward, the living, common grounds of any life systems, which always involve raucous, unsettling relationships.[9]

For our group, the basic list of possibilities for moving stably in and through broken ground actually increased. And so did each day's challenges. We had to learn to talk back. Yes, we will figure out how to reconnect this section of broken gutter. We can recycle our materials by pressing the paint store to help us. We learned that breaking ground becomes practice as we step back to listen and *then* ask more questions. We discovered we still go forward when we wobble, meaning find ourselves in a respectful debate about realignment and next steps. Breaking ground sets more than direction. It is moving stability.

Moving Stably through Failure

In Alaska, learning how to move through broken ground proved relatively easy. The changes involved low stakes. A few years later on another short-term service trip, we never fully found our footing. Arriving, by request, on a hurricane-hit island after another very long plane ride, we stepped out of the terminal to waving and welcoming hosts. The ground felt steadier. They whisked us and our gear into cars and up, up, up we went on island roads to higher ground and a gated community. We felt odd to be leaving the poorer parts of town, but better the next day as they ferried us back down the mountain and to a small city park approximately 200 by 150 yards. At the east end sat two picnic tables, a lone swing set, and two cement block bathrooms labeled, "MEN," and "WOMEN." On the west end, 2 20 x 20-foot army canvas tents were sitting on the ground. Getting those *heavy* tents up took all the strength and savvy we had, but after a long day of organizing the site, we ate and settled in surrounded by a beautiful environment. Our evening reflections focused on the next weeks' tasks of home-building for families whose houses were flattened in the terrifying winds and rains of the recent hurricane.

On the second night, some cat-calls and taunts came from a group of young men sitting on the picnic tables while we were discussing the day's work. We did not pay much attention. By the fourth night, they shouted, "Go Home! You don't belong here! You're stealing our jobs and we need work – to feed our families!" By night five, the taunts had escalated to, "You Outsiders! We don't want you here! Go Home! You destroy our culture!" The kept raising the ante and the ground grew more unsteady. A few students said they dreaded coming home to our tents. We talked about the daily struggles of the native islanders who felt pushed aside economically and physically. Outsiders kept coming and taking what had belonged to their people for hundreds of years. When the storm came, their side of the island received little help. From their perspective, which grounded in reality, first came the chain resort hotels that privatized what had been public beaches. Then the outside seasonal workers who took their jobs. Now service trip groups who again ignored their plight.

When we brought these issues to the attention of our hosts, they treated them as "usual stuff." They were not interested. Because we camped in the neighborhood hardest hit by these structural inequities, we felt the pressures first hand. Each morning at 8 a.m. sharp, we drove passed damaged homes only half-rebuilt. Adults sat on their front steps, clearly without work. Why drive seven miles to the other side of the island, closer to the high hills of our sponsors? Work needed to be done where our tents stood. All this heightened our determination to reach out to these young men. By the end of the week, a few of our group went over to the picnic tables and tried to chat. We invited them to come to the tent to join us for dinner. No success.

Reading about these tensions over land rights, economic access, indigenous groups' rights, and resort management in preparation for the trip did not prepare us for the realities we stumbled through each night. We wobbled along in what Pema Chodron, a contemporary Buddhist teacher, calls those "maybe yes, maybe no" dynamics. Maybe we could connect in some way with these angry young men, maybe not. Maybe it makes sense to be here trying to support rebuilding, maybe not. These mucky realities occupied much of our reflection time. Students vented, shared their anger, confusion, and fears. We worried about our culpability as every night the taunts rose louder. All our strategies only sunk the situation deeper–frisbee football before dinner, a shared cook-out for them and their families. Maybe yes became perpetually no.

One night when the taunting grew hotter, our hearts sunk and our minds scrambled. "We lost houses too! Why aren't you building here! We need work!" The name-calling intensified.

Three students approached with plates of food, which they took and tossed aside. Now they stood and moved toward the students, threatening. As language grew more violent and they kept moving toward the tents, other students joined the first group. Everyone encouraged cooling down. Two women students began to softly cry. Johnny and I looked at each other. We had discussed an emergency plan and as the first fist flew and missed, we went into action. He went toward the young men and I recruited three students to go with me the three blocks to a little police precinct station for help. Johnny and I worried what the turn to the police might signal, another form of outsider complicity in the suffocating system. But we felt responsible for everyone's safety and the situation had grown dangerous. The ground felt even more unstable and failing.

At the end of the second block, we came upon a different group of young local men, about the same age as the men with us in the park. Saying hello, we moved to go around them and stay on our mission. But they planted themselves directly in front of us. We stood stuck. One man flatly asked, "Trouble in the park?" We answered, "There's some tension and we think we're OK." That word tension seemed a trigger. They immediately took off toward the park, one of them even pushing aside one of the students. Something about their jump told us the situation had shifted. We did not know why, but I decided that we could not let them run to the park without following. Johnny needed to know what happened, which we could not really explain, but could report.

I told two of the students to go on to the police station and I and the other student turned back to follow this group of young men. They ran much faster than we could and beat us to the scene. By the time we got there, everything turned to sludge. Johnny stood shouting at one of the men we'd just talked to while the rest of them punched and pushed down the young men who had been with us for a week in the park. As I watched their bodies being hit and several unable to keep their feet, my body and heart sank in despair while I ran screaming toward the fighting. "Stop it! Stop it, now!" That changed nothing except the new group of young men suddenly began pushing the men we knew back toward the picnic tables and then beyond the park into a side street. As this happened a student shouted in protest, "Don't! Don't! They belong here!" One man from the new group called back, "Stay out of this! We'll take care of them"! At this very moment, a police car came up the street with the lights flashing but no siren. At the site of the police car, the newer group strongly shoved the others into the dark streets behind the park.

We stood buried in confusion and conflicted feelings. A police woman approached the two students who went to the precinct office and then ran back before she came. "What happened?" As they told what they knew, Johnny and I walked over to her. Johnny explained the rest. But none of what happened made full sense to us. She nodded and simply stated that economic and political issues were hitting the neighborhood hard. Cultural tensions were growing between natives and new people and among other groups. They were witnessing a rise in gang activity. "We're still figuring things out," she ended. Then, she shifted her attention to us asking if we were OK and did we want police regularly driving or walking by? Too overwhelmed to respond, we stood frozen and she simply stated that she would assign the park for regular duty drive-bys. We thanked her for coming. One student asked that the young men who had been in the park not get in trouble. The officer responded, "Thank you."

Our plans sunk, failed, and were stymied. Resilience might mean accepting failure and finding next steps from there. Walking back to our tents, we broke into smaller conversation groups by intuition and need. The tangled reality of our setting seemed to have left us face down in the muskeg. Too soon to discern any left-over planks or unexploited ones to shape a path forward, we called it a night. The next morning, our usual schedule took us forward but much less stably. We did our work. We came home. We ate. A few students walked to the police station asking for information. None was given, though the officer on duty thanked them for asking and for our service. We flew home three days later. We never saw any of the young men again.

Practicing Humility: Moving Stability

In both settings, the ground of our service changed our work and us. To embrace moving stability demanded humility/groundedness and non-judgment. Taking this stance helped us recognize our interdependence with our hosts and others. In contexts we could not fully control, we tried to increase our empathy for everyone, an effort to embrace our interdependence. It taught us the meaning of impermanence. I learned a great deal from these two stark experiences. Now when coordinating short-term volunteer experiences, I include additional reflection practices to help us begin to identify our reptiles. During our pre-trip orientations, I introduce basic forms of these exercises explaining their purpose and telling participants that we will be doing them while on our service trip. Once on site, these exercises gain relevance and strength through application in actual situations that we only reflectively imagined before we left. The benefit of this approach is three-fold, insights born of pre-trip expectations, insights gained in the midst of service, and insights learned by comparing the pre-trip reflections with on-the-ground service and burnout realities.

A specific practice that integrates these three insight-angles very well – and can be done before, during and after any service trip – was originally developed by the Peace Corps. It is called DIE. The practice involves: Description, Interpretation, and Evaluation; these three provide a format for information gathering and reflection in cross-cultural service settings and partnerships. This work cultivates additional insights about how our expectations do and do not match on-the-ground realities. It helps us develop skills for all the muskegs that real-world service partnerships bring. The DIE format also resonates well with contemplative approaches.

DIE has three core steps:

Remember, it is best done twice (comparatively): before engaging in service and after arrival to the service site and sharing the work:

1. Description: What I see, hear, sense (notice)
2. Interpretation: What I Think (about what I'm noticing, what analytic boxes do I use)
3. Evaluation: What I Feel (where in my body and feelings do I sense my interpretation and responses/reactions – what do they trigger, noting positives and/or negatives)

Describe invites noticing without categorizing or labeling – at least as much as we can. We put our beliefs and assumptions on hold. Use a small notebook to record your pre-service responses and carry that same notebook with you to record your DIE responses once participating in the service experience. Describe asks us to jot down observations, information, and thoughts, imagined or experienced. Try not to unpack those thoughts, just notice them. Keep track of what draws your attention and which of your senses seems most alert. Work to avoid adding layers of thinking or analyzing. If, for instance, you notice one of your own reptiles lurking but not yet moving into action, just note that. Do not try to stop those responses, including the ones we're reticent to admit. We can work with those dynamics later in the exercise.

Interpreting adds frames or boxes around what we're noticing. Think of interpreting as organizing our comments according to topic (supplies, space, etc.) and experience (confused communication with staff and local people, lacking a plan of action, etc.). After putting your descriptive data within these categories or frames take some time to sit with the information and notice what you think and feel. You might notice, for instance, that knowing something about the history of your service setting would help you understand how people relate and work. What cultural information would inform behaviors that are unfamiliar. Maybe you even misinterpreted an action, which embarrassed you and your host. Within each frame's data, feel free to add emotions that came up. Include reactions with stronger emotions.

This second step of recording our interpretations reveals how all of us color and sometimes change information we're receiving. The recording of our interpretations reveals our patterns for making sense of interactions and situations, especially the ones that take us a bit off balance. Recognizing these, even only initially, will alert us to their presence and power amid our service relationships and actions. By learning more about them, we can better track how they muck up our capacity to shift and improvise next steps in service relationships and actions. By paying closer attention to these interpretive assumptions, we may even discover that we consistently ignore certain data.

Keep all of these notations in your little notebook and regularly refer to its treasure chest of how and why I do and do not interpret basic data, descriptions, emotions, plans, interactions, etc. in the ways I do. Track how your assumptions establish your categories or frames. How do your assumptions inform your feelings and what difference does that make in the shared work? What are the sources of your fears and when do they regularly show up – are there any patterns?

Evaluation, the third step of DIE, digs down more personally. Again, I write in my notebook whenever I notice certain experiences, conversations, or dashed or fulfilled expectations that raise judgments about myself, my co-workers, or our service partners. As the instructions encourage, I pay particular attention to where feelings of shame, anxiety, defensiveness, or denial show up in my body. The thoughts are present too, but the feelings can be easier to notice and track. Sometimes my stomach churns or my chest feels crushed. I try to sit with those sensations and notice any thoughts or feelings that arise. Where do you feel anxieties or fear? My throat tightens when I'm really mad.

Have you felt similar responses in your body? Do you notice feelings of disappointment as a kind of weight on your shoulders? How do cultural and place-based expectations that differ from yours impact your experience in service? What's going on when your back tightens, when you want to argue back or change a local leader's decision that you do not like? Evaluation offers us a chance to reflect and write about the visceral or embodied impacts of our emotions, thinking, and sometimes memories. It helps us track what's going on when we find ourselves in a full sinkhole. We all have them, positive, negative, and all in between.

Especially with this last step, the DIE practice shines a brighter light on *us* in the midst of service partnerships and settings. Because we are the only ones whose behaviors we can affect or change, DIE offers significant help in shifting our weight toward the service realities with which we've partnered. DIE helps us learn to participate in change, in the scattering of our favorite reptiles, while learning to move into flexible stability. The comparative learning from pre-trip expectation to in-the-midst-of-it-reality clarifies which thoughts, expectations, former experiences, feelings, and more muck up our ability to open to the present realities and serve with others. Using DIE, we build next steps on self-reflective data, reflective realignment. Much of what we learn through DIE forwards our own creativity in giving back with others.

It's human to anticipate things running amuck in service. The stories and exercises in this chapter help us reimagine responses to different and often destabilizing scenarios as well as gain crucial insight about our own reptiles or patterns of avoidance and response. Most of us tend to walk familiar paths in life and in service and for good reasons. There are lots of positives in doing what comes easily and well. Yet part of embracing burnout as an aspect or phase of life-long resilience in service invites us to recognize that service pathways perpetually shift and change. Even our familiar settings can flood or go dry leaving us to adjust or watch burnout stagnate and destroy. Whether at home or in new service settings, the challenge is to develop the skills of moving stability and taking our service hopes and work in forward, reorganizing, and resilient directions.

Exercises

1. Think back to a short-term service experience that was disappointing and frustrating. With that reality in mind, what are the qualities of short-term service partnerships that matter most to you?

    _____

    _____

    _____

    _____

    _____

    _____

2. Bring to mind a short-term service situation which exploded your preparations and expectations. What initial demands did you as of your hosts? What initial demands did you ask of yourself? Did you try to fake compliance and

ease in the face of your situation or did your interactions ignite as your "reptiles," or habitual expectations took hold?

_____

_____

_____

_____

_____

_____

_____

3. Getting to know our "reptilian" emotions and responses:

   a. Name and write some reflections about your emotional expectations in short-term service – or draw a "reptilian" emotion or expectations in action.

   _____

   _____

   _____

   _____

   _____

   _____

   _____

Box 5.1

b.   How do they keep you preoccupied, or sometimes steal your energy? Do these resistant emotions and responses woo you into redefining yourself in their terms?

_____

_____

_____

_____

_____

_____

4.   To begin your "reflective realignment," write down some realities you did not want to face and ask:

a.   What would it take – physically, emotionally, and cognitively to move into that task, or interaction, or worksite?

_____

_____

_____

_____

_____

_____

b.   Read without judgment what you have written and sit quietly with it for several minutes. What new thoughts or emotions come up?

_____

_____

_____

_____

_____

_____

c.   Are there activities and attitudes you and/or your group might realign?

_____

_____

_____

_____

_____

_____

Supplemental Readings

Nhat Hanh, Thich and Anh-Huong Nguyen. *Walking Meditation: Peace Is Every Step. It Turns the Endless Path to Joy*. Boulder, CO: Sounds True, 2006.

Thibodeaux, Mark E. *Reimagning the Ignatian Examen: Fresh Ways to Pray from Your Day*. Chicago, IL: Loyola Press, 2015.

Notes

1   See Teresa of Avila, *Interior Castle*, I.1.8.
2   Segal, Williams & Teasdale, *Mindfulness-Based Cognitive Therapy for Depression*, 38–39. For additional insights about these dynamics, read through page 41.
3   Ibid.
4   David Carrasco's scholarship on Aztec landscapes and ceremonies, specifically Aztec intentional strategies for mapping multiple worlds in which they live, caught my imagination. Though describing a drastically different situation, I think many of us in short-term service strategize a map of our service world that we prefer to the actual world we are serving in. We too have developed mapping practices for living within multiple worlds.
5   Bondi, *To Love as God Loves,* 23. For Gregory, love was God.
6   Taylor, *Learning to Walk in the Dark,* 2.
7   Lane, *The Solace of Fierce Landscapes,* 192.
8   Ibid, 193.
9   Kearns and Keller, *Ecospirit*, 5.

References

Bondi, Roberta. *To Love as God Loves: Conversations with the Early Church*. Minneapolis, MN: Fortress Press, 1987.

Kearns, Laurel and Catherine Keller. *Ecospirit: Religions and Philosophies for the Earth*. New York: Fordham University Press, 2007.

Lane, Belden C. *The Solace of Fierce Landscapes: Exploring Desert and Mountain Spirituality*. New York: Oxford University Press, 1998.

Segal, Zindel, Mark Williams, and John Teasdale. *Mindfulness-Based Cognitive Therapy for Depression: A New Approach to Preventing Relapse*. New York: The Guilford Press, 2002.

Taylor, Barbara Brown. *Learning to Walk in the Dark*. New York: HarperOne, 2014.

Teresa of Avila. *Interior Castle*. Translated and edited by E. Allison Peers. New York: Doubleday, 1989.

Chapter 6

Not All Up to Me/All Up to Me

Taking on the Program

As teenagers, I and a group of close friends volunteered in a triangle of neighborhoods within a three-mile radius of each other and within a larger urban area. Today, I still serve with people living in these neighborhoods and others like them across the metropolitan area where I live. Many of these urban pockets of economic struggle and social systems failure have and continue to experience the relentless waves of urban development. New apartments and condominiums along with single-family homes continually edge into these communities. With them come rising costs, loss of local businesses, and eventually higher taxes. Much of the rental housing in the triangle goes through the city's housing authority programs. Individuals and families including African-Americans, immigrants, and some whites, participate in these rental subsidy programs. Numbers of them also receive some government support for food and healthcare.

While in college, our volunteer group stayed in touch not only with each other but with those still living and serving in these neighborhoods. Their ongoing work partnered with locals and leveraged political knowledge and organizing into active strategies for neighborhood change. They succeeded, failed, and lots in between. Some of the work came quickly to fruition. Other work defied best intentions and well-designed plans. Poverty trapped in patterns of race-based exclusion from viable sources of income dragged on through generations. City decision-makers did not intervene. We felt inspired by the neighbors we came to know and enjoyed hearing updates. Many of them lived on these streets all of their lives. Their knowledge of the community and how it best thrived flowed generationally from grandparents to parents to children and foster care siblings.

Despite our true admiration of the self-direction of people in these neighborhoods, we did not fully realize or respect their strategies for positive change. We overlooked how they coordinated resources and civic actions through their fraternal lodges, privately owned corner stores, and religious communities. More than a few times, we heard news of a successful neighborhood initiative, getting city trash cans placed on corners for example, but did not understand the processes that led to those "wins." Despite our ignorances, people in the neighbourhood continued to inspire us; so, we all were interested when Joey, our self-appointed ring-leader, contacted each of us asking if we would be willing to come to a meeting over our winter break. He wanted to pitch a service idea that he hoped would draw us back into these communities. We jumped at the chance.

With our semester breaks overlapping, we met on a Thursday afternoon in later-December arriving at a broad church parking lot around 6:00 p.m. Joey grew up in this church, and we had heard stories about it in the past. We knew the basic history: Stafford Memorial Church; founded 1884; now standing at the borderline between Thompson Pines, one of the three neighborhoods we volunteered in, and the newly redeveloping neighborhoods to the immediate north. Historically, Stafford ministered to the northerly neighborhood known as Middleton, originally prosperous and white. From the 1960s to the '90s, white flight took hold and suburbanization also grew. Many in the Middleton neighborhood moved out. Increasingly, African-Americans were the majority if not the sole population of neighborhoods in the city. But by now, in the late '80s, urban redevelopment was creeping back. White and some African-American individuals and families, often young and willing to take what some considered a risk, were returning to Middleton.

Floundering somewhat in the borderlands between these changes, the church searched for its new community and mission. As we stood in the parking lot facing a mostly unused but very large Sunday School building, we tried to imagine what the church had been and could be. The building looked unused and empty. Crime still brought troubles as we could see from the broken glass and needles around our feet. Increased drug and human trafficking mixed well with absent landlords to the south in Thompson Pines and the rest of the triangle neighborhoods. Yet, the church steadfastly held on. Some members accepted the status quo and focused on keeping the bills paid. A few more active members had a vision. They wanted to strengthen relationships with those new neighbors to the north of the church, but they were equally intent on stronger relationships with those to the south in Thompson Pines. Within the last year, this group co-created a partnership with Founders Memorial African Methodist Episcopal Church, a large historic Black congregation in Thompson Pines. Stafford volunteers began working in Founders' food, and clothing closets and the church also pledged a financial commitment to the newly shared work.

Now, these activists believed Joey could help them build next steps. Their plan: Ask Joey to recruit a few of his service-experienced friends to create and run a summer activities program for neighborhood youth, ages four to sixteen. Joey immediately liked the idea and called us: Lance, his best friend from high school, Janice, my friend who volunteered with me during high school, and me, who knew Joey from the neighborhood service that he, Lance, and I had been involved in. As we stood that evening facing the Sunday School building, Joey's only facts were that our possible program might be housed "somewhere in there." Obviously, nothing definite yet. As the last remnants of the winter sun disappeared, Joey's enthusiasm flowed. "I think they plan for us to use the basement! It covers the whole length of the building!"

I shot a glance toward Lance with our eyes growing bigger. Lance spoke up, "Did these people from the church suggest what we might do all day with these neighborhood children? Did they give you a budget? Maybe someone on the staff will meet with us regularly; you know, like supervise out work and guide us?" Joey brushed off Lance's questions as details to be worked out later assuring us things would be fine. Basically, the church hoped we would offer educational and fun activities relevant to the needs and interests of Thompson Pines kids and their parents. The church also hoped to lessen the parents' burden of paying for summer daycare by providing this enrichment program for a much cheaper price. The church team working with Joey suggested a Monday through Friday format, maybe 8:00 a.m. to 5:30 p.m. to match the parents' work hours.

They hoped the program would predominantly serve children from Thompson Pines, but they knew word would spread. They wouldn't exclude any child, but recruitment would begin through their new community partnership with Founders. The space could legally accommodate 90 bodies. In fact, over that summer, we offered programming to a group of "regulars" from Thompson Pines as others came and went. Usually, our daily program served around 90 children. Listening, I couldn't help but loudly breathe in and out. Joey continued. "So yeah, Lance, it's totally up to us!" But Lance was shaking his head "no." "Joey, we've never done anything this big, for this many kids and their parents or for this many hours a day. Do they have any program goals besides childcare?" Joey didn't know. In fact, Joey didn't know much. Though we all wanted in on this and we truly enjoyed working with people from these neighborhoods and their children, we felt skittish. Silenced by our pondering, Janice jumped in. "Were parents from Thompson Pines part of these conversations? Had they asked for anything specific?" Joey did not know.

In part, our questions came from our past knowledge of the other two childcare programs in Thompson Pines. One group focused on Black empowerment, teaching skills to foster a strong sense of identity among the children as well as offering educational opportunities and year-round tutoring. The second group's work rooted in religious identity and formation. Housed in a neighborhood church, its curriculum of community-service and reconciliation was based in Biblical teachings. They too provided tutoring all year round. Both programs served food. We asked Joey if either of those groups had been told about this idea. Joey did not know. All this disconnection made me worry that the program would orbit in a universe to itself and the burden would be solely on us. In fact, all of us, even Joey, were beginning to envision the complexities and problems coming our way. We had enough service experience in the neighborhood to analyze historical patterns of racially-edged public policies with economic and political consequences. The community's strengths met those challenges, including well-intentioned folks who came to serve. As white students from privileged backgrounds, our presence and actions added certain layers of tension.[1] We would discover what those were and their impacts. But for now, we found stability in the relationships we had developed in these neighborhoods.

Sensing our growing unease and realizing that our questions were beginning to weaken his resolve, Joey jumped in. He began telling us about Stafford's renewed community partnership over the last year. He felt sure the community had been consulted about this idea. Lance stepped in again noting that we only had a few months to plan the program. We stood somewhat stymied. What to do? The support for parents deserved a shot. At this juncture, Joey suggested we go see the building. Seeing the space might help us make our decision. Internally, each of us struggled to think through the real problems with this approach; while at the same time, we felt the urgency of parents needing a safe and relatively low-cost program for their children *this* summer. Surely, we would say yes? As each of us pondered these communal and personal questions, Joey moved us closer to the building.

It stood before us like a long rectangular box feathered in layers of aquamarine translucent plastic panels. Clinging to the building by silver metal hooks, these panels covered three floors of windows across the thousand-foot-long structure. The bottom floor, we would soon find out, was one giant "Rec Area." To enter that level, we moved to the back of the building where a concrete slab spread out behind it. At the back of the slab stood metal no-net, basketball goals and behind those an open, broad field of unkempt grass. Two collapsing picnic tables to the right of the slab must have regularly attracted late-night gatherings of locals and perhaps those without shelter or with business to trade. At least the trash suggested this. Joey fiddled with a key to the door facing this back area and leading into the bottom floor. Finally, he coerced it open. We walked inside.

The space held nothing except the clammy feel on our skin. Floors of poured concrete met walls of concrete block rising to meet smaller aluminum-edged windows across the top of the wall. The space felt as if it had not been used. Joey disappeared in the shadows as we heard his hands patting the walls to discover the light switch. On; then, the fluorescent buzzing! The entire summer that buzzing never stopped when the lights were on, but we eventually tuned it out. Despite our concerns, as we moved across that threshold, our excitement about this idea grew. Janice spoke first. "Wow – this is a big space. We can put almost everybody in here on a rainy day – set up various play areas – lots of options." As we tossed around ideas, the empty space came alive with possibilities and puzzles. How would we arrange the components of our program within it? What would the kids prefer? Where would we get supplies? We wandered around in the open areas pitching ideas to each other. We left about thirty minutes later hopeful that we could build something useful for the community.

Returning to our campuses, we stayed in touch as plans for the summer took shape over that spring. Families would be asked to pay $20 per child per week. Many would pay what they could. The program offered recreation, art, and educational experiences, along with field trips, swimming and swimming lessons, as well as reading and math tutoring. Janice committed to providing two meals a day, breakfast and lunch. This proved to be a major program asset to parents. We could not have imagined that by our second week, 50 to 60 children would eat a breakfast of cereal, bananas, and milk with us. By lunchtime, we grew to 90 or more children. Lunch usually consisted of hot dogs or peanut butter sandwiches along with an apple or another banana. Periodically, we splurged from the budget and cooked hamburgers on the old brick grill outside.

Our budget equaled the parents' payments plus the church's additional funding, which remained undisclosed until the week before we began. We were never told if the church was paying us for our summer work, but they did. That lump-sum amount covered most of the summer's rent for our two-story, collapsing apartment only five blocks away. By keeping our utility and food budgets at rock bottom, we made it through the summer financially only tapping into our personal savings now and then. An equally tight monthly program budget went toward supplies and food. Most days we loved the freedom to create and adjust things as we thought the kids preferred or needed. On a number of days, we wished for more supervision and guidance from the church. It never came. Because we arrived only a few days before the program opened, we had no chance to talk over our plans with parents we knew from the neighborhood. We simply went to work, crossing into new territory without a map. We just kept going day by day, and the initial parental responses buoyed our hopes. We seemed to be offering something of value to them and their children. Only later did we discover how fragile our communication lines would become, how problematic our boundary-crossing with our "all up to me" attitude would be.

Service Thresholds

To serve is to meet a need, or so the linear version of the story goes. And that's not wrong. It's just incomplete. Serving is always also partnering. Some of our partners are literally other people or creatures that join us in serving and burning out. Other "partners" are aspects of ourselves. Some aspects of ourselves we know very well. That familiar irritability when service plans change or how wedded we get to a particular policy or procedure. We're more practiced in recognizing how these assumptions and needs push us across thresholds of service breakdown. With some intentional self-care, we can soothe and support ourselves. We can pick our attitude up and get back to work. We triggered the mess; we can fix it. All up to me: I crossed a threshold into semi-collapse, but dosed myself up with a bit of extra rest and resolved determination and onward: next steps for service.

It works well enough, but this threshold-crossing self-care "all up to me" response looks a lot like a moderately skilled kayaker paddles with a group of friends when a small squall comes up. That kayaker has enough basic strokes to stay upright and move forward. She feels basic emotional relief and handles the situation all by herself. But push the squall up a step or three. The waves get higher as the wind whips them up forming white-caps. Lightning begins to strike nearby and the wind gets stronger. Tiring, she begins to hit a breakdown point in her skill sets, which she tries to ignore. Lacking skills and self-care, she's lost resilience. She's floundering under additional pressures which require a larger repertoire of self-care skills than the usual set. She needs skills at the level of self-resilience, where tools available to her can match this higher threshold of breakdown demands and tasks.

Not up to this level of breakdown, the consequences also hit a higher level. The boat flips over. She is in the water and struggles amid high waves to signal for help to the other paddlers. This is collapse of a different order. She can access very little at this point to keep her going forward into the fray. Her level of self-care is too low. It cannot meet this level of strain. She needs a stronger skill sets, one I identify as a skill sets of self-resilience that are able to meet the higher challenge. And when crossing thresholds of water and waves this complex, she needs partners, a community of paddlers with a range of resources willing to be with her all the way.

This is my metaphor for the problems we get into when we move into service with underdeveloped skills of self-resilience. To acquire those skills, we cannot serve alone. We must establish ourselves in a community of shared service and burnout, which allows us to step back from certain responsibilities while we attend to seriously needed self-resilience. I'll go back to the kayak example. I might be able to right my boat once or twice in higher waves by rolling it myself. But I will tire. When I fail, I will need to count on others to come and help me get my boat righted, help me not dangle upside down in water. I will need some additional time to recoup my strength and keep going. That deeper self-resilience depends on others. I need their community and support to keep going. So too in service, when burnout takes us deep down into its fury, we cannot restore and move one alone. At that point, to recover resilience, we count on community. It's "not all up to me."

Distinguishing self-care from self-resilience clarifies which skill sets we need when. And honestly, in service, everyone will need the stronger and richer skill sets of self-resilience and group-resilience to make it through repeating cycles of burnout. They will keep coming cycle after cycle. To develop this level of resilience skill and insight takes practice along with community. Start with pausing longer to assess your true emotional state. How has this burnout impacted you? Listen more keenly to yourself, which will help you listen more pointedly to those you're serving with. The whole community will have ideas for moving through this really rough time. So, listen more – it's "not all up to you." And speak less as a strategy for building community strength, as desert contemplatives advocated.[2] This practice begins with internal clarity that strengthens into community-oriented resilience. As individuals and service teams learn to practice this, we expand from a self-only assessment to embrace a group-also intentionality and support.

Another way to strengthen self-resilience is to pay closer attention to your body when service collapse hits. How strongly does your body react to surprising change in a service setting? Does your body keep trying to go back – the way some kayakers will keep trying to roll when their hips and arms are too tired? Notice when your body has shifted to a kind of service burnout shock. Don't panic; pause and listen to your body. Build resilience from there. Next steps cannot be all up to you. Hear your body note: I had "no idea" that these were the stakes to which I gave all my energy. Are they the best stakes, the ones that will move the work forward? Tensions in our bodies are good signals that we're in a stronger corner and more stuck than we imagined. We've crossed a threshold here that requires more than self-care. We need other bodies and minds and hearts. We need self and other-resilience.

Listening to our thoughts, emotions, and bodies helps us find the strength to discern a threshold has been breached. We're across. Self-resilience, alone and with others, is the power to honestly explore these more complex dynamics within service and burnout. Developing this level of resilience with self and others requires maturity and much practice. They take time to develop, slower analyses, and a candid look at our reactions and actions as serious problems often derailing shared service. Why have we left others out of the feedback loops we know are crucial for resilience-building? When did we embrace an "all up to me" posture, whose patching together of self-care strategies cannot hold up under this level of burnout?

Yet because what we learn about ourselves at this level of breakdown confounds us, we often resist. Patterns of assumed privilege or dismissal root deeply to our self-images and beliefs as people who give back – but give back in too solitary a way. Instead, serious rethinking and reorienting needs to be done. Broad-based, communally-engaged burnout requires new priorities of time, focus, and resources. The limits we assumed earlier in our "all up to me" world are stretched until they break. Now, we must approach burning and serving from a "not all up to me" posture that takes time to build enough resilience to move through trouble rather than skirt it. If we try to avoid this level of resilience-building, by patching together attitudes, relationships, and actions, the stability we gain will not last long. Worse, it comes at a high price for the service we're doing. Burnout will return sooner and with a viciousness.

Our preferred scenarios of service tell of individuals and/or communities moving across a threshold together in common cause from one state (we might use the term, phase) to the next.[3] We're actually not paying attention. Because when partnerships weaken or falter, thresholds signal that tolerance levels for the phase of stability have reached their maximum points. Burnout has already begun. The more serious the threshold crossing or, the more frequently and/or larger it appears, the more seriously we must attend to it. And we cannot pay attention to burn-out's thrashing across this threshold moment alone. The chaos and breakdowns will demand more rebuilding than we can do singly. An "all up to me" attitude nour-ished by surface acts of self-care will fail quickly. We must develop self-resilience born of shared work in the face of burnout.

This deeper challenge brings complex questions reflecting feedback loops of self and others and community. How did the fire of burnout get set and who helped set it? What should assessment include? When can it begin? Who can discern the gaffs and losses? When did assumed privilege twist resources toward unintended goals? These are second-order, or more complex questions that self-care thinking and doing simply do not engage. We need to build self and self-and-other/community resilience. Discerning what steps, people, goals, strategies, resources and more can be taken into this burnout recovery work and what, at least for now cannot be taken in though perhaps later, is the focus of this chapter.

What might self-resilience alone and with others look like? We cannot discern that on our own. The questions and the response toggle between ourselves and our teams, asking for serious time given to relationship-building, assessment of assets and needs, as well as determination of service goals. These questions and their responses are born of adaptive choice-making, which is nourished by resil-ience practices born of the principle "not all up to me." We would be learning this lesson, though we did not know that yet. So, standing in the early winter chill of the church's parking lot, we expected to cross some thresholds, but probably the kinds we could individually handle. We did not anticipate breakdowns born of our own lack of insight and planning. Our attempts to be responsible would feed overly-hurried, overly-autonomous responses. We "took charge" and no amount of self-care would be able to soothe the scalding of that isolation. We would need community for that. We would suffer from lack of self-resilience, which would have reinforced our interdependence with the resilience of Thompson Pines.

When It's All Up to Me

Enthusiasm for new service partnerships and programs often blinds us to the importance of developing self-resilience integrated with community-resilience, our partners' gifts and insights. As we cross thresholds of burnout, we will benefit from the community's insights and experiences, which can bolster our own resilience. We also will miscalculate assumptions and needs that are not obvious to us in our-selves and our partnering community. Taking on too much on ourselves, then, we push forward without thoroughly understanding how our decisions will impact the program and our partnerships. We are leaking the very energies and wisdom we will need to move into thicker burnout issues. We are disconnecting from the multi-source resilience we require to take next steps into the debris.

When we embrace an "all up to me" principle, the desire to believe the work is useful and good distorts our thinking and our emotions. We are blinded by our sense that this new venture will fill a truly needed gap in services; we drive forward without full participation from all parties. These distortions urge us to skip over self-reflective steps that foster questions that challenge how well our assumptions align with the community's. Interpreting trouble solely from the perspective of our resources and change-making capacities quickens the fire. Ignoring our different experiences of from access to resources to decision-making power, we plunge forward with the heat steadily rising.

Plunge forward we did, in a full-on sprint as the summer quickly approached. We leveraged resources from our families and Stafford. We gathered time, money, access to supplies, and the conviction of our own model of service. We feared tarrying and asking questions. We wanted nothing to stop this mission. We believed in it – and ourselves – obviously too much. Throwing measured judgment including deeper connections with the community out the window, we laid our paths of non-resilient service right up to the thresholds of burnout to come.

To understand the relationship of thresholds of collapse to resilience, think about the training great athletes take on to break world records. Certainly, they press and strengthen their skills by putting themselves right at an edge of collapse. They leverage limits as edges to be worked with, but not edges to burn through or over. They understand that developing new skills and better techniques will not work if all the energy is lost into total collapse or burnout. They build resilience by staying at the edge, by careful consideration of their body's limits. They also rely on the resilience and training of their coaches, massage therapists, psychologist – the whole team working with them.

Together they identify thresholds, push to the edges of them for improvement, but no great athlete in her right mind crosses that threshold by herself. Resilience is bottomed out in that case. Instead, serious athletes and wise people working with them, like teams in service tune in to their limits and viscerally, emotionally, as well as intellectually stay just back of the tipping point. They draw resilient wisdom and practical techniques for leveraging physical restoration from the whole team. They notice when working parts are misaligned and misfiring and they not only say something but also correct and pull back to assess for self and team resilience.

As we went into that summer, we generally ignored threshold-born information. In fact, we tried not to notice. We did not linger to hear voices raising concerns. We dismissed suggestions that available resources and gifts from the community were missing. All our actions were born of genuine good-will, even some distorted sense that involving the community would only add more burden to them. Instead, we would surge on ahead by taking on all aspects of the program – "all up to me." Our decisions impacted multiple constituencies from those receiving services to those sharing stakes. Many neighbors and others offered us varrious forms of in-kind support. We tended not to notice We stayed at the surface of the work, turning to bouts of self-care when we felt wobbly, a night out dancing, a dinner with meat, or sleeping in; nothing substantive. And our strategy was not and is not ours alone. Many of us in service believe so strongly that we can move forward using an "all up to me" mentality. We can't.

In part our mistaken approach roots in our worries. We worry the new service venture will not work. But instead of diving into our uncertainty, a kind of early breakdown phase in itself, we skip that step and move straight on to action, to building the new venture. No time wasted on examining problems we don't want to worry about. We push those aside often claiming we're too busy. Putting on our "all up to me" face and mindset, we believe our service can go forward fueled by determined and self-designed "good intentions."[4] That summer, we embraced this path, though we knew enough to see our situation lay fraught with political, financial, and emotional pot-holes, probably canyons. We simply went ahead assuming we could work out any problem. Hoping for the best, we made decisions mostly on the run. We didn't worry about the details or the lack of Stafford's vision for this program. We also knew that our previous service with Thompson Pines did *not* unfold like this. We shared all the planning with the community. But who had time – or would take time – to think through that difference? We had a program to build – "all up to us!"

In our earlier service with Thompson Pines, the guiding principle was "not all up to me." We attended numbers of community meetings. Decisions were shared. Supervision was regular. Our team leaders created short and long-term goals, then revised and re-revised in conversations with those we served with. Processing decisions with those living in the neighborhood took priority over speed and action. Plans often shifted as a result. Additionally, our supervisors asked us for weekly personal and ethical reflections about our work and experiences, and this information fed into the following week's team meeting. In those meetings, we tracked not only our activities and assumptions but also our personal and team levels of resilience. We had a place to tell the truth about threshold crossings and breakdowns. We were not isolated. All this experience went out the window with the Stafford program.

When have you found yourself in a similar situation, forging ahead in service in that "all up to me" style without personal and shared strategies for building and then drawing on resilience? What happened as things fell apart? How did you find your bearings? What were the impacts on the communities with whom you served? What did you sacrifice in order to just keep going forward? Did counting on the "all up to me" principle to power you through really work? Did you feel like we did, that the service you were trying to provide behaved more like services offered from a pop-up store? "All up to me" service generally doesn't last. It exacerbates burnout. We found that out the hard way.

Surviving Isn't Enough

We survived the first week. At the end of our second full week of what we expected to be an 11-week program, I lay in bed not sleeping. The roaches scurried in the kitchen downstairs making musical accompaniment to the rhythmic beat of mice banging against the inside of our walls. They liked to shuttle from the basement to the attic and back down. In my head, images of smiling and mostly happy children also shuttled back and forth. Then the problems sauntered in. Young teen women bullied each other and drew us into the fray – the way I had as a teen. One little boy kept confusing city rats with cats and trying to call them out of dark corners on the back-left side of the building. He wanted to pet them. No one on the church staff responded to our requests for rodent removal, except to tell us they got the request. We're all busy.

Our "curriculum" existed only by the seat of our pants, and we were already running out of ideas. Joey picked up some "youth programming" books, which we had spent last weekend perusing trying to find something we could do during the upcoming week. We did our planning on the weekends, supposedly a time for rest and renewal. My fatigue grew exponentially in two weeks. We gave everything we could each day, including our gaffs and goofs, which we did not hide from each other. Generally, all of us took *too* much responsibility for every aspect of the program, reeking of our "all up to me" approach. Already, I began to dread each day's

"Welcome Song" as a rising floodgate to a day of activities. Soon we'd be flooded with impromptu predicaments we would all try to fix. Obviously, coherent goals and objectives went lacking, but we suffered more from our distorted sense of universal responsibility. Why in the midst of our "all of us" talk did I feel so alone?

Still, as the children began arriving to the program around 7:30 a.m., I felt buoyed by their energy and the parents' genuine appreciation. By 8 a.m., we were "live." Lance took the higher energy kids outside for soccer or baseball. Joey shepherded the three to seven year olds into a specific area he'd arranged for them. Some could pull out little rugs and go back to sleep while others could rummage the bookshelves for books and games. Janice always went straight to the kitchen to get lunch going. When she wasn't cooking our food, she gave small classes on healthy eating. She also bought our food and handled most of the cooking. While in these sessions, our teen girls got into their nagging-at-each-other behaviors. The food Janice worked with came from stall owners at the State Farmer's Market. In two short weeks, she had established solid relationships with a number of vendors. They had already begun giving us donations, including fresh peaches just before they started to turn bad. The kids ate everything, and quickly.

I led arts and crafts activities in two smaller rooms off the main room. "Borrowing" materials from the church's Sunday School rooms, I tried to save money. None of us had a specific budget, though the church now gave us a monthly "program stipend." Joey handled that. If I really needed a specific art supply, Joey would give me the cash. I would go buy it. In one room of the two, the older kids decided to recreate their neighborhood by building a model with stuff they found from the streets: cloth, pieces of metal and glass, paper, shoe strings, popsicle sticks, whatever! The other room became the domain of slightly younger children who loved to draw and paint as well as build with clay.

I also taught swimming in the city's nearby Olympic-size pool. Twice a week, I drove the Church's three-speed-on-the-floor van to the pool and back. If it rained, we detoured to the nearby Boys and Girls Club in the only poor white neighborhood near us. The staff at the BGC provided years of experience and pragmatic problem-solving concerning running a daily program for local kids. The kids loved going there because they got to see friends they knew from school but never visited. Services like the Boys and Girls Club or afternoon tutoring programs held in church or community center basements supported many families and their children. We knew of these ecosystems from our past service. We tried to touch base with them when we could, the corner stores that kept a tab until social security or other benefit checks arrived, the school-sponsored debate leagues, and Church-based sports teams. We witnessed the shared power of these community groups, but our "all up to me" approach kept us from truly participating. We forged ahead alone.

Still unable to sleep, images of the week buzzed in my head. Where would the next needed resources come from? What about my internal resources? Did I have enough? Could I keep up the pace when already my charge forward button felt overused? Why did I feel vulnerable? How come that special treat of a movie earlier in the week didn't register as self-care? I tried to pull these thoughts back. Other than forging on, what were our options at this point? Already our teamwork had bifurcated into "just let it go" or "duplication," two typical outcomes in an "all up to me" world. If certain types of breakdowns occurred, NO jelly, NO construction paper, NO green crayons, just "let it go," do without, and try to substitute something else. When about to run out of toilet paper, at least two of the four of us would slip away without telling the others and buy the needed stuff. "Duplication," double the toilet paper we actually needed. Hence, we lost double of our budget, thanks to "all up to me."

Haven't you felt your shoulders weary from double or triple duty in service? Doing your part but quickly picking up the shovel to help someone else – even without their asking. How wearying when each of us assumes service means me – and me only. In part, I lost sleep because I crossed my personal limits so often that they seemed to disappear. Who could rest? Have you felt the difference when the old self-care niceties, a good meal or a shared coffee with a friend, offered only a short-term boost? You needed more; you needed resilience as you viscerally felt the downhill drive of the service you were engaged in. Was it your fault? Was it all up to you?

Breakdowns and Backlash

I stood aghast as the City Pool administrator told me that our kids could not just leave their towels and sunscreen on the deck chairs. Our group was too big. Groups of five or more were required to rent baskets and keep their stuff in them. The word "rent" reverberated in my head. "How much are the rental baskets?" He told me they were cheaper by the month; I dove into my pockets and pulled out my personal credit card. "We'll take two months, please." Another breakdown. Another immediate Band-Aid, "all up to me." Bypassing the urban economies I lived in that summer, I paid the bill myself. Each of us that summer did something like this regularly.

When Joey discovered early one morning that over half our library books were missing, he plunged through the shock to go straight into action. Spending his own money for books at a nearby used bookstore, he filled the shelves before too many kids noticed. We never discussed these kinds of decisions. We reacted from our own resources and authority. When parents from Thompson Pines started showing up the next day with books for the library, we knew that the kids had noticed the books suddenly changed. They figured something went wrong and told their parents. We weren't as alone as we assumed. We were in a system, but not engaging it. Rather than participate, which would have slowed things down, we bulled our way across breakdowns or thresholds to keep service going.

Those nights when I couldn't sleep, I thought about memories of my service mentors. How had they moved through the expected and unexpected demands and delights of giving back? The more I pondered this, the more I remembered that they consistently backed away from quick interventions on their own. Attuned to the community as partner, they reached out to discuss shared next steps. Taking time to notice and talk about a threshold of burnout everyone could see coming, they privileged resilience in their partnerships. That resilience helped them move across assumed lines rather than be held hostage to them. Not taking the stance of community versus program, staff versus local leadership, power versus presumed less power, they leveraged partnerships and discovered talents, treasures, and sometimes deeper tensions where none appeared to exist. They thrived as a broad household.

Our household was smaller. We counted on tricks and shaped a house of mirrors where we were the only resources. Without resilience, we – even in just the first few weeks – were seriously breaking down. We became blind to the resources at our own back door. For example, one morning Lawrence, an elder in the community who read to the children three mornings a week, told us that he would have to change his commitment to two mornings a week. Of course, we said fine, not to worry. But he went on to tell us why. A neighbor had fallen and needed assistance. Lawrence would be helping his neighbor several mornings a week. Others would come the additionally needed days and nights. Though we were surrounded by this community, we knew nothing about the neighbor's plight. We had pulled out from the web and the resilience within it. When we next saw him, he brought along the paper copy of his upcoming two-week schedule for the neighbor's care. We were amazed at the level of organization and the range of ages and genders throughout the day and night. We knew nothing of deep communal resilience in service like this.

The list also contained names of city and county offices and programs the neighbor might need. We had no such listing on our program walls, though daily we barely missed severe injury situations. We also began to note how these situations impacted the kids in our programs as well as the neighbors that came by to help. They were living in a system of shared resources and resilience. We could leverage only ourselves. Whether picking up a neighbor's child in the afternoon, for example, or providing supper, or placing flyers under doors alerting the neighborhood that Founders Memorial's afternoon program would offer extended hours during the holiday break from school, our neighbors lived service and breakdown by inter-resilience. They could move through all the cycles of serving and burnout because they did not function like superheroes. The work was "not all up to me."

Feedback Loops: Assessing Reality, Learning Thresholds

Resilience Theory calls these interdependent networks feedback loops. Through them, change can be monitored and assessed. Plans for next steps shaped and reshaped as actions are taken and then taken in a different way. When our neighbors hit a threshold of capacity or resources, and collapse loomed ahead, they took a step back, took stock of the situation, and rethought what they were doing. They worked their feedback loops, sharing information and revising plans. Intentionally moving forward, they flexed their expectations and plans according to what did and did not work. These feedback systems helped them loop in resilience-bearing information and assets. It allowed them to admit failure or misalignment and take steps to reconstruct or exploit. As a neighborhood service system, their feedback loops built resilience capacity for serving and the next cycles of breaking down.

From our dislocated, surface level self-care standpoints, we simply rejoiced that a local nurse offered to run two afternoon "check-up clinics" in our program. When neighbors arrived with unexpected cookies, puzzles, and clothing, we thanked them and asked no questions. Losing resilience, we also lost our ability to take in the webs of feedback all around us and how they would benefit our program. One catastrophic example of this came when the vendors at the Georgia Farmer's Market kept sending more and more free food. By the end of our first month, Janice drove the van instead of her car to carry back the boxes of fruit, breads, sandwich meats, and vegetables. Unable to use all of it, Janice starting giving small bags of extra food to children hanging around the kitchen at the end of the day.

That worked OK at first. But soon more children hung around the kitchen in hopes of getting the extra food. Again, we witnessed the surface pattern but strained to see the system. Even after talking about it one night in our apartment, we did not consider food distribution a community concern, part of a systems feedback loop involving system resilience. Knowing we had to do something to help Janice, who grew more exhausted with each day, we developed a plan – all by ourselves. We took the extra food Janice brought back from the Farmer's Market and packed it up to distribute to families as they picked up their children. If each of us took a few minutes here and there throughout the day to pack a few small bags of extra food, we could get it done. We sent home two flyers to tell families how this would work and that it would begin the following Wednesday. That first distribution day felt chaotic, but we distributed all the food and felt happy.

The following week, a few officers from the Thompson Pines Community Organization (TPCO) arrived during our food distribution process. They only observed, but at the end of our distribution, the President came up to Janice and asked if we could attend their monthly meeting at Founders Memorial that night. Their edged tone caught our ears. Still quarantined in our "all up to me" world, however, we were flummoxed by the invitation but immediately said yes. Stepping into their large fellowship hall at 7:30 p.m., we carried bags of peaches. They nodded but said nothing as we offered them. Then they dove straight into their questions. Why were we organizing a food market for only certain members of the Thompson Pines Community? Who appointed us to determine community food needs? Were we ever planning to reach out to them, the representatives of the community, to ask advice, to help with coordination?

The questions ricocheted in our minds? Our resilience levels, already bottomed out, went lower. Disoriented in our sequestered principle and bone-killing work, we felt initially defensive. Who could be against families getting fresh food? Silence met our question until the President of the Organization stated that we were missing the point. Then he told us the point. Thompson Pines worked as a community. They leveraged communication with feedback loops and valued processes of joint decision-making. We arrived with our privilege and ignored theirs. The bottom line became obvious: communication had collapsed. We did not know how to work within communities. He continued noting that since we arrived, we did not ask who they were or what the community had been doing and thinking – about food or anything else. His voice remained (steady and clear) as we felt the shock. Our resilience had gone bust. We were depleted and segregated by our own choice. Very alone.

They knew very well that Thompson Pines was a food desert, meaning families had no regular access to fresh fruits, vegetables, and meats. Larger grocery chains able to carry these goods at a profit would not locate in a neighborhood perceived as unprofitable, perceptions often drawn from race-based assumptions. The neighborhood depended on little mom and pop groceries for food. The floor space and profit margins of these stores could not sustain fresh perishable foods. Despite longstanding lobbying efforts with the Mayor's Office, the city had done nothing to help recruit a major grocery store chain to the neighborhood. Numbers of meetings with City Council and State Representatives proved ineffective. Now we showed up, marching into their neighborhood with fresh food and distributing it to only certain families? Who gave us the authority to pick and choose? Who were we to disregard *their* authority and knowledge?

We were flummoxed. Lance blushed as if ashamed. I felt overwhelmed. Resilient-less, none of us spoke, including Joey. Their authority and power became tactile, as clear and direct as stepping across a threshold. We would not take one more step into their lives or their self-determination. They were in charge. We were not and now we knew for ourselves how deeply burned out we were. At this point, they did not ask but explained their plan for next steps. The neighbors – everyone – would be told what we were doing. And they would be told that we did it on our own without consulting the TPCO. The next statement hit like a hammer. They would encourage neighbors to boycott our summer program. In effect, for their children to step across our threshold was to cross into a closed source of healthy food in the midst of a food desert. This felt like burnout to them. The room fell silent. Eventually, they told us that they hoped something would be done to correct the situation, but until then, they would encourage neighbors to stay away. Knowing our next food distribution day was less than 24 hours away, we reeled at this news. Our blindness and individually-driven service model created a line, us versus them, outsider-privileged students and them, white and black. The threshold now clearly marked, sources of resilience bottomed out.

Just beginning to wake up to the consequences of our choices, we wanted to say something affirmative. Yet our first attempts fell short as we fretted and tried to demonstrate goodwill by asking questions that revealed our lack of understanding. We avoided the key issues of our privileged assumptions that we could simply take the community's roles of power and authority. How could we make it better? What should we do? Again, extended silence. They took no care of us. They also did not treat us unfairly. They looked at us and said nothing, which did force us to also sit with the reality of our actions, well-meant or not: we received and delivered food to some community members and not others without *any* communications with the community. They clarified our next steps. Stop. That's all they said. Stop – and don't cross this line again. Next steps would not be "all up to us." We were in a collapse of our own making.

Economically stable whites, giving food away amid a communal food desert stung of longstanding injustices well-known in Thompson Pines. We were next invited to leave, which we did, speechless and clearer about our dislocation, our separation. None of us slept. But none of us were ready or able to change because the next morning over coffee we knew we had to make things right. It was "all up to us." When we opened the doors of our program, many fewer kids arrived. Janice went to the Farmer's Market and told those vendors that we would not be taking extra food for a few weeks, which confused them, but she did not explain. She and we knew we were at a fragile moment, but our resilience levels were so low that we struggled to find next steps. The vendors, however, had already boxed up that week's extra food and basically demanded she take it away. When she arrived back at our building, we stood flummoxed. What to do with all this food? There it was again; we felt we must *do* something, a default action that comes along with "all up to me" thinking. Making the flip to "not all up to me" service and burnout required partnership.

The TPCO had asked us to meet again with them in two days. They would share with us their ideas for our participation in their advocacy work to get fresh food to the neighborhood. We noted that, unlike us, they took a few days to think through these issues. Instead of reaching out to them in order, we thought, to honor their timetable, we went into action. Another example of "all up to me."

In a spurt of problem-solving, we set up tables at the front of Stafford's big parking lot and offered bags of food to anyone coming by. Within thirty minutes of doing that, several executive members of the TPCO arrived carrying homemade placards, which they marched up and down in front of our tables. "Thompson Pines is a Food Desert," "Who Gets Food?" "Healthy Food is Everybody's Right," "Stafford Church Ignores Bedford Pines." Other protesters joined, and the shouting got louder. The Pastor came out of his office to face angry neighbors, who quickly filled him in about our decisions and behaviors.

We were over the tipping point, out of any feedback loops with TPCO, the food vendors, and the Pastor. We stood there burning and wishing that the food would just disappear. The Pastor told us to take the food back inside. We did. He called a shelter in a nearby section of town, they came and picked it up. Then, he came downstairs – for the first time that summer. There were missing feedback loops of resilience everywhere. But now he told us our next steps with the leadership of TPCO. We asked for a meeting later that afternoon, and the TPCO agreed. They were generous and firm. We listened. Together, we committed to regular weekly conversations for as long as our program would last that summer. Shaped by the TPCO, these conversations would continue introducing us in a "not all up to us" approach. We were invited and also began attending all local and open Community Organization meetings and events. We found ourselves in a new model of service driven by the principle, "Not All Up to Me." We were discovering resilience beyond ourselves, breakdown by breakdown.

By week four of attending community meetings, we faced the end of our summer program only three weeks away. Taking in the new principle and practices proved more difficult than we'd imagined. Old habits and assumptions do not go away easily. Having a few members of Stafford going with us to these meetings provided support for our steep learning curve and an introduction for them to the community. The church pledged to a long-term relationship, set up a committee to maintain regular communication, and within a year Stafford and TPCO created a working group focused specifically on shared lobbying and community education to help alleviate Thompson Park's food desert status. Of course, it takes years of common commitment to create feedback loops for service rooted in a "not all up to me" principle and practices.

Asset Inventories: Practicing Not All Up to Me

Only later in my community-related service training and work did I learn about a community assets approach to partnerships. Like any model, this one is not perfect, as in the case of young bilingual children serving as interpreters for their parents. Clearly, an "asset" of a certain kind, these children also pay a price as they translate deportation or other serious legal documents while not quite knowing what the words mean. They do know that their parents are very upset by their words. Their assets, as described in more detail in this section, also become liabilities for these children.[5] Yet overall, the asset approach with community participation, which has been extensively researched, offers models for partnered participatory change that would have moved our food distribution approach to include community input and decision-making. This approach would have changed the assumptions and understandings we brought into our community-engaged service.

This approach resonates with some of the work we did through personal inventorying in Chapter 1. But inventorying at the communal level in cases like Thompson Pines and Stafford requires careful assessment of the impacts of choices and decisions at different levels and scales. The Assets Inventory approach to community partnerships was developed by John Kretzmann, a professor at Northwestern University, and John McKnight, a professor at DePaul University. It generally rejects community assessment models focused on needs. Shifting the lens to materials and people resources, this assets viewpoint reconceives power and contributions from a community-based perspective. An abandoned grassy area currently collecting trash, rats, and groups of unfocused teens stirs possibilities to become a recreation site. An empty warehouse long abandoned by its owner offers usable space, which communities and governments can re-envision together. Experiment with this model by walking through your neighborhood with your service partners. Notice how an assets-driven viewpoint corrects need-based assumptions empowering communities and their partners to create positive change. Healthy partnerships in service and burnout grow the assets.

Some initial shifts toward an asset consciousness began for me through attending the community meetings and spending Sunday afternoons walking the neighborhood to meet more of our neighbors. They consistently revealed sources of energy and mechanisms for community-based power and resilient change. Those corner stores, for example, not only ran a tab for locals awaiting Social Security checks but also offered their back rooms as spaces for political action group meetings. I went to one such gathering, chairs stuffed between giant freezers and stacked inventory. This meeting served as a dress rehearsal for an upcoming presentation to the Education Committee of the City Council. Their topic centered on community-desired curriculum for all grades in their local schools. Now whenever I went into one of these stores, I paid attention to other services they offered. That back room also had stacks of shoe boxes, basic school supplies, rain gear, etc. Unlike big box stores, they stocked specific goods needed by the community.

The children also taught me lessons, though, at that time, I could not absorb them fully. They consistently pointed to a few elder women in the neighborhood as sources of meals and emergency help, an unexpected overnight stay or a run to the public health clinic. I only saw them on their porches as I ran by waving hi. If I had looked more closely and gotten to know them, I would have learned what the children knew. I had taken in only what I saw and not paid attention to pursuing what I did not see on the surface. So, when these women were not tending to necessary chores or their own grandchildren, I would have seen that they served food to children whose parents decided to work a second shift. Toward the end of the summer, I asked Miss Natashia, as she told me to call her, if I could take her to lunch. She answered by inviting me to lunch in her home in two days, on a Saturday.

During that meal and two later visits before I left that summer, I learned how and why Miss Natashia gave verbal prescriptions to children as well as food. These prescriptions demanded they drink more water in the summer, stay out of the heat, and help their parents more. Of course, she always had water on hand, along with fruit and sometimes cookies, and gave them out freely. She introduced many of them to the safe biking program at the Boys and Girls Club. I suspected, with their help, she procured several needed bikes. From Miss Natashia, Miss Lucy, Mr. Werner and others in the community, I learned more about the daily trade-offs of knowledge, resources, and time required of these families to access basic services.

Practices of paying stronger attention to smaller details, listening with deeper awareness of words chosen and who said them, as well as being more present to others' embodied reactions as well as my own during interactions strengthen our capacities to fully participate in community-engaged service and burnout. The complex negotiations of service and burnout in shared partnerships requires more practice. It takes time, as noted above, to develop stronger observational skills and to learn new modes of communication. Practice time helps us let go to ideas we've never considered. Our flexibility increases as we come to trust "us" more than just me. We learn to take note of overlooked assets and by practice to support them through shared work. We're learning to turn our attention to other sources of energy and wisdom than what's familiar and comfortable to us.

What mistakes we might have avoided if we'd spent intentional time learning more about the ways people in Thompson Pines leveraged support for shared action. We knew nothing of their styles and rationales. We also missed the feedback loops they used to communicate, leverage support, and decide next steps. Unaware of the community's strategies for leveraging support and determining next steps, we learned nothing of their place and priorities. Had we done that, we might have participated with them building shared resilience in partnership. Their long-term wisdom could have taught us a lot about community assets within resilient systems of service.

As mentioned above, this asset-related complexity came home to me in my later work with community-engaged service partnerships. With the help of community leaders, I came to see how and why one identified asset might, from another angle, foster difficulty or harm. While working with a charter school focused on internationalization with intentional recruitment of immigrant and refugee children and families, I witnessed how an asset also can include deficits. Specifically, I noticed numbers of immigrant and refugee children caught in this two-way bind when asked to be translators for their families. This meant that children were hearing English language descriptions of requirements that they then had to explain to their parents in their native languages.

Children told their parents about additional monies required for uniforms. They explained the cost of lunch programs. Many families did not have funds for additional costs such as these; yet, the children were the conveyors of the information. Children found themselves caught between family loyalty and school, a tough negotiation no child should have to face. When questions turned to issues of legal residency or the address of a family's home, the children's assets became liabilities not only to the family but also to the children's emotional lives. Their language skills allowed school authorities to ask questions parents might not want to answer or might not be able to answer. The stakes are high as families negotiate their immigrant and refugee status in the United States. These intersections of language and translation assets and liabilities proved to be double-edged propositions, good and bad, for everyone to negotiate.

Over time, we discovered enough families in the neighborhoods of the school with adults who did know English. They were happy to serve as translators. Unlike my summer experience with the Thompson Pines community, I embedded myself more fully with the community. I focused on learning their forms of self-empowerment, communication, and asset leveraging. Still, the work took time, and I depended on several community members to help me learn to hear and participate. This is another demand on the community, but these mentors were willing to give me that additional time for which I was grateful. The asset-tuned world requires these feedback systems where resources of talent and time cycle through discerned limits before put into action. It's complex and pragmatic work, full of problem-solving and creativity. Any community-engaged service and burnout will benefit from diving deep into these dynamics.

A community-engaged "not all up to me" approach could have opened the eyes and minds of our young team to group-level resources and limits and saved us a world of hurt and damage. But our general blindness to such asset-resilience feedback loops remained through most of the summer. Even on the last day of the program, we received these benefits without quite taking them in. Mr. Clementane stopped by to make sure all our water pipes were fully off and all the electrical sockets and the stove disconnected. An unassuming "fix-it guy," he periodically "came by" our program, ostensibly just to chat. We paid little attention as he talked about his Deacon work at Mount Pisgah Baptist or shared recent neighborhood information. All the while, he was checking our sockets and pipes, fixing broken doorknobs and stuck windows. He embodied Thompson Pines' resilience cycles in our midst. We did not grasp his asset-driven lessons. We were living "all up to me" service. Inviting us to learn more than self-driven competency, he embodied communal *resilience*. We and our "all up to me" principle burned out. And unfortunately, we unnecessarily burned a lot of communal resources as well.

Inventories of Self-Resilience: Practicing Not All Up to Me

Resilient self and community-care born of asset-bearing feedback loops are to more and less degrees integrative systems, working like ecological systems with some sense of wholeness, never finally right or figured out or "done."[6] "Not all up to me" signaled continuing evolution, adjustment, and change. To begin learning the practices of self and community resilience asks us to shift our intentions from "all up to me" to "not all up to me." That intention-setting preferences interactions rather than self-preoccupation. It claims an intentional distinction between self-care, basically surface, and self-resilience, the deeper level work assuming interdependence. Intending to practice choice-making in community, we try to honestly sense our own deepest needs and discerningly invite others to help us think about them and possible next steps. Usually, self-resilience listens more than it speaks. It does not assume that every responsibility and decision belong to me – and usually me only. In fact, "not all up to me" makes decisions more from stability than on-the-fly reactions. It draws on a community's diverse resources and encourages pondering the "us" of community partnerships. "Not all up to me" builds self-empathy, as noted in the practice at the end of the chapter, and self-empathy feeds self and community resilience.

Ignatius of Loyola, a late medieval Spanish noble and soldier, also came to treasure the power of intentions building resilience within communities of partnered service. But the journey to this understanding did not come quickly or easily. Diving deeply into military service as a young man, he lay despondent with a major injury and illness. His "all up to me" approach to living would have to change. As he began that journey through a long series of steps, he eventually founded a Christian monastic order, the Jesuits or Society of Jesus. Among many practices Ignatius developed, Consciousness Examen remains a widely-used staple.[7] A core aspect of this practice involves examining our intentions and how they actually show up in daily life. Where are the mismatches, the struggles and what feelings are associated with those gaps? The practice also investigates our consolations, experiences where our intentions deeply connect with our actions, often building resilience within ourselves and with others. Typical of contemplative practices, this work is about me and others. It assumes interdependence.

Here's how we can use it in service and burnout to strengthen a "not all up to me" approach. To begin, settle yourself by calming your breath. Let your body weight also settle into a chair, remaining relaxed and upright, as you take a few minutes to follow your breath. To begin, ask yourself how you're feeling in your current service work. Notice places of tension in your body? Do you feel balanced in your service responsibilities? Have you taken on too much, not enough, just right? Do you feel alone? Do you sense you could reach out to others for help? Sit with these questions and let your thoughts and emotions shape the most honest replies that you can – with empathy for yourself. Return again to your breath and allow the work stirred by those questions to settle. Notice a phrase or two that you want to keep working with.

For a next step, ask the same questions but from a third-person or more objective perspective. The third-person vantage ups the non-judging we fall into when we think service is all up to us. Objectivity invites a more realistic assessment. Where are we holding on to responsibilities we could share? Why don't we know who could help us? What makes it difficult to reach out, to set limits recognizing that we cannot and need not take in all tasks and responsibilities? Again, once finished contemplating these questions, settle with the breath and note a few phrases you want to keep attending to as your return to your service.

In that first-person position, we may feel surges of self-accusation, guilt, and even anger. Try to notice the particular activities or relationships that draw out these feelings. The Ignatian form encourages us to honestly observe, but not condemn. When working with the third person perspective, we're invited to stretch our investigation toward our intentions. What did we intend in this particular service work? Did we believe we could adopt a "not all up to me" stance? Why or why not? If heroic and "all up to me," how did those intentions corner us into taking on more than we ought? From a third person perspective, who else might have shared this work? Why did your intentions exclude reaching out to create a service team?

The Examen is typically used at the end of the day, but it can be used at any point and need not take more than fifteen to twenty minutes. If you're feeling the load of service mounting or tensions escalating because you've overstepped boundaries of resources and authority as we did, you can pause at that moment, find a quiet place, and do a shorter version of this practice. Don't forget to openly investigate your intentions. You may discover the ethical intention was a good one, but the practical intention to do it all yourself, to take in all aspects of a task, in fact, breaks down the service even more.

Using this practice over time will reveal patterns in the ways you assume authority and build service from that intentional choice. Using the Examen helps me pinpoint when I begin taking in more than I can actually be responsible for. Through this practice, I've also learned the trigger-points in my service that fire off misplaced guilt and blame. Sometimes these spur me to just do something and usually without thinking of others. Sometimes they encourage a "not all up to me" stance that alters my reactive response. Learning to reach out to others before and as burnout occurs brings additional resources to bear from those various feedback loops of resilience. They help us see patterns in the rubble and move through it. The more we know about our trigger points for believing service is "all up to me," the more likely we'll learn to interdepend when giving back with others. The Examen is a great tool for sharpening this insight about intentions and actions.

The Empathy Piece: The Caring Breath

Gordon Peerman offers one additional practice that is very useful amid the hard work of discerning intentions. In his funny and pragmatic book, *Blessed Relief,* he suggests we "put ourselves into words"[8] when things are breaking down. I view this as a first step to reconnect with self-resilience. We hold up a mirror up to ourselves, which helps us more honestly assess our limits and our intentions. If our words spell "all up to me," we can choose to intend to change them to "not all up to me" and pursue resilience for ourselves and with others. Howard Thurman, the African-American theologian, and spiritual teacher, similarly links honesty with the power of self-resilience for service. By contemplatively reflecting on our honest intentions, we, as Thurman puts it, examine our "inward center."[9] Here is our deepest resilience and it is never solely reliant on the self. My inward center is me, but always also us. These two insights by Peerman and Thurman support our growth in service and burnout propelled by the shared resilience of "not all up to me." Rehearsing these intentions through contemplative practice links mind and body and heart together for better insight and action in service and burnout.[10]

As we begin reshaping our intentions toward "not all up to me," easing the self-condemnation that typically comes up is useful. No need to drain energy there, but instead to build self-and-other-resilience by "purifying" our intentions as Evagrius of Pontus, a late fourth-century Christian contemplative, recommends. Empathy helps us discern less useful distortions that drain our energy. Guilt and regret become distortions when we cannot let go of them. Honest ownership of wrongs is key, but to move into transformative change, toward "not all up to me" ease uselessly repeating guilt and despair so you can move forward to approach service differently. The practice of the "Caring Breath" can help.

I learned the Caring Breath from Margaret Pierce of Pierce Yoga in Atlanta within the lineage of TKV Desikachar (Ashram: Madras, India). The practice uses simple body movements related to the in and out movement of the breath. Begin by sitting in an upright position on a chair or cushion. Relax and breathe deeply, but not unnaturally. Draw your attention to any places of tension in the body and breathe into them, releasing tension on the out breath. Continue to breathe – no special pace required – with your palms facing up and resting on your thighs. Once settled into this rhythm, as you breathe in, lift your right hand keeping the palm up. Touch your palm to your left shoulder and breathing out return it to your right thigh. Do the same thing with your left hand, palm up, to your right shoulder and when you breathe out, return it to your thigh. Repeat this several times and let your movement settle into the breath. Now we'll add a more focused aspect of self-resilience. This time, as you breathe in, draw your right hand, palm up, toward your left shoulder. But as you breathe out, take your right palm and place it over your heart, a restorative move as if offering a dose of resilience to yourself, a kind of hug. Breathing in again, your palm moves to your right shoulder, and breathing out, your hand returns to your thigh. Do this same pattern with your left palm facing up and moving to your right shoulder. As you breathe out, take your left palm and place it over your heart. Breathing in again, your palm moves to your left shoulder and breathing out, your hand returns to your thigh. You may repeat this pattern as long as you wish.

Open yourself to positive, caring thoughts about yourself as your hand moves to your heart. Don't rush. Don't fake any feelings. Just let the motion and the breath do their work. If guilty feelings come up, so be it. Keep with the practice as a clarification of your intention to service interdependently. Build resilience by intending care and recognition for all beings, including yourself. Through the practice, tap into a physical, emotional, and bodily clarity of care, "it's not all up to me." Tough times will challenge us into the false sense that the work is "all up to me." It is not. Deeper awareness and practice of self-resilience and team-resilience helps us embrace the time and focus to press beyond self-care into community-born resilience. This is time well spent. The kind of time born of the clarity the Christian desert mothers and fathers developed; what Thomas Merton describes as getting "a foothold on solid ground."[11] From that stability in humility, as in breathing, listening, letting go to what is now, we can learn and flex within communities of service. Not the saviors, but the participants, we build resilience from a stance of "us" instead of "all up to me."

Exercises

1. When your well-intentioned "all up to me" approach left you needing more than self-care, could you turn for self-resilience to your service group? Why or why not? Or to put it another way: what does it take for you to own up to the fact that your own emotional and embodied self-care in service isn't enough?

    _____

    _____

    _____

    _____

    _____

    _____

    _____

    a. Can you remember when an individual turned to the team for shared support? What did you notice in that act; think about intentions, interactions, and/or outcomes?

        _____

        _____

        _____

        _____

        _____

        _____

        _____

2. How do you respond to un-surety in your service; not just mental unsurety, but the un-surety held by tense shoulders, misplaced anxieties, or trigger-point irritability? Write a few short phrases on the first line below, then pause, put down your pen/pencil, and breathe. Now write or sketch; what else?

_____

_____

_____

_____

_____

_____

3. Bring to mind a time you crossed a threshold upsetting and/or angering service partners. How did you find out?

_____

_____

_____

_____

_____

a. What were your first responses – thoughts, words, body, emotions, defensiveness/openness?

_____

_____

_____

_____

_____

_____

b. Did you go through more conflicts before you responded to the stakes of your partners? What shifted so that you could move into the collapses born of your "all up to me" approach?

_____

_____

_____

_____

_____

_____

_____

4. What differences might an asset-based approach offer your service?

_____

_____

_____

_____

_____

_____

Notes

1 For more insight into these dynamics and their impacts, see Lipsitz, *How Racism Takes Place*; Harvey, *Social Justice and the City*; and Powell, *Critical Regionalism*.
2 Nouwen, *The Way of the Heart*, 29–41.
3 *Merriam-Webster Online*, s.v. "Threshold," accessed March 15, 2018, www.merriam-webster. com/dictionary/threshold. Please see the first definition of "threshold" listed.
4 See Illich, "To Hell with Good Intentions" for a relevant and insightful critique of well-meaning service ventures.
5 Gratitude for this insight to the graduate level class I co-taught with Professor Vialla Hart-field-Méndez entitled "Partnering Communities and Universities: The Transformative Power of Community-Engaged Research, Scholarship, and Teaching." Daniela Hernandez offered this specific scenario. Any confusion of her content or intention is my mistake.
6 Odum, *Fundamentals of Ecology*, 5–9. See Odum's descriptions of these interdependent inter-relating levels.
7 For more on the Examen, see Ignatius of Loyola, *The Spiritual Exercises of Saint Ignatius*; and Thibodeaux, *Reimaging the Ignatian Examen*.
8 Peerman, *Blessed Relief*, 90.
9 Thurman, *Jesus and the Disinherited*, 21.
10 Siegel, *The Neurobiology of We*. Daniel J. Siegel, M.D. of UCLA Medical School, explores how the brain is also impacted in response to relational skill building.
11 Merton quoted in Nouwen, *The Way of the Heart*, 24.

References

Harvey, David. *Social Justice and the City: Geographies of Justice and Social Transformation*. Athens, GA: University of Georgia Press, 2009.

Ignatius of Loyola. *The Spiritual Exercises of Saint Ignatius*. 3rd edition. Translated by Anthony Mottola. New York: Doubleday, 1989.

Illich, Ivan. "To Hell with Good Intentions." In *Collaborative Futures: Critical Reflections on Publicly Active Graduate Education*, edited by Amanda Gilvin, Georgia M. Roberts, and Craig Martin, 75–82. Syracuse, NY: The Graduate School Press, 2012.

Lipsitz, George. *How Racism Takes Place*. Philadelphia, PA: Temple University Press, 2011.

Merriam-Webster Online, s.v. "Threshold." Accessed March 15, 2018 www.merriam-webster.com/dictionary/threshold

Nouwen, Henri J. M. *The Way of the Heart*. New York: Ballentine Books, 1981.

Odum, Eugene P., and Gary W. Barrett. *Fundamentals of Ecology*. 3rd edition. Philadelphia, PA: Saunders, 1971.

Peerman, Gordon. *Blessed Relief: What Christians Can Learn from Buddhists about Suffering*. Woodstock, VT: Skylight Paths Publishing, 2008.

Powell, Douglas Reichert. *Critical Regionalism: Connecting Politics and Culture in the American Landscape*. Chapel Hill, NC: University of North Carolina Press, 2007.

Siegel, Daniel J. *The Neurobiology of We: How Relationships, the Mind, and the Brain Interact to Shape Who We Are*. Boulder, CO: Sounds True Audio Learning Course, 2008.

Thibodeaux, Mark E. *Reimaging the Ignatian Examen: Fresh Ways to Pray from Your Day*. Chicago, IL: Loyola Press, 2015.

Thurman, Howard. *Jesus and the Disinherited*. Boston, MA: Beacon Press, 1996.

Chapter 7

The Edge of Earshot

A first step into the soaring lobby of City Hospital opened the gates to a flood of noise and movement. In this surging sea – a massive hydra of clinics, research hubs, patient rooms, and specialty units – the public, especially the poor, received a full range of healthcare services. Locals referred to this place as Cities – plural because there are many hospitals within Cities. Baby Clinics, HIV/AIDS Clinics, Diabetes Clinics, and the Emergency Unit, a hospital unto itself in many local lives. In each one of these places within Cities, people found treatment and care. I came that day to co-lead a new therapeutic intervention group using a meditation-based protocol. My co-leader was a post-doctoral fellow working in the Out-Patient Psych Unit. To a limited degree, I trained in group process through a hospital chaplaincy program and my work in an addiction treatment center. My co-leader brought the group process heft. I brought life-long study and training in meditation practices, specifically, in this case, several years of experience with a new compassion-based meditation protocol, which was becoming a more commonly-used intervention in this area, Cognitively-Based Compassion Training®, commonly called CBCT®.

Created by Professor Lobsang Tenzin Negi,[1] CBCT® integrates two well-known Tibetan contemplative teachings, Lam Rim and Lo Jong, with insights from contemporary neuroscience, evolutionary biology, and psychology. Part of the larger work of the Center for Contemplative Science and Compassion-Based Ethics, the version of CBCT® used on our unit was slightly altered to meet the needs of our population of suicide attempters. The protocol was taught in six sessions, one theme per week for six weeks. The take-away life-learnings for group members emphasized retraining attention for present moment analysis. The sessions posed questions like: What's my emotional, physical, and mental state right now? How are my inner reactions impacting my relationships with others? Can I disengage from negative emotions and body tensions to mentally discover and reframe choices that sustain a healthy and compassionate life? Rooted in appreciation of self and others fueled by non-judging empathy, these six sessions reflected a secular framing of practices that foster compassionate acts. Similar to this book, CBCT®'s protocol also welcomes practitioners from religious traditions.

Our version of the protocol, specifically tailored for the population served in the Psych Unit of Cities, taught the following six core concepts, one per week: Attention and Mindful Awareness; Self-Compassion; Cultivating Impartiality; Appreciation: Gratitude, Affection and Inclusivity; Empathy; and Compassion.[2] After each week's meeting, group members were given paper copies of homework related to the session's lesson. We used their experiences with their homework as part of our check-in at the beginning of the next week's session. This design emerged from conversations with Professor Negi and Dr. Chuck Raison, an evolutionary psychiatrist also helping to shape and study this intervention. Brendan Ozawa-deSilva,

Associate Director for SEE Learning in the Center, and others contributed to our work, including some suggestions I offered specifically for the Cities script. Tim Harrison,[3] another member of the Center's team, has steadily supported our use of the protocol. But none of this would have come to life without the insistent and smart advocacy of Professor Nadine Kaslow, the Chief of Cities Out-Patient Psych Unit. She and Professors Negi and Raison recruited me to co-lead the first group with one of the Unit's Post-Doctoral Fellows. Only our third time through the protocol, she and I felt the pressure of the intervention's hefty learning curve for group members and ourselves.

As I waited at the elevator, I rehearsed the key points of the day's lesson, Lesson Four: Appreciation: Gratitude, Affection, and Inclusivity. The diversity of cultures, classes, economic statuses, and identity-groups at Cities surrounded me. A group to the left of me chatted while clustered around a teenager in a wheelchair. Metal rods, post-surgery, shot out of his right leg. Not far from them, a group of young Spanish-speaking mothers held their babies and discussed vaccinations. Suddenly, a loud clamor pulled all our attention in one direction. A young woman burst into the area talking non-stop to her friend. "We have to find that place! My baby! We have to find her – we have to find that place!" she exclaimed.

Standing near the upset women, a nurse asked, "What's happened? How can we help?" The mother shouted out bullet points, her own personal crisis protocol: "A candle. Hot wax! All over my baby's arm! Screaming! 911 took her! I have to get to her. I have to go now!" The script delivered, the nurse responded, "Of course." She turned her head toward a nearby physician who moved closer. "We work in the Burn Unit," she said. "We're headed that way now. You're at the correct elevator. Let's go together." The ding of the elevator bell punctuated their next steps as we opened a path for them to get on. The door closed as the young woman kept repeating her protocol script, like a mantra: the candle, the burn, the scream, 911, get to her now.

Protocols

Ancient Greece first used protocols to literally mark the initial sheet of a papyrus roll. Glued to the outside of a manuscript case, this flyleaf bore the date of the roll's manufacture and a description of the contents. Over time protocols evolved into more detailed records of texts, such as minutes of a diplomatic meeting or negotiation. Today, most of us link the word protocol with a list of steps or procedures to be followed. These can be social codes for human interactions[4] or particular procedures used for conducting experiments.[5] Like most hospitals related to research-generating schools of medicine, Cities uses protocols for patient-intake information, employment processing, charting, and studies. Protocols shore up consistency in any process and offer a reliable map, from beginning to end, that anyone can trace or retrace.

In therapeutic service led by volunteers or helping professionals, whether related to healthcare or not, protocols provide consistency in content delivery. That regularity guarantees reliable data for research assessment if and when that's being done. In our case, as people enrolled to join our therapy group, they were informed of their rights. The steps of the intervention protocol were explained. Then participants would be invited to begin a research process starting with an intake interview, which included taking several psychological scales tests. These initial protocol steps helped the unit determine if the person would be best served by participating in our group or if another group would be better for them. Once graduating from our six-session group, a participant would participate in an exit interview within a few days of finishing and take some additional psychological scales tests. A final follow-up assessment would be given three months later. The whole process, repeated by each participant, provided reliable and consistent data about the effects of our intervention. Other researchers could follow it and compare outcomes. A protocol process like this typified the approach of the Out-Patient Psych Unit at Cities, known for its innovative and reliable research as well as its nationally renowned NIA Program for African-American women.[6] "Nia" is a principle of Kwanzaa, meaning "Purpose."

The mother's panicked protocol still rattled around the elevator bay as I noticed the time for my group quickly approaching. The clear steps of our intervention mattered not only to the researchers but also to people like that mother. It offered them a clearer mental map of steps toward healing and skills for reappraising behavior choices and healthy emotions. Our protocol also increased research funding at Cities by indicating successful interventions for patients. That funding offset some of the high costs of excellent medical and therapeutic care. These mental musings triggered by the distraught mother's cries were interrupted by an older African-American woman standing next to me. Her cousin's burns were "blessedly healed" in that Burn Unit, she explained. "I just know they'll take care of that baby," she assured me. I nodded yes. My response complied with the social protocol and expectation at Cities. We listen to each other.

The inter-relational emphases of conversations at Cities kept its heart beating. Though unwritten, people were expected to interact, to comfort, to actively help, to care. Behaving as isolated automatons while waiting for an elevator or standing in line to pay a bill broke accepted norms. One got a chance or two to learn, but then, one best step up. And step up named the core value as witnessed in the response to that mother. If someone asked for help, give it if you could. If not, find someone who could. Go the extra mile. Behave kindly. Speak respectfully. Act as if it might be you next time who needed help and compassion. At Cities, strangers talked familiarly with people and families they had never met. Patients chatted with staff people, sometimes sharing health information though the staff person knew nothing of their situation. But staff listened, and if they could respond with explanations to questions the patient might ask, they did. This people-taught code of conduct or protocol assumed everyone's voice counted. Mostly it worked, and it explained how healing took on a communal, often participatory style here. Now, the ring of the elevator bell brought me back from these thoughts. I stepped in, pushed the button for my floor and wished a good day to the African-American woman who had spoken to me.

Simultaneously, the man beside me in the elevator offered a hardy "Afternoon!" Even in Cities' elevators, the social protocol held. Unlike the usual silence and separation that reigned in most elevators, people here did not fiddle with their phones unless they needed to. Most riders chatted or observed with interest. When the doors opened, and people got off, by foot, stroller, or walker, they bid the rest of us goodbye. "Everybody have a great day." "Careful for this afternoon's thunderstorms." Similarly, as people got on, greetings were shared. "Appreciate you making room." "How's everybody doing today?" Once the doors closed, comments unfolded about local sports teams, weather, or how busy certain clinics were that day. At the next floor, we squeezed in more bodies and up we went. Sure, some days the chatter irritated me, especially if a tough situation from our unit was playing out in my mind. But narrowed attention did not match the tacit script, the protocol, here.

A Group Intervention

With many floors to go, I thought about the ways active listening upped the potency of communities in service. Some contemporary scholarship on the development of human communities historically confirms the advantages of humans living and working in groups. Though we continue to bicker and fight, the evolutionary evidence points to group formation as a key factor in our sustainability and emotional support. We top out as the ones doing it the best – so far.[7] By helping individuals regulate behaviors, interactions, and emotions, groups not only tighten our safety nets for survival, but they also expand our inventive potential. Studies like those done by Haidt and Damasio confirm these findings. They also helped me make sense of the mutual care that developed among the people participating in the suicide attempters' group. Often members thanked others for listening to their stories and encouraging them. If members had to miss a week, others warmly greeted them upon their return. Sometimes, the power of belonging welled up so strongly for returning members that they could not speak their gratitude in response.

The CBCT® protocol reinforced these behaviors and insights. We learned to experience our group as a resource. Learning how to pay attention to commonalities, to offer kindness and empathy to each other, we grew a group feeling mirrored in the CBCT® protocol and the community sense of Cities. Specifically, we practiced skills that helped us notice others' struggles to keep their emotions regulated and healthy and support them in those attempts. That work increased group members' self-compassion turning blaming and guilt into recognition of destructive thoughts and ways through them. The practices taught group members to step back or pause when tensions arose. We came to the conclusion that tensions will come and go – it's life! By returning thoughts and body (often using walking meditation) to the present, participants regrouped themselves in the humanness in all of us. Over our six weeks together, group members described feeling happier and less burdened with shame and self-judging.[8] They now had access to alternate principles and concrete tools that helped them choose different perspectives and actions. They had new direction and insight.

Most group members were referred to us by the Emergency Unit. They were brought in by friends, family members, or the police calling an ambulance. Their lives had grown so unbearable, isolated, and despairing that they felt they could not go on. The sources of their despair often involved life traumas, especially physical and/or emotional violence – often as children, a horrible turn in circumstances, mental illnesses, and/or addictions. Once stabilized, they were interviewed, referred to this group, and then began interviews required by the program's intake protocols. Once accepted into the group and participating, many still faced serious struggles to find reliable and decent housing and food as well as employment. Typically, they moved from one night shelter to another, to shared public housing with strangers as roommates, followed by a few days with a family member, and then out again on the streets. Their phone numbers continually changed. Sometimes, they got a better job and moved one. Sometimes, they disappeared. Their life circumstances often appeared to work against everything this protocol could offer.

Yet, they kept coming whenever they could. They expressed encouragement through being with the group. They told stories about the new skills helping them pause before choosing behaviors they knew were dead-ends. They felt some new support for getting through tough times. The weekly lessons about responding and behaving differently would encourage them, we hoped, to claim different stakes for finding happiness. By learning to recalibrate their typical responses to everyday incidents and usual tensions in relationships through the principles and practices of CBCT®, life could feel and be more flourishing. They could choose happiness.[9]

Having survived a suicide attempt, they understood the direct consequences of choice-making when cornered by pain, aloneness, and uncontrolled emotions and memories. Not to deny the deep pain in the lives, this protocol focused on possible ways out of those familiar dead-ends. They experienced and talked about how in using CBCT®'s practices, they could settle, see options, and take new steps through and beyond their pain. They supported each other's efforts to live a more heedful life; one intensely focused on self and other care. They could learn to opt for life-giving choices. Our research protocol was designed to provide data about the effects of CBCT® as a healthcare intervention.

My co-leader and I tried to follow the prescribed CBCT® script as close to the letter as possible. Reliability not only meant solid research, but published articles, which we hoped would foster new conversations about responses to this urgent treatment need. We hoped for better outcomes; life lived by our group members and others. Careful research also would increase our chances for additional funding to keep the study and the group going.[10] For ourselves as co-leaders, the regularity of the protocol provided stability in the up and down interactions of group work in mental illness treatment. The protocol provided a map articulating a path and a rationale for staying on the path.

We took few liberties during the first two groups making only slight adjustments to the protocol in response to specific questions and requests. Looking back, now eight years later, our willingness to adjust and adapt steadily grew. Dr. Kaslow, our unit chief and strong advocate for this treatment modality, highlighted two outcomes of the CBCT® intervention. Number one, that group members learned that more good came to them if they could learn to choose compassion towards themselves and others. Number two, that women grasped how the daily demands of their lives – child-care, providing food, and running a household – left them little energy for kindness to themselves, and too often to anyone else. Interactive energies sparking shared joy, common affection, and appreciation, basically went missing. After eight years, we now know that CBCT® helps group members soften that self-judging and tone down their judgment of others. The protocol fosters choice-making. It encourages honest self-discernment while building social support for living a healthier and happier life. But in that first year, we focused most on learning how to effectively deliver the basic protocol with hopes that it would be helpful to participants. Each week, we learned new things through the group's responses. But that first year, we tried to stick to the protocol for the sake of consistent research

Scripts We Serve With: Choices We Make

Serving as a group process leader (for example, someone running a community center's sharing group for young mothers or a Stop the Violence support group for men who batter) or as a psychotherapist following a formal intervention (for example, a research-oriented group or a protocol-based group like DBT, Dialectical Behavioral Therapy) demands training. Group leading also brings choices in the delivery of that protocol. All types of volunteers and helping professionals (psychologists, nurses, clergy, or social workers) know this. Consistent work with a protocol develops therapists' insights and confidence. They learn more about best uses amid the push and pull of group member's individual needs and histories. Facilitators and therapists must balance emergent characteristics and dynamics in the group with the expected steps of a therapeutic plan or protocol. Over time, this balancing act of choices impacts the delivery and perhaps some aspects of the outcomes. Group numbers, socio-cultural and economic contexts, as well as size of the unit also impact process and outcomes. Add the factor of a new protocol or intervention, and all these dynamics typically become more complex.

We faced that same balancing act. For example, our group began as a one-hour intervention. But after the first three weeks, we shifted to one hour and fifteen minutes because transportation issues often made group members late. We planned to move through one lesson of the protocol each week for six weeks. Then we would begin a new group and go through the whole protocol again. But early into the work, we determined that many in our groups could not meet our expected week-by-week attendance. Their lives unfolded irregularly. They had doctor appointments or required meetings with a social service agency, a family crisis, or loss of transportation or housing that demanded immediate attention. They would miss group one week, perhaps two or three. We adjusted accordingly, encouraging group members to come as regularly as they could.

A group member might attend Lesson One and not return until Lesson Four. She might go missing again to reappear for Lesson One, at the start of the next round of six lessons. "Just keep coming" became our mantra. Typically group interventions following a protocol expect regular attendance. But even in less stressed populations, this regularity breaks down. We, like others, adjusted, though we discussed the possible negative impacts on our research data. We had no choice if we wanted people to attend. We did. They did. Bottom line: those attending when they could, learned some basics of our meditation protocol and how those related to their emotional and practical daily life. They got baseline messages: kindness to self and others expands choices for happiness; the skills of empathy and gratitude increase resilience, the capacity to move through breakdowns and recover. Some group members directly told us that hearing the lesson a second time made it stick. They understood it better. We noticed that the repeaters asked the most useful questions.

Staff burnout in support or therapeutic groups like this one can result from breakdowns born of already existent staff problems. These can be camouflaged initially by the challenges of implementing a new protocol. Arising frictions may appear related to the new group, but in fact, the tensions and misaligned power dynamics were well established within the staff. In these cases, what appears to be the group going off the rails is actually due to explosive forces unrelated to the new protocol. This breakdown or burnout will not, of course, respond to changes in the protocol. The staff needs to do their own work for rebuilding resilience. These next steps can impact group functioning because the protocol is not hijacked by staff divisiveness. One round of protocol rebuilding for the group is lost, but the gains in staff functionality are well worth it.

Another version of burnout and rebuilding also impacted our groups. By the middle of our second six-weeks, we knew we were facing it. Though not well understood and typically not discussed, I call this version, a self-imposed breakdown. This burning intentionally breaks apart specific elements and assumptions of the protocol script and activities themselves. A demolition project, this work may reroute sections of the protocol's already mapped therapeutic trail. Or this self-chosen collapse may respond to a formerly overlooked set of issues. They must be addressed – a trail built to them – before the work or path of the original trail can continue. This self-imposed burnout remains connected to the broad intention of a protocol while remapping routes to the core goals or destinations. It's a tricky balance, requiring teamwork. Unlike typical breakdowns portrayed in this book arising from warped principles that deny burnout-born resilience, or stuck practices that willfully resist rebuilding amid the rubble, the burnout we learned in this protocol was of our own making. We created it. It did not come from outside our cycle of service. It did not happen *to* us. It happened *because* of us. This chapter uniquely describes a *very* different kind of burnout than has been discussed in this book so far. We intentionally struck the match. This burnout was born of our own doing.

Choosing Self-Started Burnout

Heedful, closely tuning into the present-moment work of the group and work within ourselves, we discovered certain pieces of the protocol had been jettisoned. As the stories below convey, we had made changes in content. We had adjusted practices and their order. Sometimes, the protocol changes were small and inconsequential. Other times, they drove us into territory that demanded a reconstruction of the protocol's path in alternate directions – maybe still in view of the original script, but notably distant. To do this, we had to strengthen our own equanimity or capacity to hold steady in the presence of whatever arose. That balance sharpened our awareness to the point that we could pause and question the protocol. Our litmus test for "let's try a change" was compassion. If altering the script upped the group's capacity to more fully engage the weekly lessons to build empathy and act compassionately, we made the change. We made choices born of inner stability and outward concern. Cautious and aware, as if walking a narrow edge of a cliff, we drew on our deepest skills and the core contemplative principles of the protocol we were teaching: awareness (internal and external), non-judgment, appreciation, empathy, and engaged compassion.

As if bushwhacking, then, we and members in the group crafted an alternate trail as phases of reconstruction. That reworking often revealed other resources or insights we never considered and/or never exploited. For example, a woman in the group off-handedly commented one day that she only found solace in her plants. Startling herself and us, the comment sparked others' memories. Quickly, we were surrounded by stories of plants and gardening and especially the comfort and joy growing things nurtured. Suddenly the day's lesson derailed into a lesson we taught two weeks before, Nurture and Self-Compassion. Bending back to connect to that earlier lesson, revisiting its key points kept us within the protocol's broad infrastructure, but the discussion took precious and limited time from the lesson we were supposed to cover that day. This can happen in group work; a previous lesson finds sudden traction in a later one. We, like many, felt some pressure to redirect the conversation back to the lesson of the week. But the animated stories of gardening made the redirection only interrupted newly found traction in the ideas of self-care.

As the group discussed angles on nurture and self-compassion we and the protocol never considered, we sensed something deeper was happening. Group members' investment in the work grew. The plant narratives needed to be told and heard. Group-born lessons of plant-caring brought up new angles on empathy for others and how empathy actually fueled kind actions. A later explicit lesson, the smaller signals of this linkage in the protocol had gone, so far, unnoticed, even resisted, until now. Suddenly, they cut a trail through stories of plants that set up the core journey. They could keep working with compassion, a seriously difficult topic for suicide attempters because they found the link in plants when they needed it. Our order did not cut the trail. We watched them come alive with each other, egging each other forward, laughing, crying, all about plants and gardens and family.

Unable to reroute the conversation back to the day's lesson, we co-leaders could do nothing other than follow. With about twenty-five minutes left, the group seemed done with that path and agreeable to turning back to the day's script on gratitude and affection. But soon the trail to gratitude and affection took a pig-path turn back to the newly cut path of nurture. Grateful for plants! Love my plants, and they love me! My co-leader and I began to settle into what was arising while noting the learning pattern they demanded we follow. Would we shift the order of the protocol's lessons, cutting a path from nurture and self-care straight to active compassion? Or at least intentionally take that loop trail to compassion to return to the expected order of the protocol moving from self-nurture to affection and gratitude? What should we do if we found ourselves typically off-trail or cutting new trail? What would happen to the reliability of the new protocol? After group, my co-leader and I commiserated. Normal wobbly just went hyper. We agreed that the group and we as facilitators did what needed to be done that day. But next week, we needed to work harder to hold to the given script. We would try to avoid such a major breakdown in the order of the lessons.

This chapter asks if as helping professionals and volunteers, we call it therapeutic service when it happens by misdirection or by chosen breakdown? How far can we push a protocol? Should we choose to trigger a service phase of collapse by notably disrupting the map proposed for healing? Can we reach our destination this way? And if so, how far can we burn that edge without fully collapsing the intent of the protocol's therapeutic outcomes? Or is that third step into burnout too much? Is it different for different settings? What about in yours? How might cautious attention, heedfulness, in these decisions leverage our and the group's equanimity, or open balance, toward creative work for therapeutic good via a protocol broken and reconstructed?

Have you done this; and if so, what happened? Was the choice intentional or did you find yourself drawn off-track by the group? Was it a full-on break-away, or a slight side trail within view of the main script's agenda? Do you burn your protocol often or only in certain situations – and why? These collapses happen in many forms and to different degrees; what's most typical for you? How do you resist? How do you not resist – and do you worry about allowing the group to go off-trail too often, to regularly burn out the script? Can you find your way back to your protocol's big ideas? Go to the end of the chapter to work with some of these questions.

Questions like these bothered my co-leader and me especially during those early groups when we felt more pressure to maintain this newly minted protocol. We had no models for choosing to burn the service offered to and with others. We struggled to listen with balance to the group member's scripts, which left our protocol's scripted words.

The trail-breaking made me anxious, particularly as a volunteer co-leader. Though my career involved working with groups including therapeutic ones like this, I was not a degreed professional. But having worked with them for many years, I learned that the shifts and alterations in therapeutic processes are normal. However, our group work took this to a breaking point level. Group members urged us to pursue a break-out path, not an adjustment. We came to believe this intentional choice-making would bring us to a relevant and accessible destination for healing.

Setting Fires: Heedful Resilience

During that next round of the six-week protocol, the group continued to struggle with the concept of self-forgiveness, one segment within the nurture and self-compassion session. They continued to break off and return to that content. Consciously and unconsciously, they were determined to find the keys to unlock the doors of their life-long prisons of self-hatred. We, as group leaders, felt failure in their repeated returning to this previous lesson. Of course, all helping professionals and group leading volunteers feel failure and actually fail. Not fatal. But it stalled us. Yet the group, also feeling failure and the muck of remaining in their deep-rooted self-images of unworthiness did not leave it there. They kept turning back, kept trying to find something like a key out of that prison. By week four, one group member who graduated from the previous six-week class again disrupted the current lesson to turn back to self-forgiveness.

He drew our attention to the bank of windows in our group therapy room, high above the street. Miffed and worried that we'd somehow shaped a group whose primary work seemed to be undoing the protocol script, I tried to intervene and redirect back to the lesson at hand, but he continued. He liked looking out the windows. The view, so many stories above the chaos and debris of the ground level below, gave him a different perspective. "There's so much beautiful blue sky up here. Sky I can't see when I'm down on the street. Down there, the high buildings block my view. I'm stuck struggling. It's like I live in a small box when I'm on the street." But up here, he went on, even when the sky was covered in clouds, he knew the blue was there. He had seen it. This perspective freed him from his box. Then, he delivered the punch line, "I think we – each of us – is like the blue sky. Clouds come and go – tough times, bad choices, daily struggles for food and shelter, life in a box. But the sky, the blue sky is always there. It don't go away just 'cause I can't see it. I am the blue sky."

It was his own mantra of self-forgiveness or remembering the deep good that was in him, which he delivered to our group. This phrase became a major mantra for every group afterward. We even put it on the posted list of "Key Ideas in CBCT®." "I'm capable of being a happy person. I can learn to forgive myself. I'm capable of being the blue sky; we all are." Once he said it, "I am the blue sky," the room sat in silence looking out the windows as clouds appeared and moved on while the blue sky remained. He admitted he'd never understood what we were talking about when we encouraged forgiving ourselves. He did not believe he could do that. We made his confusion worse, he added, by suggesting everyone could better regulate those self-hating emotions. None of this connected. But as he watched out the windows, this idea came to him. He could remember that deep down he was "the blue sky" rather than the clouds.

Was this emotional regulation to focus on the positive instead of the negative? "Clouds come and go. Troubles come and go. I got to focus on my good self when I get down." Another group member had been trying to jump in and finally did. "When you keep choosing to cover yourself with clouds – you can't see the blue." Still another voice chimed in, "I never thought about the fact that the blue is always there," she paused. "That my kindness, my goodness is always there." We were off script again. None of this came from the page, and hearing it this first time stirred the same uneasiness in me. Finding their own traction and cutting a path *back* to a lesson four weeks ago, the group pursued issues "off script." We became our own trigger or tipping point, flipping into adaptive resilience, not minor adjustments.

Especially in those early months, the choice to choose to burn the protocol's path lay just beyond my earshot, just beyond my imagination. I struggled to hear the intentionality of the group. I wondered if they weren't just stalling or confused about content. I couldn't let the changes in though I heard the soft crackling of the fire they set that was just catching. Initially, I and my co-leader kept looking for water to douse it, kept harkening back to the protocol as we should hear it in group. The examples below make this conflict concrete. They tell of our journey to work through the group's refusal to remain cornered and to join with them in learning to set fires. But one point needs to be underscored as you read on. Over the last eight years, we've done as much burning as stabilizing, and yet, we've always arrived by week six, on Lesson Six, right at our destination.

Flexibility Became Our Mantra

When I stepped on to the elevator that day, I reflected on how I never imagined the scenes and choices described above. When we set out to run this group, it never crossed my mind that we would derail the script as we were doing. I assumed we would follow it to the letter. Heading to the next to highest floor, I was one of the last to get off and I'd migrated to the back. Next to me, another man, still waiting for his stop, stood staring at the floor. I tried to match his stillness, using the focus to think through the key points of today's lesson. Upon arrival to my floor, I would connect with my co-leader for a quick chat about our day's plan before group members arrived. She worked full time on the unit and could update me about group members' past week: new hospitalizations, shifts in meds, new housing, reports from their personal therapists (if they had one), etc.

By the last two floors, only the man and I remained. Unexpectedly, he spoke, though he still looked at the floor. "I know how bad it is to hurt your own child. That mother – screaming. It's so bad – the pain – seems endless. I hope they can help that baby." I did not remember noticing him as we witnessed the mother's panic on the ground floor. The candor of his statement left me speechless. I only nodded in agreement. Then, the "ding" of the elevator signaled our arrival at my floor, and running late, I quickly bid him a good day and hurried down the cavernous hall to meet my co-leader. She already sat in the group's room looking over the list of expected attendees. When I opened the door, she turned, smiled, and said. "We should have a new member today."

Sitting down opposite her, I joined the circle of chairs for group. We chatted briefly about a few group members and who would lead which parts of the protocol materials. As we were finishing, the group's undergraduate assistant arrived with paper and pencils. Before each group, every attendee took a short self-assessment on their psychological state that day, a suicide protocol. Sometimes, we had activities that required pencil and paper as well. With everything readied, our undergraduate colleague opened the door to the room. Group members came in and sat down.

After our first six weeks, in a stroke of genius, our undergraduate assistant created a poster listing each week's lesson headings and key points. Each week, we put this poster on the wall with masking tape to orient us for each session. As a reminder, the core components of the protocol were: Attention and Mindful Awareness; Self-Compassion; Cultivating Impartiality; Appreciation: Gratitude, Affection and Inclusivity; Empathy; and Compassion.[11] At any time in the session, we could refer to the poster and review the connections between one lesson and another. The list also helped group members focus on the day's topic. My co-leader and I referred often to the poster, and over time, group members did too. By the end of a six-week course, regardless of the specific lessons attended, each graduate received a formal graduation certificate, which we signed. As we gave them out with due congratulations, smiles grew everywhere, and there was often clapping. The certification completed, a journey taken for the sake of their own health and resilience, the graduates expressed their hopes for better times, including more acts of self and other kindness. We all knew – in some ways now more than before – that their hopes would require daily work.

On this particular day, six group members arrived on time. We assumed our missing member had a transportation issue or an unexpected conflict. Starting, as usual, with a check-in, each member offered a short initial update about how things were going. Many included discussions of their homework, which we encouraged. As the last person began her check-in, a man peered through the window of the door to our room. I recognized him, the quiet man from the elevator. Already up and inviting him in, my co-leader greeted him as he apologized for being late. "I had trouble finding the room," he said. "Yep, all of us have trouble finding the right room on this floor," piped up a group member, who pointed to the chair beside him and said, "Have a seat." As the newcomer took his place across from me, I heard again his words in the elevator, "I know how bad it is to hurt your own child. That mother – screaming. So bad – the pain – seems endless. I hope they can help that baby." At some point, his pain must have felt too much to bear. "We're so glad you're here," I offered.

At the Edge of Earshot

Into later rounds of the protocol that first year, we came to expect some sparks that would alter or change our process. The day's lesson, Lesson Four: Gratitude and Affection, called for an early, short sitting practice to help settle the group, since this topic typically drew confusion and critique, if not derailing. We made that adjustment. Life had been very tough for most of our group members. Their parents' struggles too often left them without basic resources. Violence and trauma took its toll. Gratitude and affection stirred irrelevance or rage. We hoped the sitting practice would settle people's minds and perhaps open up some additional space for memories of kindnesses and gratitude.

As I began explaining the basics of sitting meditation, LaRhenda, a graduate from our first group who continued to attend, interrupted. "Could we do walking meditation[12] instead? It calms me down better than sitting meditation." My gut tightened at her unexpected request. Wouldn't walking keep the group stirred up and distracted, something we didn't want with this lesson? How I wanted to say no, as I heard my voice responding, "Sure, we can do that." I chose – again – to break with the protocol. She nodded her thanks as I, still bewildered by my own response, looked at my co-leader who stared back. I got up from my chair and asked the group to remain silent while following me out the door and down the hallway to the right. I wondered if some in the group also questioned this decision. Do walking meditation in a hospital hall? But no one said a word. They simply followed me as we turned left into a quieter hallway intersecting with ours.

I noticed my body relaxing as we walked. Maybe LaRhenda was right. A few feet down the hall, we gathered as a group, and I explained that even a bit of mindful walking in silence could help our brains and bodies calm down. I sensed the contradiction as the hospital's hallway chatter, clattering laundry carts, and mechanical room engines competed with me for group members' attention. "Let's begin," I said, feeling resigned to the situation. I asked everyone to stand still and pay attention to what standing feels like. We focused on the weight of our bodies dropping and settling into our feet. We tried to relax a bit more by breathing more deeply. I offered Thich Nhat Hahn's image, "Give it to the earth," as a way of encouraging us to feel the weight of our bodies through our feet. "Let your body drop and relax. Also, our hearts and minds, drop and stabilize, like an anchor." We stood and breathed, trying this practice of reliability in the midst of the hospital and life's constant change.

They were right with me, so I transitioned into shifting our body weight from side to side. I encouraged them to focus on the feeling of tension at the edges of our feet as the body's weight shifted. Where does the balance give way? How far can we push the edge without losing it? "There are life lessons here," I claimed. As I felt my shoulders release and my face relax, my mind started to return to the debate: sitting or walking. You too might turn to this practice when someone has altered your script or when you're the culprit of change. In the break from expected steps, try pausing and settling. You can do this in a bathroom or in a corner of your own office. If you can find quieter places outside, try it there. Do not wait for emotional or intellectual confirmation, just try taking an even-keeled stance in the present and then test it, push it, learn the edges of it. This standing practice steadies us amid anxious debates and decisions about changing the protocol and much more.

We then walked the 50 yards down to the end of the hall stopping at the single window, which looked out over the city. I asked for initial comments about the practice. *All* of them were positive. Internally, I shook my head in disbelief. Calm minds born of walking in a hospital corridor? Nothing to do but keep going. I explained a few more aspects of the practice, and we walked back down the hall paying more attention to specific points of pressure on the foot as it shifted from heel to mid-foot to toe. I encouraged us to sense the swing of the leg and that moment of first contact by the foot. With these basic instructions, we returned to the place where we began and stood in silence. I noted how focusing on just a few more details, as we just did, increased our mental focus while maintaining our bodies' relaxation. I suggested that we were walking fully in the present when a group member added, "Don't do that very much . . . that being in the present." "Neither do I," I responded. You might try it too.

We returned to our room in silence as my co-leader unlocked the door and everyone took their seat. Before I said another word, a quiet murmuring took over the room. Neighbor to neighbor shared positive reactions to the practice. Bottom line: everyone liked doing the walking meditation. Inside, my agitation continued. We were off track. We had walked off the protocol's map, not far, but still, it unbalanced me. One usually quiet woman shifted in her chair. Well-known for nursing her rage, I thought, finally, I would hear a seething critique. She suffered under the heavy obligation of caring for her bed-ridden mother, a mother who beat her regularly when she was a child. "When I walked and breathed, my mind let go. It just let go – like I was – and I don't know how to say it – part of the movement. I could focus just on that. Seemed like all the other stuff could wait. I just walked in the quiet."

Another woman grabbed onto her words saying she too felt something she'd never felt before – her feet! Everyone laughed out loud. "I wobbled," one man admitted. "I almost tripped and fell," another man piped up. More giggles and nodding heads as a different woman explained her struggle to stay balanced in her job, a free association that caught us off guard, but led to talk about jobs and being fired, and the importance of work for mental health. We were drifting from the script's version of gratitude and affection, but we were experiencing both as a group. Straight ahead on a trail, we were burning as we spoke. Clearly, I thought to myself, we will be doing walking meditation again next week.

I felt some comfort in making a pre-emptive strike, breaking next week's protocol before we were into it. Would such disorder impact the reliability of the research? By now I could not deny that we had burned a number of new side trails that did and did not connect back to the script's mapped path. Still, I worried; I pushed back. "Aren't the hallways too noisy for meditation?" LaRhenda quickly responded, "The din in the hallways matches the howling in my mind." Others nodded and went on to talk about how the literal task of walking became the edge of their attention, a sharp demand that they could heed because the other noises of the hall and their minds canceled each other out. They described the process as "walking it out," another phrase that went on our weekly posted list, a side trail.

For the first time, the youngest group member spoke. "When I walked it was like everything in my head focused on my steps. My mind felt clearer than it has in a long time." The session ended with an overweight group member describing how much easier it was to focus on her breath when walking instead of sitting in a chair. Breathing in a chair made her feel panicky because she couldn't get a full breath. Walking meditation at this point again collapsed a portion of our protocol, small, but notable. What would these changes mean to our outcomes? I had begun to shift my definition. Maybe outcomes told us more about reworking the trail than the results of sticking to it.

Burning for Redirection

We continued following the protocol and break off pieces of it to redesign them, collapse content into other sections, and/or ditch them. What initially fell beyond earshot began to be heard by us as co-leaders. We began to resist our own tendencies to avoid breakpoints and reconstruction. We even began to listen to alternative paths born of our own experiences with the group. Less and less did we try to over-speak, to talk down ideas that pulled the group in alternate directions. But leaving identified and stable intentions and information held in the protocol kept us always slightly off-balance – as if group work doesn't do this anyway. But with a protocol, I believed I was balanced and stable, like good service. That distortion faced serious challenges as we learned to hear and respond to them. Not clean, nor easy. But the usual messy, exploitative work of resilience born of collapse.

Being the most experienced with the compassion training aspects of the protocol, I felt more anxiety when departing from it. As helping professionals and therapists, you face similar situations and dynamics every day. What if you began to keep a "protocol burnout diary," a regular record by which you could map your decisions to flip an intended path in a different direction? Why not record your experiences, trying hard not to judge the action, stay just with the facts as you notice them? What do you notice?

That question helped me more honestly come to terms with my own penchant for avoiding resilience, the breaking apart and rebuilding work of protocol change. Did the changes generally foster less or more insights? This question is not asking if the goals of the protocol were met. Were the reconstructed paths relevant to the main work of the group or not? This question is not asking if the reconstructed paths were completely relevant to the protocol. How protocol-relevant should reconstructive moves be? Did you allow yourself to be with the process in motion, choosing to go along and perhaps reinterpreting protocol elements to match the new path? Did they? As a model, resilience theory helps us engage systems moving into collapse and the early adaptive sparks of recombinations. Resilience theory also signals that systems in collapse can flip into something quite different. Control is not consistent, or in some cases possible. Learning to be with this process is tough work. Practice helps because we better seize what's being undone or replaced and early signs of the consequences. Keeping a diary of these "irregularities" or trail-breaking points will give you a more honest record of the process and your responses to it.

With this information, we see our typical responses, resistances, attempts to redirect (more or less), or surrender without direction. But what if we used these tipping points to enrich our skills for listening even more intently to what's at the edge of earshot. A concrete record identifies the match, the striking, and the impact of change. Knowing those elements of the break will help us track consequences, the twists, and turns of new trails or altered next steps through the protocol as it is emerging – the protocol we've chosen to burn. Alongside the facts of our decisions to change the path or not, I tried to keep an emotional record that emerged and sometimes fed my choices.

Did anxiety about a slow uptake of a particular lesson urge me toward breakdown? Did I fear asking more questions of a group member who just ditched the path we were on because I'm afraid of some part of her story? What's driving the change? Where are you and the group really needing to go, to burn a new path? Tracking as honestly as we can, the recruitment of burnout in therapeutic processes is demanding work. Keep a record. Trust the process of burnout to move the group and you into something useful, even if in the end it involves a rejection of the newly broken trail. As my co-leader and I began moving past the edges of our deafness to hear the group's and the protocol's work as alive, as a life system, we discovered choices, which moved in many directions. The choice to move into, to trigger, some breakdown of the script and process was one of those. Some examples bring this approach to life.

We certainly tried to teach the protocol's elements as prescribed, of course, but with intentional practice, we learned to lean into the edges off script. For example, while trying to teach Lesson Five: Empathic Concern in relation to strangers, not just friends, we rarely had luck engaging the group. But during one round of the protocol, while on Lesson Three: Cultivating Impartiality, we were discussing the importance of recognizing that everyone struggles and we all hope for a happy life. We're interdependent – in this together. At that point, an irate group member brought up his problem with empathy for a stranger.

He described how his "supposed new friend," actually a stranger at the same shelter, stole his money while he was asleep. That "guy" left with it the next morning before our group member woke up. "And it might be a good thing too – I'm mad as hell at him." He continued saying he felt too angry to participate in group that day, and, he sure didn't care about everybody struggling – "whatever that word is, imparti . . ." We got it. Rather than ignore this break in the flow of our week's theme, my co-leader suggested we pause and do a brief practice involving standing and simple arm movements. So, we stood in a circle, moved our arms in simple up and down motions and breathed. We returned to the day's topic after that.

But during our post-group chat, my co-leader and I wrestled with his resistance to empathic concern. How many others in the group felt the same and likely for similar reasons? At that point, we realized that the spontaneous turn by my co-leader to a shared body practice might provide an alternative path for introducing empathic concern. Shared movement might be a better path than shared words. We all did it, and in the doing perhaps it brought us some embodied sense of resonance or caring and belonging. We decided to think more about that and see if we could build from there. A new practice for one lesson learned in the midst of a different lesson. We were learning to catch sight of new paths for different days while remaining mostly on script. We were coming to trust the process of letting go of stability to move into reconstruction at will.

Over the Edge

Choosing to set the fire and move in a different direction with a week's lesson or allow the group to continue working on an earlier concept became more normal. Many times, of course, we followed the map as given. The protocol, though new and untested, taught us each time we used it and its collapsed elements. Thinking our way through it with empathy and kindness toward the group and ourselves gave us flexibility. That tone, being willing to let our shared work leave the prescribed trail or go over an edge, also nurtured an honesty among group members. These authentic stories, some of which we might not have heard without choosing to set the protocol afire, confirmed the usefulness of this approach.

Ardo's story is but one example. That day, we pretty much followed the script's steps. But leaving it if we needed to for the sake of engaged compassion in our group work remained a possibility. Ardo was a 20-something Hispanic man born in Texas, who shocked us by returning for his second session. He spoke not one word during his first session, other than his name. This day's lesson focused on Impartiality (Lesson Three), the recognition that everyone wants to thrive. The script described our tendencies to relate to others and ourselves using labels like friend, stranger, and enemy. Emotionally and mentally, we tend to define our fundamental needs and hopes as somewhat uniquely ours. Perhaps family and friends share similar ones. But others, if we think about them at all, fall into various categories of wants and needs emotionally and mentally different from us.

This worldview crushes endearment, a caring approach to all persons and beings that share our desire for happiness and thriving. Instead, it breeds a false understanding that links happiness with performance, doing what can be judged by self and others as worthy or right. This lesson on non-judging and avoiding labels based on performance of assumed goods did not ignore the impacts of structural inequities and injustices. We discussed those as they played out in group members' lives. Still, in the end, usually, the assumption that enemies don't deserve happiness reigned. People "like that" don't do or think "right," meaning they are not like us, so, they are judged and set aside. Endearment goes out the window. Yet, too many in this group had been "thrown away," had been judged. They knew their own hopes for happiness. Perhaps their enemies had hopes too. Our core message that everyone wants to be happy and thrive had become fundamental to the group.

I explained impartiality pretty much per the script. Then everybody turned to an exercise designed to bring out the way we label ourselves, the ogre of self-judging. Each of us wrote down our list of bad-me labels, Then, I asked for a list of good-me labels. Ardo did the practices but shared nothing. Others talked about how many negative labels came to mind and quickly. An alum repeated a poignant story of self-judging involving her addiction to buying things in order to feel happy, to re-label herself as worthy. But when she got home with the stuff, she still felt empty. Her buying addiction only put her more in debt. How to escape from the self-judging and its very negative consequences? As others offered understanding and support, she shared that she was learning through CBCT® that she could make other choices for happiness. She had begun to believe she could let go of some of the negative self-labeling.

By now, Ardo's frame steadily shook. His left leg bounced incessantly, moving up and down like a piston. Still looking at the floor, he almost whispered that prison would be a good place for him. He deserved that label. Any label of goodness, any self-forgiveness wasn't in the cards for him. "I done too much." He paused. The group waited. He then described how his neighborhood valued toughness. "You do better with a gang than without. That label matters. Get some income (we never knew the source). People got your back." At first, he told us, he'd been eager to fight. Gang-against-gang violence was the norm. He felt especially good if the fight involved retaliation. "'They's' not like me." Those others, yeh, they gone now. His voice got quieter. Another long pause. "But I don't want it no more."

Two men in the group nodded in understanding. Then the oldest one said, "That's a big problem, huh? You know that other gang. They're just like you." My co-leader and I would have never been so direct. Ardo repeated the phrase, "Big problem. Big problem." "How come?" an older woman in the group asked. Ardo started talking and told us a lot more about life in local gangs while keeping details vague. "Someone," he said quietly, "got to be responsible: call the fights, strategize, win. Money on the line; blood too." His leg pumped relentlessly now as if churning out what he had wanted to tell someone for a long time, about his life, about his labels gone bad. Some in the room couldn't relate. Others nodded their heads as if they'd shared some of his experiences. It seemed that their solidarity fueled his opening up. When a mid-thirties male group member began to interject his experiences,

Ardo put his hand up signaling "stop," and went on. The words, seemingly, had to get out. They kept tumbling over the edge of earshot into raw labels that defined his life and told us something of his story.

After a few minutes of setting up scenes of gang-on-gang fights, he slowed down. He looked as if his mind had been transported somewhere out of our room. "Leaders have to do things. They tell other people *they* have to do things." The labels now signaled life or death with no way off that path of violence. "So, I'm the leader. I do what I have to do. Same thing for myself, I kill." Ardo's suicide attempt almost worked, but the EMTs got him to Cities just in time. So, he failed. Another failure. Another judgment and label. "I'm not good at nothin'." Then the words stopped, though his leg did not, and we sat for a minute in silence until an older man in the group broke it. "All of us done things we can't live with." A few shook their heads in agreement.

Though following our lesson plan, we had moved way beyond our expected topic path. Labels, sources of violence and pain to the point of death, this did not explicitly show up in the protocol. One could imagine overhearing this insight in conversations about labels. But we heard it directly and personally. A tangent that turned out to be a system flip, a jolting reorientation about how we try to live in ways that increase healing and happiness. The narrative reached into our bodies and emotions, this young man so enmeshed in death. Ardo set off a fire in the room, a chaos we'd all held tightly under control. Ardo drew us over the edge, and we heard him.

We were both on the prescribed path of the day and yet so deeply in it that it felt like a newly burned path. The lesson of impartiality and non-judging, a matter of actual life and death. For this group, the lesson to learn. Probably at some level for all of us. As the first burn of Ardo's words eased, we found our way back to the original lesson. Others shared their experiences of labeling and self-judging. But no exercise we prepared could register the visceral lesson on impartiality Ardo delivered. "We've all done things we can't live with," my co-leader repeated. Self-judging could not imprison us in isolation. That togetherness might become a step toward impartiality. Thanking Ardo for sharing his experience with labels, my co-leader announced that the group's time was up. Ardo left quickly, though he said goodbye on his way out. He did not return to the group.

Re-Tracking for Resilience

Just a bit over two years out, we developed a regular homework protocol to go along with our script,[13] assignments that helped us take account of what happened to group members during the week between sessions. A set of practices for each week and a daily grid with spaces to write down their daily practices and briefly reflect on their impact, these maps gave us direction. We could document, even partially, where they went with our lessons, and the impacts of practices tried. The hand-written phrases on the homework sheets also signaled areas of concern, confusion, accomplishment, and rejection. Often, we saw how deeply self-judging shaped the lives of our group members – and ourselves.

In addition to the sheets, we heard verbal homework reports as part of our check-in, and those stories took us back to an edge we had missed or under-heard. If a group member said he struggled to figure out how to open his heart toward a stranger, a homework suggestion, we learned first to ask the group if they'd had similar experiences or insights they might offer. Sometimes feedback from a group member proved so disorienting to our theme or plans that we turned to the newly proposed trail. We stayed on it long enough to sense if the intentions and content could foster restorative thriving. Sometimes group members stopped our progress or pushed it further. Sometimes we did. Homework, check-in, and the sessions themselves helped us sharpen our listening skills and increased our courage to strike a match to some part of that day's protocol lesson, let it burn a bit or a lot, or not strike a match at all.

During one homework discussion, for example, a female group member shared that she'd developed a new practice over the week. She simply sat and breathed for two or three minutes – no more. She did this many times a day, not just once or twice. She felt she needed multiple calming moments a day to cope with the stresses of moving in with her daughter. With two children of her own, the daughter already felt over the edge. She often grew impatient with her mother, who struggled with self-destructive feelings. When such a tilting point happened, the daughter often screamed at her mother, belittling her in front of the grandchildren. This response only fed the mother's already self-destructive issues. But the mother found a way through it, by leaving the room and going somewhere else – the porch, the bathroom, wherever.

She would sit there and breathe for just a few minutes. By doing that, she found she could settle herself and think rather than only emotionally react. Self-care, she called it. She could wait and reorient her focus toward appreciating that she had a place to stay. She even felt some empathy for her daughter. Occasionally after hearing this report, we used this practice when someone in the group described a similar experience of finding themselves at an edge. Rather than miss the lesson, we heard it, and all took a moment to sit and breathe. We labeled the exercise: "breathe your way back to stability." As alums heard or saw in group how useful the homework assignments could be, they began thinking of other improvements to our protocol delivery.

Calling a meeting, the alums asked us to rethink how we taught the entire first lesson, that pivotal point: Attention and Mindful Awareness. Rather than use the traditional images of a calm mind as a flowing stream not stuck in its own debris, they suggested we find another image, one more relevant to their lives. They reminded us that many in our groups feared the water and never learned to swim. Public pools were rarely funded for their neighborhoods. Some older members who lived through legal segregation associated water with death, a form of lynching. We heard them and knew we needed to burn a new path. The changes took several meetings, but they helped us rewrite the script so that it resonated with their daily experiences as urban people.

This revised script used images of walking downtown streets, encountering strangers at a free lunch site, finding new clothes and shoes at a clothing center, and obtaining a necessary document from a government office. Using this version provided real-world scenes for learning to shift attention from the melee of life to deeper intentions for calm awareness and healthy choices of self and other caring. Group discussions of homework focused on the previous week's lesson now revolved around actual life experiences. Intentional choices directly linked to their experiences of failure and despair as well as chosen joy and stronger relationships. Group members learned how to drop their stress levels by practicing during their daily movements through the city's noise, jostling, and sometimes hostile interactions. They could choose to walk around the potholes of their emotions. They took new direction to foster healthier relationships. They offered assistance to others needing help. The protocol took new life from the lives of those trying to practice it.

Learning to hear beyond earshot – beyond what we wanted to hear for the sake of keeping the protocol and ourselves intact took time and energy. Eight years later, it still does. The protocol remains in progress, and we've learned to trust the burning more than repeated iterations that don't meet the needs of the group. When we choose breakdowns, they work, and they don't. That's part of the process too. And research, we discovered, can continue, but its emphasis expands not only to outcomes but also to what we are learning about new side trails and original paths burned and reconstructed. One concrete practice that nourished our commitment to hearing the group more deeply and thoroughly came from a co-leader who turned to African folk-tales for inspiration. Using a tale about the strength of a spider's carefully and caringly made web, we used this as a group activity emphasizing the power of interdependence, the web of our lives. Sometimes we used this group activity to work with impartiality, sometimes for gratitude, and still other times for endearment and empathy. Group members consistently found it helpful for concretizing the power of interdependence as strength for life.

The activity in one form, begins by asking every group member to think of a difficult situation faced in the last few days or week. One person takes a ball of yarn and holds it while sharing a story of difficulty or suffering. Others listen intently without commenting. They do not interrupt. Once that person finishes, we sit in silence until another group member asks for the ball of yarn. Receiving it, with the yarn unwinding to reach from the thread still held by the first speaker, the second person tells their story of difficulty from the last week. The second person asks to tell their story next because the two stories link through circumstances, key issues, persons involved, emotions, or something else. Then another person asks to tell a story and is given the ball of yarn. Soon a visual web of connectivity through listening, shared life, and caring emerged. Our lives are interdependent with linkages we may not know or easily see. Differences remain, we are separate; yet, we find linkages. Some we expect. Others astound us.

This web exercise became the visible concept of "just like me," a phrase that recognizes difference while embracing points of connection. The web practice also helped us embody non-judging and empathetic listening and living. Through yarn woven among us, we showed the reality of what often lay just beyond earshot. Now we could see it and practice sharing difficulties and insights brought to life by the protocol lesson for the day. But we also noted the fragility of this web, how easily it could tear. And we saw that sometimes the threads of our shared web needed more tension. Maybe that was honesty or appreciation. Some group members discussed the need to break out of certain webs or relationships. All these lessons emerged as we broke the prescribed trail to leave aspects of our protocol behind.

Learning to release a rigid notion of protocol to hear what falls beyond earshot did not come quickly to us. Releasing the stability of the printed page to a verbal or emotional sign of redirection or reorganization takes courage. As helping professionals and volunteers, we practiced a new meaning of protocol, one more like a script unfolding, a map still in the making, an unexplored trail shooting out of the side of an established route. We didn't avoid these brush fires and larger collapses and accepted their offered resources or dead-ends. Like other protocols at Cities, including medical care, urgent help in a hallway, and elevator chatter, ours listened carefully for life beyond earshot in a suicide attempters' group.

Exercises

1. Think of a time when dynamics in a difficult or complex group urged you to let go of a significant portion of your protocol (for that day, or more) – *not* simply adjust it.

   a. What thoughts, feelings, and/or embodied responses first arose and which ones helped you go with the change? Did specific group interactions in that moment or earlier impact your decision?

   _____

   _____

   _____

   _____

   _____

   _____

   b. Repeat this exercise, but thinking of a less difficult or complex group. What thoughts, feelings, and/or embodied responses first arose and which helped you go with the change? Did specific group interactions in that moment or earlier impact your decision?

   _____

   _____

   _____

   _____

   _____

   _____

   c. What positive, negative, and/or middling results emerged from the change?

   _____

   _____

   _____

   _____

   _____

   _____

2. What's your process when a protocol shift is needed? Do you listen to a range of ideas (staff's and participants')? Do you pay more attention to feelings (emotions or embodied) (staff's and participants')? Do you sit with the idea (sometimes procrastinating) or do you dive in? Something else?

_____

_____

_____

_____

_____

_____

_____

3. Think about the ways energy flows when your group works with their *usual* protocol. Consider flows of energy around ideas, stories, exercises – what else.

   a. In the boxes provided: Draw two energy maps (See Figure 4.1 for an example): Map one: Draw the energy map when working with *the usual protocol.* Map two: Draw the energy map *after a protocol change.* If drawing doesn't appeal to you, write your responses to each situation in the provided box.

Box 7.1 Two Energy Maps

b.   Use the following table to compare the two drawings. What similarities and differences do you notice? What ideas and emotions arise for you as you compare the two maps/situations?

Table 7.1

Drawing 1	Drawing 2

4.   How might the chapter's suggested practices help or support you amid the changes?

_____

_____

_____

_____

_____

_____

_____

Supplemental Readings

Emory University. "Center for Contemplative Science and Compassion-Based Ethics." Accessed March 14, 2019. http://compassion.emory.edu

Emory-Tibet Partnership. "CBCT Compassion Training." Accessed May 31, 2017. https://tibet.emory.edu/cognitively-based-compassion-training/index.html

Johnson, Suzanne, Bradley L. Goodnight, Huaiyu Zhang, Irene Daboin, Barbara Patterson, and Nadine J. Kaslow. "Compassion-Based Meditation Among African Americans: Self-Criticism Mediates Changes in Depression." *Suicide and Life Threatening Behavior* 48: 160–168.

Kleinman, Arthur. *What Really Matters.* New York: Oxford University Press, 2006.

Pace, Thaddeus W.W., Lobsang Tenzin Negi, Daniel D. Adame, Steven P. Cole, Teresa I. Sivilli, Timothy D. Brown, Michael J. Issa, and Charles L. Raison. "Effect of Compassion Meditation on Neuroendocrine, Innate Immune and Behavioral Responses to Psychosocial Stress." *Psychoneuroendocrinology* 34, no. 1 (January 2009): 87–98.

University of Wisconsin-Madison. "Center for Healthy Minds." Accessed March 3, 2019. https://centerhealthyminds.org/

Notes

1   Professor Lobsang Tenzin Negi, with a PhD from Emory University and an equivalent final degree, the Geshe degree, through Tibetan Gelupka monastic training, developed the protocol: Cognitively-Based Compassion Training® (CBCT®). He is now on the faculty of the Religion Department at Emory University. The first research on the protocol was initiated by Dr. Chuck Raison, an evolutionary psychiatrist, and Thad Pace, an immune systems researcher. Dr. Nadine Kaslow, Chief Psychologist at Cities and Director of the Psychology Postdoctoral Fellowship Program in Professional Psychology, as well as the NIA Program, asked to bring this intervention to Cities.

2   These elements reflect "CBCT® Core Skills and Insights" (handout) April 2018, developed by Lucy Albaugh with my assistance. They also are specifically adapted for use in this group with Professor Negi's permission. Our script for each Module provides detailed teaching notes, exercises, and homework. To serve as a group facilitator of CBCT® requires training courses and certifications. See "Center for Contemplative Science and Compassion Based Ethics." Emory University, accessed March 14, 2019, http://compassion.emory.edu.

3   Currently, Tim Harrison serves as the Associate Director, of the current CBCT® Program within the Center for Contemplative Science and Compassion-Based Ethics at Emory University.

4   *Merriam-Webster Online*, s.v. "Protocol," accessed August 2, 2018, www.merriam-webster.com/dictionary/threshold.

5   The World Health Organization offers one particular format, which serves as an example of this type of protocol. See "Recommended format for a Research Protocol," World Health Organization, accessed February 12, 2019. www.who.int/rpc/research_ethics/format_rp/en/.

6   "Grady Nia Project," Emory University School of Medicine, accessed February 12, 2019, http://psychiatry.emory.edu/niaproject/.

7   See Haidt, *The Righteous Mind*. For a somewhat different evolutionary perspective, see Damasio, *The Strange Order of Things*.

8   See Zhang et al., "Self-Criticism and Depressive Symptoms"; and "Shame and Depressive Symptoms."

9   In the CBCT® five-day retreat, summer 2018, Professor Negi linked this sense of self-observation and shifted response as learning to maintain a sense of heedfulness in daily life, making circumspect decisions; to work to sustain disengagement from triggers of self-damaging and other-damaging behaviors.

10 Now at the beginning of our ninth year of running a CBCT® group on the unit, numbers of presentations have been given at national conferences about this work. The unit has received research and foundation funding, which remains necessary.

11 These elements reflect "CBCT® Core Skills and Insights" (handout) April 2018. They also are specifically adapted for use in this group with Professor Negi's permission. Our script for each Module provides detailed teaching notes, exercises, and homework. To serve as a group facilitator of CBCT® requires training courses and certifications.

12 Details of the practice explained below.

13 Huaiyu Zhang, PhD, developed these take-home assignment sheets: description of the practice on one side and weekly calendar to check-off completed homework with room for comments.

References

Damasio, Antonio. *The Strange Order of Things: Life, Feeling, and the Making of Cultures.* New York: Pantheon Books, 2018.

Emory University. "Center for Contemplative Science and Compassion-Based Ethics." Accessed March 14, 2019. http://compassion.emory.edu

Emory University School of Medicine. "Grady Nia Project." Accessed March 2, 2019. http://psychiatry.emory.edu/niaproject/

Haidt, Jonathan. *The Righteous Mind: Why Good People Are Divided by Politics and Religion.* New York: Pantheon Books, 2012.

Merriam-Webster Online, s.v. "Protocol." Accessed March 15, 2018. www.merriam-webster.com/dictionary/threshold

World Health Organization. "Recommended Format for a Research Protocol." Accessed February 12, 2019. www.who.int/rpc/research_ethics/format_rp/en/

Zhang, Huaiyu, Erika R. Carr, Amanda Garcia-Williams, Asher Evan Siegelman, Danielle Berke, Larisa V. Niles-Carnes, Bobbi Patterson, Natalie N. Watson-Singleton, and Nadine J. Kaslow. "Shame and Depressive Symptoms: Self-Compassion and Contingent Self-Worth as Mediators?" *Journal of Clinical Psychology in Medical Settings* 25.3 (February 2018): 408–419.

Zhang, Huaiyu, Natalie N. Watson-Singleton, Sara E. Pollard, Delishia M. Pittman, Dorian A. Lamis, Nicole L. Fischer, Bobbi Patterson, and Nadine J. Kaslow. "Self-Criticism and Depressive Symptoms: Mediating Role of Self-Compassion." *OMEGA: Journal of Death and Dying* (September 2017): 1–22.

Chapter 8

Naming the Unnamed

Engagement Cracks Open Conversations

A long table, covered with a dark green tablecloth boasting the navy blue "Parkston University" seal at its center, sat on the auditorium stage. People wandered in and took their seats anticipating the celebration of the restored university-community partnership between Lewistown, an urban neighborhood literally pressing against the east wall of the campus, and Parkston, a mid-sized university founded in the Midwest in 1823. To the right of the stage, four people stood chatting among themselves: Sharie Lewis, president of the Lewistown Community Organization, Sammy Landers, co-director of the partnership from the Parkston side, Mark Benson, the other co-director and history professor, and two students just finishing their semester-long course through the partnership. Alicia Borden, a university-paid partnership program assistant, greeted a range of stakeholders coming through the auditorium doors: community internship supervisors from Lewistown and the campus, faculty teaching classes working at various community sites, staff members from Campus Life, Student Services, and the Career and Counseling Offices, participating students, and a few upper level administrators. Pods of community members sat in clusters throughout the auditorium along with currently involved students, interested students, faculty, and administrators from both communities.

Music played as images of partnerships were projected on a large screen behind the table. Some attending witnessed the complete collapse of the Lewistown-Parkston Community-Engaged Partnership three years ago. Tonight would be, everyone hoped, the great comeback, though most wondered about the past failure. Would that happen again? Community-engaged partnerships require so much energy. Can they really work? Adding two new half-time positions from the university side should help. One worked in the Lewistown Community Organization office and the other coordinated placement decisions and daily programming/problem-solving on the university side. Sammy Landers and Sharie Lewis worked with the partnership when it collapsed and stepped up again for this round. They were linchpins in the program's survival. As the music faded, Landers led the panel to their seats on the stage.

He welcomed everyone emphasizing the happy rebirth of the program. With support, he acknowledged, from local staff and colleagues working with staff and faculty involved in the American Association of Colleges and Universities' "Civic Learning and Democratic Engagement" Program as well as the AACU's "Bringing Theory to Practice" Programs,[1] this next iteration already stood on more solid and shared ground. He thanked supportive administrators at Parkston who "believed enough in our renewed partnership to dedicate necessary resources," and he thanked Sharie Lewis, the dedicated leader of the LCO. Sharie Lewis had enthusiastically applauded each name and office. A believer in civic partnerships, she pushed for needed changes in communication and decision-making. She too believed the revised program would bring success.

Her commitment to civic engagement drew on the strategies of her great grand-father, The Rev. Samuel Lewis. An African-American minister and prominent community leader, he led a famous city workers boycott in this small mid-western city. His and the community's strategies pressed government and other hiring offices to listen to and negotiate with workers, most of whom, at that time, were African-Americans. Creating the Lewistown Community Organization (LCO), Sharie continued his work tirelessly pursuing fair and equal treatment for the citizens of Lewistown and other urban minority communities struggling with economic and political exclusions. Without Sharie Lewis' advocacy, the community might not have agreed to consider, much less attempt, another partnership with Parkston. Having taken that next step, the room at Parkston now swelled with hope that the evening would be a grand celebration.

Smiling broadly, Landers explained the varied activities of the partnership from classes working on specific community-based projects, to internships, to a few special projects instigated by LCO and fully supported by Parkston. Each venture began with a proposal from either or both partners. Most engagements involved community members, students, and faculty, ranging from mutually-beneficial research to training, and/or program delivery. All involved some sort of assessment. Whether studies focused on city zoning laws or elder education events at the Senior, the projects drew participants from both communities helping to rebuild trust through mutual engagement, and lessons learned via the program's past rubble.

As Landers spoke, he often turned toward Lewis describing their shared perspectives on the successes and dangers ahead. He named some causes of the breached commitments from three years ago. He warned that the walls between Lewistown and Parkston had grown even higher since that collapse. The university's addition of more professionally-oriented degrees pushed more students away from Lewistown placements into businesses, nursing homes, and hospitals across the city. Initially, Lewistown welcomed the new degrees hoping that students would be placed in training sites in their community. But the university did not choose their sites for a number of reasons beneficial to the school and less so to Lewistown. The community felt betrayed needing the care the new degree training opportunities would provide. These conflicts, Landers warned, must not be swept aside for the benefit of Parkston as they were in the past. As he finished, Sharie Lewis stood up and continued the theme.

She challenged the university community to look more carefully at the increasing numbers of students moving off-campus into Lewistown to save housing costs. Properties in Lewistown that formerly housed people using city housing allowances were shifting to serve this high-paying student population. Suddenly, long-term renters were out on the streets struggling to find places to live in their own neighborhood. Following the students were numbers of new chain restaurants and bars. Longstanding neighborhood mom-and-pop businesses were struggling to compete. While the neighborhood became a first choice for cheaper living, students did not seem interested in volunteering in school programs for children and young adults. Classes including placements to teach English as a Second Language in Lewistown struggled to get enrollments. "What does engagement really mean when major areas of concern for the community get no traction in Parkston?" Lewis asked. She and Landers let the silence settle over the room. They wanted to name the sticking points still in play while they had everyone's attention and goodwill.

With that accomplished, Landers turned the page. "Tonight, we commit to a growing and better university-community partnership between Lewistown and Parkston." Turning to the students at the table, he said, "Tell us about your experiences with our *new* Lewistown-Parkston Community Engagement Partnership?" Armando, a psychology major with a human health minor, spoke first. With immigrant parents who came from El Salvador to South Carolina, he needed almost full funding for college. With the scholarship he received from Parkston, he tried to take advantage of every opportunity and give back. During the fall semester, he took a sociology seminar that volunteered two times a week with an after-school tutoring program in Lewistown's Elementary School. Helping African-American and Latinx children work on their language skills and homework not only made him feel good but provided a way he could support other minority students to consider college as a viable choice for their lives. He also demonstrated to the university, the power of broadening assumptions about college-readiness and the resources offered by a diverse study body.[2] The following spring semester, he interned with Father Manny, short for Manuel, at the Our Lady of Grace Roman Catholic Church, about five blocks from campus. Reverend Manuel Rodriguez, a Roman Catholic priest, had served this congregation for the last six years, and Armando felt lucky to serve in his own faith tradition.

Originally an African-American parish, the church now also served a large immigrant community from Mexico, Guatemala, El Salvador, and other Central and South American countries. Through the internship, Armando helped organize a public health fair at the church that offered free vaccines for children provided by the city's Public Health Office. Calling a meeting for information-sharing and planning, Armando also brought together various stakeholders to coordinate additional neighborhood meetings to assess and discuss needed health services. As community members requested more fairs, Armando involved the human health faculty and other students in the minor. The hopes to expand these fairs had not been as successful as Armando and Lewistown members had hoped. Unsure about the sources of this apparent lack of interest, they would keep pressing. But one exciting result of the health fairs was a new pain management group supported by Father Manny's church. Teaching specific mindfulness-based practices to elders suffering with pain, a campus volunteer found his interest in neuroscience contributing to people's lives. Overall, Armando reported, these various partnerships were working well for everybody.[3]

He ended his remarks by thanking the community members who had taught him so much and faculty members who welcomed linkages of classroom learning to communities. At that point, Father Manny, sitting in the audience, shouted out the community's gratitude to him and named that the church planned to hire Armando after his graduation. "We count on this partnership," he added as the audience burst into applause and Armando smiled broadly. A "win–win," Landers stated as he thanked Armando and introduced the next speaker, Jana, a sophomore whose community-partnered work fulfilled a project requirement for her urban sociology class.

Jana began describing an after-school program at Sanders Elementary School where she worked with other Parkston students. In teams of four, one team coming each day of the school week, Parkston students provided reliable after-school activities including tutoring, outdoor physical activities, creative arts, and music. As a sociology major, she explained how social concepts about the impacts of resource-access on education came to life through their work with the partnership. Enjoying getting to know the children so close to her campus, she expressed appreciation for families determined to find resources for their children's thriving. Planning to continue volunteering with the school after the class, she hoped to pursue a master's degree in education and become an elementary school teacher.

At the end of her remarks, she thanked the Counseling Center staff. One staff member helped Jana connect a child's parent with a local community mental health center. This experience also encouraged Jana to meet with a counselor for a few sessions to talk about issues in her own life, including her struggles when facing the lack of resources available to children right outside the walls of her university. The room again fell silent. Did students need this kind of support while working with the Partnership? Where the resource gaps between Parkston and Lewistown that severe? Where did people living in Lewistown turn for mental health support? Landers broke in adding his personal and the program's thanks to the Counseling Center and other offices in Campus Life.

He knew very well that many students turned to them after working with communities living with the effects of long-term inequities. The Partnership involved real people with a range of assets and struggles. Participants from both groups directly faced unexpected and unacknowledged assumptions that impacted their shared work. With the help of Parkston's Student Services professionals, the Partnership assisted Lewistown residents in finding the help they needed as well as connecting students and faculty with requested resources. "We dare not ignore the full range of human tensions and emotions that arise amid community-engagement partnerships," he said. Turning to Jana, he thanked her for raising these issues and the rest of her remarks. As she moved to sit down, she paused. "Actually, Professor Landers" she continued, "I'd like to say one more thing."

She spoke about the Partnership's lessons on "setting limits," a term, she noted, the Counseling Center taught her. While doing her community-engaged work, she found limits she could not overcome or ignore. One, she explained, involved recognizing that no matter how much she strove to understand the lives of students she worked with in the school, she could never fully fathom their experiences. "We continue to talk and share, but many of my assumptions about life and choices simply were not available to the students I work with." She encouraged any student thinking about working with the Partnership to pay attention. "No matter how well designed the project or well-intended we are, we do not share the same 'lived experience', as my sociology professor calls it, as those we partner with." She continued by highlighting differences in assumptions only made more complex because most students worked with Lewistown people for a very short time, a semester or two. Then she thanked Professor Landers and sat down. Landers then introduced Sharie Lewis.

Lewis began her remarks by giving full credit to other local leaders for encouraging the restart of the program. She also thanked Parkston for recommitting with the neighborhood to bring shared resources to people facing serious roadblocks to their health and thriving. "Partnership is our way forward to support each other and take next steps." She restated LCO's full commitment to those steps and called for growth in the restarted program born of renewed and stronger commitment. The tone of the room shifted back again toward trust and hope while remaining mindful of the serious caution Jana raised.

Pushing her issues a bit further, Lewis then asked if the university were ready to begin a series of university-sponsored listening sessions with various Lewistown Partner offices. The LCO felt this was a necessary next step for program development. Some initiatives the LCO wanted to discuss included: students helping members of the Senior Citizen Center to create a neighborhood recycling program – good for the environment and a sustainable source of neighborhood education and funds for the Center; a new physical fitness program for elementary school children who suffer with obesity; and a "College-*Is*-for-You" initiative. In addition to naming areas available for next steps in the partnership, Lewis' question heightened the stakes of the partnership. Was Parkston really committed to long-term, ongoing initiatives? Were new resources available for additional community-engaged change from permanent recycling bins to summer athletic camps for Lewistown youth held in Parkston athletic facilities?

She challenged the room to celebrate what had been accomplished through relatively small amounts of resources, space, and time while envisioning more. She wanted to take the partnership to the next level. This is the serious and often hard reality faced by university-community partnerships. They best thrive when imagination meets commitment, when shared experience continues to unfold and shape new work. Or would Parkston remain at the first level of community-engagement, repeated activity, not life together?

As Lewis sat down, small clusters of people in the audience quietly discussed issues she introduced. Landers again stood up and opened the floor for questions and comments, which sparked several Lewistown locals to ask how their organizations could apply for student interns or programmatic help related to a class. Borden, the new Program Coordinator, stepped forward and outlined basic steps, which matched a PowerPoint slide now appearing on the screen. Several stated their hopes to talk through aspects of their setting in addition to filling out forms. "Who could we talk with?" asked one neighbor. Borden responded that she would be happy to talk with any Lewistown person about possible partnerships, but offered no details. As these questions faded, a few students raised their hands adding positive testimony to the power of these partnerships and encouraging Parkston to up its involvements.

Then a community member raised his hand while stating that he hoped to offer a few summer internships to help with an LCO-sponsored college prep program. "When does the summer session begin," he inquired adding that LCO would provide youth small stipends to participate, a necessary strategy since all young people in the neighborhood had to work in the summer. He hoped Parkston students would participate as part of a class, not needing payment. "So, the start of our program depends on when the Parkston students are available." Lewis picked up on the theme, naming a list of organizations also needing to know the start date for Parkston's summer session. Landers and Borden recognized the problem. Most Parkston students went away during the summer to work as interns or camp counselors. Many went home or took internships related to their future careers. They too needed money to pay for school. Faculty also left for the summers. "We are looking for additional grants to fund summer internships, which we hope might keep some students here," Borden stated quietly. To change the realities of no summer support would require the long-term commitment, creativity, and work Lewis advocated only minutes before. Summer support demanded serious institutional change.

Pockets of Lewistown residents began to murmur, and the room again turned tense. Lewis pressed on, "Our young people struggle to find employment and useful activities to occupy their time. The Partnership is critical for this, especially in the summer. Are there no opportunities?" A photography professor in the audience interjected stating she could offer a workshop or two for Lewistown children and teens. More silence. Then, a staff member from the Health Center expressed willingness to sponsor a simple health fair for the community. "Perhaps some of the neighborhood young people could help us design and organize that." Landers spoke up, emphasizing his hope that other opportunities like these would emerge. But the Lewistown neighbors knew there were no guarantees. One LCO Council member stood up and said, "We have to learn how to be "all-year-long" neighbors." That phrase caught the ear of a first-year student interested in taking a course through the Partnership. He raised his hand, and Landers called on him.

"I'll be a sophomore next year," he said. "I'm thinking about taking a community-engagement course. But I hear the neighborhood is dangerous after dark and by 4:45 p.m. it's already so dark that street lights are turning on." He continued explaining that he hoped to take a Spanish class at Parkston, which included volunteering with the English as a Second Language Program in Lewistown. But the required cross-language conversations happened in Lewistown between 6:30 p.m. and 8:00 p.m. "Isn't that too late in the day for students like me to be walking around in that neighborhood? I've heard students get robbed, sometimes attacked. Is this true?" As he spoke, Lewis leaned forward in her chair. The upbeat tone of the room sank again. "We hear you," she quickly interjected. "But our angle on what's happening is different from yours. We share your concerns – but our concerns are about *you* being in our neighborhood after dark." Her voice now took an edge.

She then described Lewistown's worries and anger over Parkston students encouraging a drug and sex trade that put Lewistown neighbors at risk for health and safety. Until Parkston student dollars stimulated the markets, Lewistown did not have middle-men dealers on the streets. "Do you think *our* community members have the cash for drugs or sex? Very rarely! Parkston people have those resources." She returned to earlier comments about gentrification literally displacing long-term residents. Lack of access to jobs and no sustainable local economy were strangling Lewistown and especially the future of local youth. "Our young people are trapped like prey in new economies that Parkston is strongly contributing to. These economic decisions impact our daily experiences." The room went utterly silent as waves of tension swept over it. Fury across her face, she sat back in her chair.

Community members in the auditorium nodded their heads in agreement. Many knew the histories of economic and periodically race-related exclusions that undermined successfully shared ventures. Would this renewed Partnership really make any difference? Could the unnamed and ignored struggles of Lewistown be named and addressed? Looking at the audience, Lewis realized that the staffs of the Health and Counseling Centers knew many students' stories of addiction and dangerous sexual behaviors played out via time and money spent in Lewistown. So did Campus Police and other Student Life Administrators. All this had remained unnamed, but now, thought Lewis, the naming would begin – and quickly – in the student paper, community news outlets, and across the web: Parkston students contribute to the drug trade in Lewistown; Lewistown gentrification pushes long-time residents out; sexual predators. There were more unnamed matters that would come forward through the Partnership's new start – now also full of rubble.

Speed, Cycles, and Anchoring in Kindness

When naming the unnamed happens in service communities, whether planned or unplanned, it speeds up collapses already in progress, the way a structure of blocks suddenly implodes once the tipping point is reached. Additionally, other nearby and ready-to-burn factors, sometimes on nearby levels or the same level of the partnership, get swept into this ratcheted energy. That evening at Parkston, the heat kept rising as partners exposed the precarious and inflamed stability of their shared work until it tipped. Formerly dismissed incidents now sparked acknowledged and sometimes deeper problems of miscommunication, mismatched energies, and hidden agendas cornering the work of this service household. Finding next steps through the breakdowns born of naming the unnamed would require work, but even more, courage.

The work of naming begins with identifying frictions, sparks, and full-on fires. Insight emerges slowly from the ashes of good intentions when well-meant rescue operations only reinforce denial of deeper problems. To move forward by naming the unnamed, we commit to next steps into these tougher spaces. Rebuilding relationships is core to this work and difficult. Trust lost is a painful experience. Communication ignored or warped feels like betrayal. As the naming continues, so will the pain, mistrust, and ambivalence. Add differences in experience, background, and social status and the conversation gets tougher. In many ways, the most important first step of naming is not leaving. It's staying with the heat and the damage, looking at it as closely as possible before even starting to consider moving through it. This is a kind of contemplative stance. Just be there. Stay there as openly as possible.

There are more stories to hear. Those triggered by naming the unnamed brought out other stories from the past when aspects of the work went unnamed. These also must be heard and often heard again. But with the openness of awareness paying full attention, sparks of hope will still burn, and partners can see and note them. These are the sparks of newly named elements of the relationships and possibly the work. To pay attention to those sparks, be diligent about keeping participants together. How? Listen more. Ask for more details. Stay focused on these necessary issues. Slow down those wishing to charge ahead toward some renaming or rebuilding fix. Encourage those who linger too long over the damages to slightly pick up the pace. Use your grounded attention to discern this group's pace for moving through the damage and taking note of possible resources. The process is a layered complexity, and includes fast and slow moving segments, different levels, and varied partners.

Community-engaged partnerships are multi-level service systems by nature. When multiple factors are triggered into collapse, certain levels of the work spin faster into burnout. The graphic below shows how these speeded up levels ignite and accelerate change. Our impulses in partnerships can urge us to intervene quickly. But such responses ignore the other aspect of this graphic, the slower moving, "remembering" cycles of the partnership. Though the "revolt" or breakdown heightens trouble and loss, recovering is within the system, offered in part by the existence in memory or in the future of remembered stability. Count on that. Remind each other of that. The work is about listening to awareness amid the speeding collapse born of that stability from past experiences (when they worked) and anticipated ones. (Figure 8.1).[4]

There's creativity at all levels. Attend to it by remembering it and pointing it out. As the revolt phase unleashes breakdown, it also releases new information. Some very hard to hear and accept. Often new levels of the partnership come into view, those previously denied. Again, tough to take in, but very useful for rebuilding or exploitation. Blaming and fault-finding grow less important when our attention taps into these multi-leveled systems. Discovering when and how to isolate blame becomes tougher, which also dampens fault-finding's importance. Though responsibility-taking remains crucial in these relationships at whatever level(s), the emphasis moves to the work of moving into what burnout or collapse reveal.

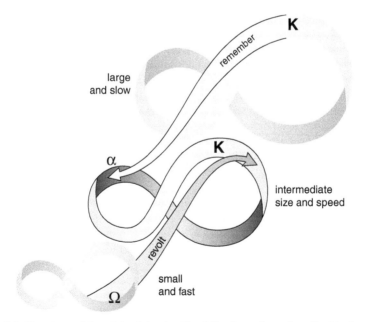

Figure 8.1 Creating and Sustaining Adaptive Capability. From *Panarchy*, edited by Lance Gunderson and C. S. Holling, Figure 3-10, 75. Copyright 2002 Island Press. Reproduced by permission of Island Press, Washington DC. For additional information, see Resilience Alliance: www.resalliance.org. Accessed June 29, 2019.

Serious attention goes to the newly-unfolding questions and issues opened by burnout. The energy moves forward rather than getting stuck in the past and its accusations.

As listening and early conversations begin, pursue honest identification of sources of destructive and morally-suspect behaviors. Stick with concretes and specifics. These are the possible sources for rekindling the fires of shared community-engaged service. The participation of as many partners as possible in this work of moving into multi-layered burnout will help assure that no level is overlooked or intentionally ignored. This inclusive, dive-deep approach will take more time and likely additional frustration, but the multi-leveled thickness of community-partnered engagements simply require this steady and complex work.

Practices like the Caring Breath described in Chapter 6 support self-care as partners move into such tough, often extended and honest conversations. Building from that self-care practice, we can expand to offer loving-kindness to others, in this case, our community partners – at whatever level. Pay attention to the different levels. To do an expanded version of this practice, start with a few rounds of the self-care Caring Breath. After settling into that mode, when you move one hand from your leg to your shoulder breathing in and then to your heart breathing out shift your intention to sending heartfelt concern and care to your partner(s). Hold them tenderly in your heart, offering support for their struggles and work in the rubble of breakdown. As you breathe in again moving your hand back to your shoulder, keep your concern for them centered in your mind and heart. As you release your breath and move your hand back down to your leg, intend that their pain may be released or eased.

As you do this, elements from their perspectives in the partnership may come to mind. Integrate them into the practice: may they be relieved of that difficulty; may they experience kindness and tender support as they work toward next steps. Stay focused on their perspectives and roles in the partnership from a kind-hearted standpoint. Before a difficult meeting or even in the midst of one, we can visualize (rather than literally do) this practice of self-care and partner-care. This practice helps us resist our natural defensiveness and remember that we're working together for shared service. Using this practice also helps us look more honestly at issues we've overlooked or denied. The self-care aspect helps us avoid flipping into defensive guilt or ineffective self-blaming. The practice can help us draw energy for tough conversations as we now speak from a place of compassion for self and others.

I think of this practice as strength-conditioning for the courage to loosen our grip on the interactive and inter-relational work of acknowledging faults, apologizing, accepting, and forgiving. We can choose to be in the ruptured unfolding of demanding accountability, remaining wary, and whatever the real relational work requires, without resorting to defensive resistance. Like any other practice, it requires repetitive use. You will get better at it. This practice refocuses our minds and intentions toward rebuilding honest and caring mutuality. Its simplicity also makes it effective amid the speed-up phases of multi-level burnout typical of partnerships.

Finally, this practice helps stabilize our attention and intentions when things are breaking apart all around us. It allows us to move into now-named elements that increase our anxiety (that's why we resisted them) and defensiveness. The practice encourages listening rather than talking because it views the present moment as operating from kindness – not silly niceness but kindness born of healthy-boundaries and relational commitment. We gain a bit more space for taking in accusations, including unfair accusations, without resorting to old patterns of domination. Correcting wrong information can be done without repositioning our group as the one in control. Loving-kindness highlights the deeper commitments in the partnership – that blue sky behind the clouds mentioned in Chapter 7 – and these impel us toward healing and reconstruction born of mutually-agreed upon next steps, including termination.

Of course, these contemplative practices will not magically do away with the serious conflicts now named. They will refocus attention on the rubble, understanding it, and working to repair relationships. It's often slow and halting work. But the intentional pace helps us return to the cycle's inherent slow-mode stability while still determining realistic options for next steps. We're learning to live with the realities that community-engaged partnerships are not predictable. Partners' contributions and struggles in the work are not fully understandable. Things – meaning resources, people, situations, and groups – change. But intending kindness and trying to reconnect with the slower stability also linked at different levels to burnout creates better environments to figure out if, when, and how the partnership can be rebuilt. This is the pace and context of new naming, whatever that might bring.

Don Michael, a public policy expert trained in psychology and sociology, contended that moving into difficult and tumultuous work while acknowledging and confronting the deep uncertainty reveals the "inevitable fact of our ignorance" in a complex and fast-changing world.[5] Though we feel a helpless weightlessness when struggling to begin moving through the burnout phase of naming the unnamed, it is useful to ground ourselves in the realities of "don't know anything about the next steps, but I can care about us." The complexities of multi-paced nested hierarchies or levels of the partnerships cannot be understood much less solved quickly. What we can do is settle into this reality and drop down into its smaller cycles of relationships while also being aware of or even engaged with larger cycles.

Aware of multi-leveled hierarchies, we move forward even though our next steps remain unclear. Michael's research on predicting the future of systems taught him the importance of finding stability even amid degeneration at ever increasing speeds. We are learning to live into the process with kindness rather than control, and this is crucial for community-engaged partnerships. Kindness toward self and others fosters present-moment courage to remember that service and burnout phases tend toward renewal.[6] Though the future feels deeply unsettling, as Don Michaels says, we drop down into our bodies, minds, and hearts to re-set our commitment to serve as partners with "both feet firmly planted firmly in mid-air," which he also cleverly titled his chapter.[7]

The Weight of Collapse: Practices for Staying with the Pressures

This approach matters because the weight of collapse amid naming the unnamed hits with a fury. To make this more concrete, think back to our evening program when one now-named issue led to a string of other unnamed, now-named issues. Once released, their pressures not only turn us topsy-turvy (feet in the air) but also highlight serious challenges that have been denied or dismissed. The layers, often involving hierarchies of power and resources from volunteers to board members, can overwhelm our capacity to re-imagine or respond. Trying to reorder expectations of access to power and resources for next steps, even steps deeper into the rubble, can quickly overwhelm partners. As happened in the program that night, a single issue, drug selling for example, became a tipping point to a vast cascade of interrelated levels of activity, access, and accountability. How can useful and serious next steps emerge?

It can be helpful to think of the newly named as a needed inventory of areas of strength, weakness, or problems in your own community's commitment to the partnership. As newly discovered issues and dynamics, some might be more immediately contributing to increased understanding and positive change than others. Before moving into shared conversations with your partner, pause to think more about your issues. Learn to bear the weight of your own failures, denials, and misjudgments as well as gifts and places of growth. What were the protective strategies at work in your particular form of denial or no naming? Why was the need so strong to explain away difficulties and/or injustices? When was it expedient to turn your head and avoid that tough subjects or problems? Again, not every newly named issue must be dealt with in the present. Another cycle of collapse will come. But move into this breakdown to leverage the opportunities in it.

One way to work with these newly named elements is to draw your version of the partnership as a body. Yes, a literal body. In the practices section at the end of the chapter, you will find space and opportunity to make a first try. Having done some initial thinking about your defensiveness and avoidance, the exercise will bring out additional angles and dynamics that you had not initially considered. This is the gift of art-based exercises. This individual work will also prepare you to do this activity with your community partner, taking a next step in your insight and inventory-building together. To begin, use a large piece of butcher paper and together draw your "shared body of service partnership." In some situations, that image might look like two overlapping bodies. Be creative! Again, the idea is to place descriptive words, emotions, categories onto particular areas of the body. Where does anxiety show up? How does long-term shared practice appear? Let your imagination teach you more about your partnership's capacities to move through breakdown.

Of course, no body drawing will be complete. If there's notable disagreement within a group, note that on the body. Where do different assumptions show up? How does this exercise expand individuals' or groups' awareness of stakes as well as gifts and capacities? Have certain body parts or embodied capacities become stunted or even missing? Did strengths show up that we had overlooked or forgotten? Where are the confusions, the resource mismatches? For all community partners, this work helps us take in who we are, what we offer, and what has, is, and will be happening through partnered service. Taking periods of stillness and reflection while doing this work will elicit additional insights and questions. This work is about each partner's experience or sense of their presence in shared service and implicitly the impact of shared engagement.

This initial set of exercises can be followed-up in a variety of ways. The goal or intention is to offer communities a different avenue or experience for naming themselves in the partnership. If embodied, what are their experiences, capacities, struggles, frustrations, gifts, and more? This artistic or creative approach often opens new avenues of thinking, emotion, and experience. It can affirm the work of new naming. To follow-up, groups might focus on one particular area of the body.

They might ask questions about the reasons for limits or capacities. They could emphasize embodied potential for connection to others. They can signal their aspirations and what blocks those. They might depict sources of anger and optimism. This approach can be especially helpful in highly divisive situations where tensions are high. Verbal descriptions at these times can easily devolve into accusations. The options for using this practice should best suit the needs and interests of partnership members.

Finally, if used over a series of weeks, this artistic approach can help articulate if and how paths of next steps might take shape. Which shared concerns and resources arc available to move into the rubble? Versions of these activities can support community groups and their partners through cycles of burnout and reconstruction. When words seem to send partners back to their corners, this approach may loosen the grip of denial and dismissal. It may encourage movement into less "me" and a bit more "us."

Another Case Study – Into Burnout: Muddled Intentions, Named Resentments

Looking at a case study of a newly-forming community partnership takes a different slant on these issues of not naming and new naming. A colleague and I discovered this when asked to serve as consultants to a small liberal arts college – we'll call it Continuum. Continuum's history emphasized community service, but those volunteer-based good works had never birthed ongoing community-engaged partnerships. They were ready to take that step and believed it might also help with student recruitment. Even in our preparatory phone calls, we heard this mixed message: commitment to partnership *and* more student bodies. They knew particular histories of communities near the campus, but nothing comprehensive. They knew a certain faculty group expressed interest, but they did not know if interest spread beyond this group. They did not know what communities around them thought or felt about them. Muddled intentions hamper community partnerships.

We arrived and stood on the 151-year-old quad amidst towering trees of the coastal southern United States. We would work in these stately academic buildings for the next two days consulting with faculty, Campus Life staff, who had created volunteer-based opportunities in the community, and administrators. We met only once with students. Literally going from one group to the next, the conversations felt narrowed. One particular and talented administrator projected a specific model into our conversations, which we tried to soften, if not avoid. By the end of the day, we suggested she hold off on presenting her plans so that we could hear more from the different constituencies. What did they envision, want, and need? We added two meetings with secretarial level staff involved in the volunteering programs. They gave us an ear-full! Do not forget to talk to all parties who work daily "in the trenches" of community-engagement.

The few identified faculty interested in engaged teaching and learning with local communities brought their stories and excitement. Each told their experience and with enthusiasm expounded ideas they believed would work well. Others did not appear to listen to them. Partnership on the Continuum side felt solitary, detached. It was as if my colleague and I were riders on a subway car, seeing one station just long enough to catch the name and then the subway car barreled to the next.

Most of the faculty descriptions related to their coursework and had little to do with the community, except for one faculty member who had been involved for years in a community-empowerment program. Except for him, we heard almost nothing about the community. They seemed unaware of actual potential partners. These are typical signs of imagined partnerships rather than real ones. The work of relationship-building had not begun. We knew that without this, nothing else could happen.

Throughout the day we heard many vague descriptions of "desires to help." Class-based learning objectives appeared to expect communities to provide what the professors needed. Again, the actual knowledge of the community proved to be so poor that the faculty and most staff could not have identified actual matches between community and campus goals. This campus' intentions for engagement could not begin to approach the serious work of Parkston and Lewistown. To build community-engaged partnerships would require more effort and time on the campus' part to understand their own goals and objectives more clearly and then to begin to develop actual relationships. From their position alone, much work needed to be done.

The event we most anticipated was the evening dinner with local community leaders and service directors. We were eager to hear about their interests in community-engaged partnering with the campus. Did they have goals and specific objectives? We wondered if they knew much about the campus and quickly found out that they knew much more about the faculty and school than the school and faculty knew about them. The faculty member most engaged with the community had sent the invitations for this dinner. Twenty-five guests arrived, and all but two were African-American. From the moment the meal began, we observed the strong relationships among these community members. They knew each other well and had worked together on numbers of initiatives often partnering well with local businesses.

More than half worked in a range of neighborhood-based programs offering tutoring, after-school care, sports, art, and athletics. A few worked in direct service-delivery organizations. They represented religious, community-based, and service organization groups. Five attendees lived in a small neighborhood literally across the street from the south end of the campus. They reported that the campus referred to their area as "the less developed end of the town." We chatted among ourselves during the meal then shifted for a more focused, shared conversation after each attendee identified themselves. Already one image had repeatedly emerged: an unbreachable trench between the campus and the neighborhood. In that trench lay a list of issues never named to us by anyone in the college. Most attendees felt that these issues would not be viewed as crucial to a service partnership by their college partners They, however, viewed them as very important.

The issues revolved around recognition and respect, the first two elements of building community-partnerships. They often go unattended. The neighborhood members reported that only a rare few from the college stepped onto their streets except for occasional volunteering. They felt as if their homes and streets were shunned and dismissed. Naming this, from their perspectives, provided a first step to building a partnership. They wanted to talk about being invisible. Why had the college never embraced their political activism, for example, their campaign with City Hall to increase funding for public housing repairs? Why were their talented high schoolers never recruited to visit the college? Why were no scholarships available for local kids like theirs? Some students were willing to consider attending an almost all-white campus if they could easily return home for support. When the community sent invitations to the college inviting them to their block parties and religiously-sponsored bake sales supporting local projects, they never heard back. The tone sank below disappointment to frustration and anger. Invisible and unheard. Now named. Yet, the college was not in attendance. It did not hear.

Back in my room that night, I developed a short list of core concerns and questions emerging from the evening's discussion. I shared it in my meeting the next day with a group of campus administrators and faculty identified as the Leadership Team for this community-engaged initiative. I expected expressions of confusion and surprise. I expected to see some bodies in the room tighten as these concerns hit emotional chords. But their responses remained intellectual and fact-based. They knew of no bake sales. They assumed the neighbors' talented teens wanted to attend the state university. That's where most students wanted to go. They'd never heard of Mama Jackson, the woman who lived literally across the street and knew the coastal tradition of basket weaving. They had no idea her baskets were in the state's museum and in other museums across the country. When new naming happens in community-engagement, pay close attention to the responses. Notice particularly if any relational aspects emerge. In this case, they did not. Just the facts – as the campus saw them.

Of course, these responses are not unique. Most of us in community engagement understand that knowing a community well takes years – even if one of the community members is a superstar of sorts. Developing relational understanding happens in that multi-scalar complexity described earlier. Partnerships emerge from these complexities, as do shared learning goals. It's easy to think relationship-building will just come along naturally. Story-sharing will just happen as the teaching, learning, and service unfold. But they do not. Partnerships begin with, require, and end with relational care and commitment. Born of intentional work requiring emotional availability, time, and clarity of goals, partnering for shared engagement is a slow movement across many shared concerns, differences, and intentions. It takes long-haul work and kindness.

During the rest of our consultancy with this school, we tried to keep coming back to the basic issue of relationship-building. How might the university engage with community-based interests and activities? What were the community's concerns that the College could share? Could they offer partnerships for enrichment of assets already existent in the community? Might, for example as one community member suggested, the school create baseball camps or other sports workout session led by the school's coaches? By building relationships in these ways, other bridges might be built across classrooms, political involvements, and jobs. Learning more about each other would support naming the unnamed, including naming when a program no longer served.

This campus and local communities had not begun the work of establishing relational links for building a "story of us," as Marshall Ganz, a Harvard innovator of public community-building and engagement, describes it. From such a shared story, he adds, communities can develop engaged partnerships of collective action and education work.[8] Where are you and your potential or existent partners on this spectrum from the not-yet-begun partnership of Continuum to the very real and ongoing work of Parkston and Lewistown. In both partnerships, the work of creating and sustaining a "story of us" involves ongoing practices of awareness and deeper attention. They require listening and listening more. Attending to the details of dreams, successes, pain, dismissal, leveraged power, rejection, creative problem-solving, and more, we cycle through service and burnout drawing on kindness born of the deepest understanding we can muster. Do not forget the power of sharing stories about the unnamed, naming them, and moving forward into the rubble and beyond.

Moving Toward a Story of "Us"

Think back on your own memories and dreams of engaged partnerships sharing community service. Choose an experience of a partnership that came to life, something relatively small. Pick a time in that partnership when certain behaviors and attitudes you expected went missing. Try to go back in your memory to that scene of breakdown. What did you feel? What did you think? How did your partner fail to meet your assumed shared commitment? Had you ever discussed these expectations? Why or why not? What other questions or issues come to mind as you think about this situation? It's in small moments like these that we discover elements of the partnership we wished we had explicitly named. Try going a bit deeper. Did any of these unnamed elements reflect or relate to your social and cultural position? Do you perceive them reflecting or relating to your partner's social and cultural expectations or position?

Don't be shy. We all have our assumptions about styles and content of communications, timely responses, reliable outcomes, follow-through, verbal agreement as real agreement, and more. These assumptions are elements in our story of shared service, though sometimes – often? – they go unnamed. When unnamed, they contribute to the collapsing of this cycle of the story of us. Yet no amount of reflection and naming will keep us safe from collapse due to unnamed issues and forces. This is part of being in a relationship. As we grow and learn about each other in the shared planning, work, and evaluation, more naming takes place. More unnamed elements also surface. So, naming the unnamed or new naming is an ongoing process.

Once you've got a list of honest naming you'd like to share with your partner, take a piece of paper and write down some of your phrases, words, even sentences. Reflect on how they help you identify points of tension and potential breakdowns in your partnership. Now let your memory conjure some of the emotions that came up when these unnamed breakdowns happen. Are judgments of yourself and/or your partner part of the experience? Do you feel the consequences of unnamed sources of collapse in your body? Pay attention to tightness around your shoulders or around your eyes. Does that smile you try to keep on your face amid your despair or rage wear you out? Did the pace of your breathing shift during telephone conversations with your community-engaged partner? Take notice of the broad range of how your story, your responses to the unnamed, shows up when working with a community-engagement partner upon a relatively small collapse.

Now as we've done throughout the book, take those memories, perhaps conflicted feelings rising from the now-named behaviors and attitudes, on a walk. But in this case, as you walk move your breath into those tight places in your body. Let the tensions release. You might just walk in your room. Or you might go outside where you can more easily notice that life all around you shares in conflicts. Some are obvious. Many are harder to take in. But as you walk and breathe with this naming work in mind, you'll notice more of these tiny human breakdowns and tensions. The walking is not about erasure. The walk helps us discern which parts of the naming now must happen. What are the priorities? Where's the emotional heft coming from, the overlooking of you as a person of equal worth or is it more that a project you cared deeply about got short-changed? Walking helps us focus and discern, what do we need to name and what new naming is now required?

Even a simple truth-telling practice like this one helps us remember that we and our service partners will always have unnamed issues and dynamics emerging in our partnerships. We need to name these and more importantly work together for new naming, for next steps, without judging but born of kindness amid tension. The more we know about our own patterns and triggers in the face of unnamed collapses, the more we can bring to our shared work for naming the rubble and discovering together what might be salvaged, rebuilt and newly named – all without guarantees, with our feet in the air. Next is another activity that helps with this process personally or with a group.

Rebuilding the "Story of Us": An Adapted Practice of Lectio Divina

This last approach to walking into and through rubble for naming and new naming focuses on strengthening our skills for listening. Learning how to listen to our own and a service partner's story requires practice. One form of practice is an adaptation of a contemplative exercise called Lectio Divina. This can be done among individual partners in community-engaged service or among service groups. It's useful as an intervention practice but is more useful when regularly done among service users or groups. Lectio Divina's specific format for telling and hearing stories as well as responding to them provides a step-by-step path, marked by fully heard blazes that name the unnamed in service and burnout while putting us on the trail toward new naming for reconstructing and moving on.

Lectio Divina draws on a long tradition of Christian contemplative practices rooted in texts or stories.[9] The steps in this adapted version draw from that tradition, offering a structured reflection process adaptable for individual or group use.[10] This reflective practice "grows" the story, you might say, hearing it into its next forms by opening space to receive the story and engage it as much as possible alone and/or with others. Lectio Divina works well at many scales, smaller and larger. Just be clear about the scale you wish to prioritize. Aspects on other scales may show up, but keep your focus where you and your partner most need it. Lectio Divina can adapt to slower and faster-paced service and burnout processes.[11] It can accommodate different vantage points. Individuals or groups using it can narrow how little or how much of a story is being engaged. Focus most on the unnamed elements that most stymie the partnership.

In preparation for the practice, a single team or both teams are asked to write a one-page narrative of an unnamed issue fueling burnout in the service partnership. Again, in very heated and quick-sparking collapses, a paragraph or two may be enough. Our example will focus on the one-page version of the practice, which urges participants to focus on two or three aspects of that single unnamed issue. Questions that can spark a group's writing process include: What's the setting and who is involved? When did the unnamed issue or action spark into conflict and/or collapse? Why was it unnamed until now – who benefitted? What two or three things should everyone know about the unnamed? What needs to happen and how can it? Of course, partners can shape questions that better fit their relationships and service. The one-page narrative should focus only on the burnout. This work is not about rebuilding or reorganizing.

This adapted form draws on the four basic elements of the traditional practice of Lectio Divina: reading a text or story, (*Lectio*)[12]; reflecting or meditating on that text – asking what the story says to the reader's life right now (*Meditatio*); responding to the text (*Oratio*)[13]; and finally, sitting quietly with the text and the process up to that point. Notice what, if anything else, comes up (*Contemplatio*).[14] Throughout the practice, participants *try* to approach the story with as few assumptions as possible. Each person tries to let go of their version, lower their defenses. Although the facts and claims of no-name burnout benefit from more detached analysis, the practice highlights human experience and interaction with the issue(s). This work draws out the impacts of partners' different histories, life stories, and challenges. As noted before, building and rebuilding a story of us begins with growing relational honesty and strength through a truer telling of the partnership. Once relational strength begins to grow, the practice can be used for more investigative problem-solving. Initially, this practice is not about problem-solving.

Facilitators require training in and experience with, the practice. They should be familiar with the local service partnerships, but they need not know specific details. Ideally, they will have experience in using this practice to work through partnership breakdown and conflict. A session opens with everyone introducing themselves and their role in the partnership. I encourage the use of art or other creative processes for these introductions.[15] Before everyone reads the one-page narrative, facilitators explain the basic steps of Lectio Divina. The story is first read aloud by the facilitator, then individuals read it for themselves. Take about ten minutes for introductions and reading, then spend thirty to thirty-five minutes working with the story, with to ten to fifteen minutes for final conversations and sharing. Again, the purpose of this practice is not for fixing or next steps. It's for moving into the burnout fired by naming the unnamed. Set time frames that work for you, but set time frames.

If the practice focuses only on one text, the whole process can unfold in an hour or less depending on the severity of the collapse. If the practice involves two texts, it can unfold within one-and-a-half to two hours. Agree to a time limit before you begin. If the time allotted is not enough, arrange for a second meeting unless the participants quickly and unanimously agree to continue working. Remember that the first use of Lectio Divina often reveals other unnamed issues and dynamics. Note those for later consideration, but stay focused on the work at hand, recognizing, clarifying, and possibly prioritizing next steps into the debris. The offered time frames for each step in this practice are suggestions. As you and your partners use this practice, determine the time frames you need.

First Step: Lectio

The first step of this practice, *Lectio*, engages the story of a partner, individual or group, has shared. Heard aloud, and then read by each participant, this step focuses on taking in the story as shared. Hold off objections, questions for clarification, and rebuttals. Remain as open as possible to listening to the story. It is the life and service experience of team members or partners. Notice any differences in this description and your own experience of the service setting and work. What's been added or left out from your version of the story? Was there new or unexpected information? Were you surprised by what was named or by the angles taken on that issue – different assumptions, unexpected sources of conflict, prejudices you suspected but didn't know how to address or didn't choose to? Try to hear this story without fixing it to match your own.

The facilitator then invites participants to spend two minutes jotting down words, phrases, or scenes arising from the text. What's now named? How did this story impact you and your story in this service work? Starting a list of key terms can be helpful. Focus on words or emotions (then put into words) that surfaced for you from the two or three issues the shared story named. These words can later remind the writer of first responses, which may change as the practice continues. The list also can contribute to a later group process of shared terms, issues, emotions, or concepts that help map next steps into the debris of no naming. Putting down pencils and pens, participants then spend another two minutes in quiet reflection, letting the work of this first step be present.

Second Step: Meditatio

The second step, traditionally called *Meditatio*, stresses reflection on the presented text or story written by a partner. Remember, each participant has been given a written copy of the story. At this point, each participant again silently and unhurriedly reads their story at the pace of relaxed breathing. As you read after hearing the text read aloud, what draws your attention most? Circle those parts of the story? Do certain phrases or words confuse or confound you? Do they make you curious for more explanation? Does something in the story frighten you? As the story unfolds, can you follow the steps of developing tensions and/or resolutions? Do certain words, like blazes, stand out to you? Are there words used early in the story that explain or amplify words used at the end? Is something named you never imagined? Does something draw out resistance in you? Do particular questions come up? These are possible sources of reflection; find and follow your own. If your mind begins shaping rebuttals or denials, put down the pencil or pen and breathe. Wait. Then return to reflecting on the text.

As teams learn to work with Lectio Divina, skills for reflection grow. Participants learn to trust words and emotions that are not self-judging or dismissive of felt experiences. They learn to sit with their responses and not push them back, especially not into categories or rationales that contributed to no naming. They develop skills for letting go to what arises without judgment or dismissal. As with any practice, this one matures over time. As facilitators gain experience with service groups and this practice, they can encourage this maturing. The step of *Meditatio* invites deeper *recognition* and understanding of the differences that culture and identity, economics, politics, and ethical constraints[16] make in service partnerships. Reflection provides intentional time to sit with these contrasts and gain insight about how they contribute to no naming. Memories also may suddenly show up from past no name service, but try to stay focused on this work. In *Meditatio*/reflection, we can notice what we tend to avoid, fear, and leverage into burnout.

Third Step: Oratio

By the third step of Lectio Divina, *Oratio*, participants shift their energies from taking in and reflecting on now named facts and dynamics to response. This is the first step in responsibility-taking. They can begin creating a map of intended and unintended behaviors as well as attitudes that foster avoidance, denial, or rerouting of unnamed issues and interactions in the partnership. How does this mapping fit with or diverge from the reflective map of step two? What feels at stake when choosing new directions and leaving old habits behind? What emotions do you experience, where in the body and heart? How do your preferences in service show up? Are first steps of reimagining priorities, staffing, and budgets possible? Participants work with this step to clarify and differentiate their typically taken paths from ones now being named and imagined or reimagined. The work with this third step of response depends on maintained honesty, including truth-telling about levels and scales: what alterations and/or changes are really possible; who can assume responsibility for next steps, etc.? This overlaying of maps, meaning shared histories, attitudes, resources, and expectations then and now creates an emergent story of breakdown, adaptation, and next steps. These overlaying elements are the initial steps forward for identifying pathways that foster resilience. If/when confusion or resistance happen in *Oratio*, pause, put down pen and pencil and regain some stability through following the breath. Then go back to responding.

Oratio claims space for internal shifts from defensive avoidance or excuse-making to active engagement, from "tell me more" to "I have an idea we could consider as we move deeper into the trouble." This is a point in the practice when literal details are useful. Concretes help, but do not need final forming. In this version of *Lectio Divina*, this step works through partnered reading, reflection, and response. This is the step transitioning from a story of me to the first work of shaping a different story of us, one moving into the cinders of the no named. As partners use this practice more frequently, this third step can become an important space to honestly name willing openness and remaining resistances. Now at an individual level, but later during shared discussion after the fourth step, the work of this third step opens new insights. We may gain deeper understanding about hurts and resentments. We also may gain new insights, new naming. This step provides insight and energy that can reconstitute a differently designed mosaic of altered thoughts, histories, emotions, and expectations learned through burnout,[17] usually discussed at the end of the full process.

Oratio's work of response should focus only on issues highlighted in the one-page narrative. This is part of the classic work of *Lectio Divina*. As Evagrius, a Christian contemplative from fourth-century Egypt described it, the power of response to any full reality at hand draws us to engage not what we wish for or what affirms our sense of stability and control. We respond or work with what is directly at hand, this one-page story. This response is the first step of diagnosis. We know more now about how tightly our mind, body, and heart withholds energy from certain aspects of service and from our partners. We sense more deeply how much we want to maintain the status quo, which no resilient life system can tolerate. By responding with new openness, we release to the reality that collapse has happened. We begin moving on into new naming by opening to alternate questions and concerns. Evagrius describes this response step as leaving the cemeteries of our own making and keeping.

We let go in order to move forward toward restoration, not perfection.[18] Not perfection. Service is a life system with cyclic collapses. No naming will return as will new naming.

Fourth Step: Contemplatio

The realizations born of the response step urge action, stepping into new or altered thinking, recognizing emotions with balance, and moving forward to work with others on the now named dynamics or issues. This is difficult work drawing partners into the tough realities of impermanence, that core contemplative teaching now realized in service and burnout. Our work with and for others is not static. Having seriously listened, reflected, and responded, we now contemplate or take in the breakdown that now also describes our service together. Hoped-for outcomes happened. Some hoped-for outcomes got cornered and burned. Deep values of service came to fruition and also failed. In specific instances, communities worked well together, and in other instances communities caused division. The fourth step provides a space to take in the positive change and understand its inherent impermanence. Pieces of it will break off; some will burn up.

At this last step, facilitators ask that all writing-related materials be put away. Everyone is invited into a quiet space of open awareness that tries to take in the conflicts, learning, and insight of the first three steps. Without pushing it to concrete next steps or mentally reconstructing some aspect of *Oratio* or *Meditatio* you did not like, just be with the process as it unfolds and breathe. No planning. No slight adjustments. Try to stay with what is. Practice an attitude that can sit with the now named difficulties and/ or injustices. Now is not the time to plan resolutions of the issues. If your mind keeps going to that future work, refocus your attention on a word or phrase linked to the now named. Stay with the process that is happening now. This will be an important skill once partners begin to actually move into the burnout of naming the unnamed.

After three minutes of silence, the facilitator reads aloud the narrative, one last time. The room continues to sit for two more minutes. The facilitator then ends the *Contemplatio* step reminding the group that this practice investigates insight or understanding. Through listening, reflection, response, and deeper awareness in the present, service partners are invited into impermanence, the reality that the shared service is changing, collapsing, burning. Together through the practice of Lectio Divina, a map is emerging that can move groups or partners into service realities that were denied, dismissed, or covered up. There will be more stories to be told as reconsideration and rebuilding begins. The cycle will continue and through this practice, hopefully, so will useful insights. The facilitator ends this last step by announcing a two- to three-minute break. Some may choose to get up and stretch. Others may write.

The group reconvenes to answer the question, "What did we do?," another strategy developed as part of the Pre-Texts approach and training through Doris Sommer's Cultural Agents program.[19] Participants keep track of the people to their left and right, making sure they have space to speak or ask to "pass" before others speak for a second time. A short break should happen between this dialogue and the next one-page story if there is a next one. Participants should be encouraged to remain focused (no turning to their cell phones) and generally quiet. No next step discussions; instead, have a sign-up sheet available for people to register their interest in follow-up conversations.

How Lectio Divina Helps

Linking a one-page narrative naming the unnamed with Lectio Divina encourages teams and partners who avoid tough conversations to pause and reflectively respond to the issues rather than jump into fix-it mode. It also creates a repository of one-page burnout narratives, one kind of history within groups or between partners. In subsequent cycles of burnout, these narratives are available for additional insight. To use them as punishing tools in subsequent conversations of failed efforts or ethics is unfair and unproductive. The reflective nature of this practice intends to grow insight within teams or between partners about the unheard, ignored and/or feared.

The one-page narratives also provide a historical inventory of now named conflicts, prejudices, and misused power dynamics. Whether consciously expressed or not, some participants may resist the existence of such an inventory. It is hard to have a record of missed opportunities to dig deeply into service partnership inequalities and tensions. For some, the unfamiliarity of the process itself slows down their trust and interest in using it. Every named broken promise, leveraged unfairness, and missed opportunity urges immediate action. This process can feel like a slow-down but used well, it builds stronger bridges of self-understanding and communication and first steps toward restorative resilience. With repeated use, Lectio Divina helps partners better distinguish levels, scales, and people contributing most strongly to burnout factors and dynamics. Over time, this practice and its process can become a default way of working in community-engaged partnerships, meaning, its steps of listening, reflecting, and responding through deeper awareness show up in daily interactions. This process builds partnerships able to engage the unnamed with accountability rather than judgment or blame.

Adapted forms of Lectio Divina, such as this one, structure pathways of participatory insight born of a story and/or experience shared in community-partnered work, classrooms, and/or workshops.[20] It can foster insight even when only segments of groups or partners participate. Their willingness to move into the wreckage will strengthen their voices to tell the stories not named without a tone of accusation. They share the story they now understand more fully. Even certain aspects of rebuilding can begin from these groups or teams. As they move into a fuller story of us, alternate or new possibilities within other versions of the story come to light. Allow the resisters their experience and rather than waiting for full participation, go forward with those that are ready to name what must be named for full resilience.

As is always the case in service and burnout, initial steps into this revised or new story of us may be small and not very new. Partial resistances may remain. Old wounds may continue festering. It's OK. Do as much honest story-telling and reflective responding as possible and see what else you learn about your collapse. Keep trying to build the shifted or now named story. This practice works well partially and with repeated use or practice because it slows down our panicked and often semi-blind responses in the face of burnout. It focuses on discovering what is real now, including the really painful and broken. This is viewed as a step forward in this version of Lectio Divina because it is the story or text of now and us. At whatever level and scale, this practice helps teams and partners intentionally investigate present-moment behaviors in service relationships that confuse or break-down well-intended work.[21]

James Finley, a psychotherapist who spent years at Gethsemani Abbey with Thomas Merton as his Novice Master, underscores the difference between listening and engaging or doing, a distinction at the heart of Lectio Divina. Hearing what others name as significant to them and their service can be hard to take in. We need all our energy just to listen and reflect on their version of our shared service. When we avoid this work, Finley believes, we heighten the potential for damaging our relationships as well as maintaining our distorted vocabularies. The infrastructure of our stories gets weaker, which proliferates seeds of ignorance and injustice. They will bloom as partnerships take in fear, biases, and/or narrowly-grasped views. We are only adding more fuel to the eventual fire of burnout that will come.

Be prepared to dive into the listening as a first and serious preparation for action. The practices of self-naming and listening for other-naming in this chapter provide useful maps for moving into burnout's territories and finding next steps.

Exercises

1. Remember a public conversation naming the breaking points of a community-engaged partnership you worked with.

    a. Write some details: who, the issues and stakes, explanations, what else?

    _____

    _____

    _____

    _____

    _____

    _____

    b. Sit with these memories, letting the details come and go. Notice if areas of your body have begun to tense – stomach area, shoulders, upper chest, where else? Jot down how your body feels in that area and if any particular emotions arise in connection to that area.

    _____

    _____

    _____

    _____

    _____

    _____

c.   Can you connect those emotions to particular aspects of/information about the partnership? How have you related to those aspects/that information?

_____

_____

_____

_____

_____

_____

This level of self-awareness will inform and enrich your contributions to the partnership body-drawing practice suggested in the chapter.

2.   Think of a burnout experience you had involving a shift in levels and speeds of your partnership. Decisions required quick action and resources. How might the expanded Caring Breath practice strengthen your resolve to move forward with honest conversations about tough and unpredictable issues?

_____

_____

_____

_____

_____

_____

3.   To prepare for the body drawing practice, think about a few newly named aspects of your partnership – points of tension or miscommunication. Inventory those, meaning think honestly about your initial thoughts (defensive?). How do you emotionally response. Get your perspectives on paper and then consider how your responses/reactions might be contributing to breakdown.

_____

_____

_____

_____

_____

_____

a. The inventory here prepares a partner to realistically draw the body of their partnership, specifically assets (example: active participation: write that phrase in the arms) traits (example: enjoyment: write that word in the heart area), and problem places (example: lack of attendance: write that work in the feet). Continue playing with these ideas, "embodying" what your community brings to this partnership.

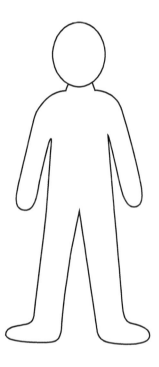

4. During the processes of building a "story of us," which issues or relationships (perhaps only parts of them), urge you to return to "unnaming." What or who signals that this has happened?

_____

_____

_____

_____

_____

_____

_____

5. Think of a current tension shared by you and your community-engaged partner. The *Oratio* step includes willingness to let go of issues and emotions you've protected or translated into terms more comfortable for you: stories of "me." Before the *Lectio Divina* process begins, write down what you know of these self-protecting areas.

_____

_____

_____

_____

_____

_____

a. Identify, if possible, for later additional work, issues and emotion too deep to engage in a first, perhaps even second-time use of *Lectio Divina*.

_____

_____

_____

_____

_____

Figure

From *Panarchy*, edited by Lance Gunderson and C.S. Holling, Figure 3–10, 75. Copyright 2002 Island Press. Reproduced by permission of Island Press, Washington, DC. Holling C.S., Lance H. Gunderson, and Garry D. Peterson, "Sustainability and Panarchies," in *Panarchy: Understanding Transformations in Human and Natural Systems*, edited by Lance H. Gunderson and C.S. Holling, 63–102. Washington, DC: Island Press, 2002.

Notes

1 See American Association of American Colleges & Universities, "Civic Learning and Democratic Engagements (CLDE);" and American Association of American Colleges & Universities, "Bringing Theory to Practice (BTtoP)."
2 See Hartfield-Méndez, "Community-based Learning, Internationalization of the Curriculum and University Engagement with Latino Communities" for additional analyses of cross-cultural community-engagement partnerships and their impacts.
3 The teaching strategies used in these classes drew aspects from the following community-engaged teaching and learning models: See Welch, *Engaging Higher Education*; Clingerman and

Lockman, *Teaching Civic Engagement*; Owen-Smith, *The Contemplative Mind in the Scholarship of Learning and Teaching*; American Association of American Colleges & Universities, "Civic Learning and Democratic Engagements (CLDE);" and American Association of American Colleges & Universities, "Bringing Theory to Practice (BTtoP)." Also see Imagining America, "Artists and Scholars in Public Life."

4   See Resilience Alliance. From *Panarchy*, edited by Lance Gunderson and C.S. Holling, Figure 3-10, 75. Copyright 2002 Island Press. Reproduced by permission of Island Press, Washington, DC.

5   See Michael, *In Search of the Missing Elephant*.

6   Holling and Gunderson, "Resilience and Adaptive Cycles," 41.

7   Michael, *In Search of the Missing Elephant*, 65–81.

8   See Ganz, "Public Narrative, Collective Action, and Power."

9   See Burton-Christie, *The Word in the Desert*, for a thorough history of the uses and meanings of scripture and other texts in the formation of early Christian contemplative communities.

10 See Dysinger, "Accepting the Embrace of God: The Ancient Art of *Lectio Divina*." The basic form of the practice used in this chapter draws from the work of Benedictine monk Luke Dysinger in *The Art and Vocation of Caring for People in Pain*, edited by Karl A Schultz.

11 Think back to the earlier graph and discussion of hierarchies or levels within systems at different phases.

12 The words in italics are the traditional words of the *Lectio Divina* Practice.

13 In traditional Christian contemplative use, *Oratio* involves response to/with God, which can inform responses and communications with others.

14 Traditionally, this last step involves gained insight taken in deeply enough to spark at least a reorientation to a text or story's content. Ideally, that reorientation informs changed behaviors and actions.

15 See Cultural Agents for examples of activities.

16 See Cannon, *Black Womanist Ethics*. Katie Cannon analyzes how and why the contexts and stories, socio-cultural relations, and spiritualities of oppressed groups' lives can shape alternate ethical frameworks in comparison to dominant group's ethical norms.

17 See Holling, Gunderson, and Peterson, "Sustainability and Panarchies," 89. The authors borrow Levi-Strauss' (1962) term, *bricolage*, to describe this process of recombining existing elements and new mutations and inventions to form something novel that solves a newly emerged problem or creates new opportunity. It is the adaptive cycle that accumulates those elements as potential and then, for transient moments, rearranges them for subsequent testing in changing circumstances.

18 Evagrius of Pontus, *The Greek Ascetic Corpus*, xxxi–xxxii. Elements of these ideas are explained by Sinkewicz in his translation of Evagrius' writings.

19 See "Pre-texts," Cultural Agents.

20 See Patterson, "Sustaining Life."

21 The Mind and Life Institute's work offers one example of leveraging this kind of insight into real world problem-solving. Through their mission "to alleviate suffering and promote flourishing by integrating science with contemplative practice and wisdom traditions," Mind and Life studies and teaches these approaches for leveraging the elasticity of perception using contemplative practices to improve common live and service. For more information see the websites for Mind and Life Institute and specifically Mind and Life Digital Dialogue.

Supplemental Readings

Bringle, Robert G., Patti H. Clayton and Mary F. Price. "Partnerships in Service Learning and Civic Engagement." *Partnerships: A Journal of Service Learning and Civic Engagement* 1, no. 1 (Summer 2009): 1–20.

Gunderson, Lance H. and C. S. Holling. *Panarchy: Understanding Transformations in Human and Natural Systems*. Washington, DC: Island Press, 2002.

Harkavay, Ira and Lee Benson. "De-Platonizing and Democratizing Education as the Bases of Service Learning." *New Directions for Teaching and Learning* 73 (Spring 1998): 11–20.

Leffers, M. Regina. "Pragmatists Jane Addams and John Dewey Inform the Ethic of Care." *Hypatia* 8, no. 2 (Spring 1993): 64–77.

Patterson, Barbara A. B. "Practicing Reconciliation in the Classroom." In *Roads to Reconciliation: Approaches to Conflict*, edited by Amy Benson Brown and Karen Poremski, 211–230. Armonk: M.E. Sharpe, 2005.

Patterson, Barbara A. B. "En/Countering the Other." In *Religion and Service Learning*, edited by Richard Devine, Joseph Favazza and F. Michael McLain, 55–68. Washington, DC: American Association of Higher Education, 2002.

References

American Association of American Colleges & Universities. "Civic Learning and Democratic Engagements (CLDE)." Accessed January 21, 2019. www.aacu.org/clde

American Association of American Colleges & Universities. "Bringing Theory to Practice (Bttop)." Accessed January 21, 2019. www.aacu.org/bttop

Burton-Christie, Douglas. *The Word in the Desert: Scripture and the Quest for Holiness in Early Christian Monasticism*. New York: Oxford University Press, 1993.

Cannon, Katie G. *Black Womanist Ethics*. Eugene, OR: Wipf and Stock Publishers, 1988.

Clingerman, Forrest, and Reid B. Locklin, eds. *Teaching Civic Engagement*. New York: Oxford University Press, 2016.

Cultural Agents. Accessed March 3, 2019. www.culturalagents.org/

Cultural Agents. "Pre-Texts." Accessed December 9, 2018. www.culturalagents.org/pre-texts/

Dysinger, Luke O.S.B. "Accepting the Embrace of God: The Ancient Art of *Lectio Divina*." In *The Art and Vocation of Caring for People in Pain*, edited by Karl A. Schultz. Mahwah, NJ: Paulist Press, 1993. 98–110.

Evagrius of Pontus. *The Greek Ascetic Corpus*. Translated by Robert E. Sinkewicz. New York: Oxford University Press, 2003.

Ganz, Marshall. "Public Narrative, Collective Action, and Power." In *Accountability through Public Opinion: From Inertia to Public Action*, edited by Sina Odugbemi and Taeku Lee. Washington, DC: The World Bank, 2011. 273–289.

Hartfield-Méndez, Vialla. "Community-Based Learning, Internationalization of the Curriculum and University Engagement with Latino Communities." *Hispania* 96, 2 (June 2013): 355–368.

Holling, C. S., and Lance H. Gunderson. "Resilience and Adaptive Cycles." In *Panarchy: Understanding Transformations in Human and Natural Systems*, edited by Lance H. Gunderson and C. S. Holling. Washington, DC: Island Press, 2002. 25–62.

Holling, C. S.,, Lance H. Gunderson., and Garry D. Peterson. "Sustainability and Panarchies." In *Panarchy: Understanding Transformations in Human and Natural Systems*, edited by Lance H. Gunderson and C. S. Holling. Washington, DC: Island Press, 2002. 63–102.

Imagining America. "Artists and Scholars in Public Life." Accessed January 21, 2019. https://imaginingamerica.org

Michael, Donald N. *In Search of the Missing Elephant*. Dorset: Triarchy Press, 2010.

Mind and Life Digital Dialogue. "Ubuntu." Accessed March 15, 2019. https://ubuntudialogue.org/

Mind and Life Institute. Accessed September 9, 2018. www.mindandlife.org/

Owen-Smith, Patricia. *The Contemplative Mind in the Scholarship of Learning and Teaching*. Bloomington: Indiana University Press, 2017.

Patterson, Barbara A.B. "Sustaining Life: Contemplative Pedagogies in a Religion and Ecology Course." In *Meditation and the Classroom: Contemplative Pedagogy for Religious Studies*. edited by Fran Grace and Judith Simmer-Brown. New York: SUNY Press, 2010. 155–162.

Resilience Alliance. Accessed November 6, 2018. www.resalliance.org/

Welch, Marshall. *Engaging Higher Education: Purpose, Platforms, and Programs for Community Engagement*. Sterling: Stylus Publishing, 2016.

Index

Note: Page numbers in *italic* denote figures.

Milton Keynes UK
Ingram Content Group UK Ltd.
UKHW011313040224
437236UK00008B/38